THE CHRISTIAN RIGHT
IN AMERICAN POLITICS

Religion and Politics Series

Mark J. Rozell, John C. Green, and Ted Jelen,
series editors

THE CHRISTIAN RIGHT IN AMERICAN POLITICS

Marching to the Millennium

Editors
JOHN C. GREEN,
MARK J. ROZELL, AND
CLYDE WILCOX

Georgetown University Press
Washington, D.C.

Georgetown University Press, Washington, D.C.
© 2003 by Georgetown University Press. All rights reserved.

Printed in the United States of America
10 9 8 7 6 5 4 3 2 1   2003

Library of Congress Cataloging-in-Publication Data

The Christian right in American politics : marching to the millennium / John C. Green, Mark J. Rozell, and Clyde Wilcox, editors.
    p. cm. — (Religion and politics series)
Includes bibiographical references and index.
    ISBN 0-87840-393-0 (hardcover : alk. paper) — ISBN 0-87840-392-2 (pbk. : alk. paper)
    1. Christianity and politics—United States—History—20th century.
2. Christians—United States—Political activity. 3. United States—Church history—20th century. I. Green, John Clifford, 1953– II. Rozell, Mark J. III. Wilcox, Clyde, 1953– IV. Religion and politics series (Georgetown University)
BR517 .C47 2003
320.5'5'097309048—dc21   2002014309

CONTENTS

LIST OF TABLES AND FIGURES

Tables

Figures

The Christian Right's Long Political March

John C. Green, Mark J. Rozell,
and Clyde Wilcox

THE CHRISTIAN RIGHT HAS FASCINATED PUNDITS, JOURNALISTS, and social scientists for more than twenty years. As one of the few conservative social movements to achieve significant political influence in the postwar period, it has repeatedly defied conventional wisdom. Its initial appearance in the late 1970s surprised observers, and its persistence over two decades was unexpected. Indeed, there have been numerous obituaries for the movement—followed by dramatic revivals of its fortunes. The 2000 election is a good example: while many observers touted the decline of the Christian Coalition, the broader movement helped George W. Bush win the Republican nomination and the White House. Bush repaid this critical support by choosing former Senator John Ashcroft, once the favored presidential candidate of the movement, as U.S. Attorney General. Indeed, the Christian Right has been engaged in a long and torturous "march toward the millennium," from outsider status into the thick of American politics. Here the "millennium" represents a date rather than progress toward the movement's goals—which remain largely unfulfilled.

This long political march has spurred extensive research on the Christian Right. Scholars have described the religious communities that form the core and peripheral constituencies of the movement (Wilcox 1992; Leege and Kellstedt 1993; Kohut et al. 2000; Layman 2001), and the attitudes and activities of leaders of these communities, especially pastors (Jelen 1991; Guth et al. 1997). A great deal is known about the social characteristics, religious doctrine, and political beliefs of Christian

Right activists (Wilcox 1992; Rozell and Wilcox 1996; Green et al. 1996; Green, Rozell, and Wilcox 1998). Scholars have also investigated the impact of the Christian Right on public policy, often in conjunction with the activities of movement opponents (see Wilcox 2000). Much of this research has focused on the national level, but there has been some work on the local level and in the states (Oldfield 1996).

We have edited three volumes on the Christian Right in state elections, beginning with *God at the Grassroots* (Rozell and Wilcox 1995a) and followed by *God at the Grassroots, 1996* (Rozell and Wilcox 1997) and *Prayers in the Precincts* (Green, Rozell, and Wilcox 2000). In this regard, we have served as informal conveners of a community of scholars who have tracked the movement's political march in particular states in the 1990s. Indeed, eleven scholars have participated continuously in the project since its inception, and twenty-nine have appeared in one or another of the publications. In this volume we welcome several new colleagues.

During the 1990s, the movement was especially focused on electoral politics. The Christian Coalition sought to build precinct-level organizations and claims to have distributed tens of millions of voter guides in churches. Activists worked within state and local Republican parties to try to influence nominations and party platforms, and in general elections to elect candidates to national, state, and local office (Rozell and Wilcox 1996; Guth et al. 2002). Thus it is appropriate to begin our study of the Christian Right's role in state elections with 1994, when the Christian Right helped the Republicans gain control of Congress for the first time in forty years. In 1996 and 1998, the movement was a net contributor to GOP success in congressional and state elections, and it aided the party's very slim victories in 2000.

By 2000, the Christian Right had been active in American politics for some twenty years. In 1990, Pat Robertson told activists at a Christian Coalition convention in Washington that his goal was to elect a profamily Congress by 1994 and a profamily president by 2000. With these basic goals accomplished, it seems appropriate to take a longer-term assessment of the impact of the movement, on politics, policies, and democracy. Thus, we asked our contributors to this volume to focus not merely on the 2000 elections but upon the activities of the Christian Right in their states since 1980. We asked them to describe the resources of the movement and the organizational ecology in which it operates: the religious groups in the state, party organizations, and supportive and opposing interest groups. And we asked them to assess the impact of the movement on state policymaking during this period. This volume, then, is both an epilogue to past research on the movement and a prologue to its next stage.

MARCHING TOWARD THE MILLENNIUM: TWELVE CASE STUDIES

The twelve case studies in this book were not chosen at random: they all represent states where the Christian Right was especially active between 1980 and 2000 in one way or another (see Green 1995, 1997, and 2000). Thus, these cases represent a basic level of organizational success: the movement was able to mobilize a minimal level of resources and then deploy them in politics on behalf of its goals. For at least a brief period of time the Christian Right was "in contention" in these states, competing against and/or cooperating with other interests, usually in elections but sometimes in other venues (see Green, Rozell, and Wilcox 2001). This fact is important to keep in mind because the movement failed to achieve this minimal level of organizational success in many of the states not included here (for examples of states where the movement was not in contention, see Rausch and Rausch 1997, and Spitzer 2000).

Once in contention, the movement's activity has varied considerably among and even within the states over time. Sometimes the Christian Right adopted a strategy of confrontation, zealously advancing its own candidates and its narrow agenda, with no concern for compromise, accommodation, or progress. Movement "purists" were usually at the forefront of confrontations. At other times the movement adopted a strategy of consolidation, supporting a wider range of candidates and a broader conservative agenda. Consolidation was the special province of movement "pragmatists" (Green, Rozell, and Wilcox 2001).

Overall, confrontation was most often associated with movement failure at the polls, although the Christian Right did achieve some gains by this means, especially within Republican committees, on party platforms, and in nominations. Also, confrontation often aided in building and maintaining movement organizations. In contrast, consolidation was more often associated with movement success at the ballot box, where the Christian Right helped Republicans and conservatives attract voters, win elections, and control government institutions. However, there were often costs associated with this strategy as well: the movement frequently had to settle for politicians and proposals that fell far short of its substantive goals, making it difficult to amass and sustain resources.

Despite this high level of activity, the Christian Right enjoyed very little success in changing public policy in these states or at the national level (Wilcox 1999, 2000). Although these case studies do not focus on policy, none find evidence of extensive success in achieving the movement's substantive goals. Of course, one must be careful to not adopt an unreasonably high standard in this regard: the American system of decentralized government, separate executive and legislative powers, and an independent judiciary makes it quite difficult for any movement to change policy quickly. Still, the Christian Right's very limited success in policymaking in these states presents a contrast to its organizational success and mixed electoral gains.

The case studies in this book are arranged according to the level of Christian Right influence in state politics, combing organizational, electoral, and policy success between 1980 and 2000. Readers may decide for themselves if this ordering is persuasive, but the value of the case studies will not be diminished by a different judgment. These cases highlight different aspects of movement and its long political march.[1]

Southern Strongholds

The Christian Right has been the strongest in the South, and thus we begin with Vinson and Guth's account of the Christian Right's "advance and retreat" in South Carolina (chapter 1; also see Guth 1995, 2000; Guth and Smith 1997). They note that the "movement appeared earlier, manifested more variation, and sustained greater influence in the state than almost anywhere else." However, a great deal of complexity lies behind the Christian Right's impact on state politics, including its potent role in the state Republican Party. The authors chronicle good examples of both confrontation and consolidation over some thirty years of South Carolina politics. Although a "force to be reckoned with," the Christian Right faces numerous limitations in a state that is becoming increasingly diverse.

In many respects, Virginia is the birthplace of the Christian Right; it is the home of both the Moral Majority and Christian Coalition (chapter 2; also see Rozell and Wilcox 1995b, 1996, 1997, and 2000). In Virginia, the movement "has evolved from a marginal player in the state's once small Republican Party to a major faction in a party that . . . has largely dominated statewide elections since the 1990s." This development has included bitter confrontations and successful consolidations. Although the Christian Right has gained considerable influence within the state GOP, learned to be effective in elections, and obtained the ear of officeholders, its impact is circumscribed by an array of opponents.

Lamare, Polinard, and Wrinkle arrive at similar conclusions in their description of the Christian Right in Texas (chapter 3; also see Bruce 1995 and 1997; Lamare, Polinard, and Wrinkle 2000). The movement appeared in various guises prior to the 1990s, but came into its own with the Texas Christian Coalition (TCC), which was one of the Coalition's strongest state affiliates. Thanks in part to such organizational resources, the movement gained considerable influence within the Texas GOP. Consolidation and confrontation have both occurred, producing more modest impacts on elections and public policy, respectively. The power of Christian conservatives is constrained by the increasing economic, cultural, and ethnic diversity of the state.

Wald and Scher describe the Christian Right in Florida as having "gradually developed from an outsider social movement to a conventional interest group to a durable faction within a major party" (chapter 4; also see Wald 1995; Wald and Scher 1997; Wald, Tartaglione, and Scher 2000). They note that in terms of access to decisionmakers the Christian Right has been a "remarkable success," partly because of consolidation within the state GOP. However, the movement has failed to change policy to any significant degree, largely because of its reliance on confrontation. Regarded as a "necessary annoyance" by mainstream Republicans, the movement has influenced the tenor of politics rather than policy outputs.

Midwestern Battlegrounds

Shifting to the Midwest, Smidt and Penning report that the Christian Right has enjoyed "mixed success" in Michigan (chapter 5; also see Smidt and Penning 1995 and 1997; Penning and Smidt 2000). Diverse movement organizations have obtained a significant role within the state's Republican Party, and in turn, the success of the Michigan GOP has given the movement considerable access to government—but only modest impact on public policy. Located in a highly diverse and competitive state that is characterized by many well-organized interests, the Christian Right has practiced more consolidation than confrontation.

Racheter, Kellstedt, and Green describe Iowa as a "crucible" for the Christian Right (chapter 6; also see Mayer and Nesmith 1995). Well known for Pat Robertson's unexpected success in the 1988 presidential caucuses, the movement has since then developed effective organizations, a strong presence in the state Republican Party, and growing influence in the state legislature. Although there are good examples of confrontation, the movement has largely practiced consolidation, adapting to the limitations imposed by the state's highly competitive brand of party politics.

Cigler, Joslyn, and Loomis describe the role of the Christian Right in Kansas, with a special emphasis on teaching of evolution in public schools (chapter 7; also Cigler and Loomis 1997 and 2000). The movement precipitated a bitter confrontation within the state Republican Party in the mid- to late 1990s. In a pattern that is reminiscent of other states at other times, the Christian Right took control of the state party organization, then lost it, and gained control of the state school board and lost that as well. In both cases, it was moderate Republicans who defeated the movement activists. Despite these defeats, the movement did succeed in moving Republican officeholders to the right. Overall, the authors conclude that "although the Christian Right remains a major force in Kansas political and social life, its triumphs have been limited."

Gilbert and Peterson conclude that the Christian Right has a "strong bark and weak bite" in Minnesota (chapter 8; also see Gilbert and Peterson 1995, 1997, and 2000). They note that "for nearly three decades Christian Right groups have worked assiduously, progressing from political outsider status to insider role, to seize control of the state Republican Party and guide its policy stances." Despite a history of confrontation, the movement has helped the state GOP draw nearly even with the Democratic-Farmer-Labor Party. However, the Christian Right faces serious opposition on cultural issues within the GOP.

Western Frontier

Turning to the West, Zweir describes the Christian Right in Colorado, where the movement was bolstered by large-scale migration from California, including the arrival of Focus of the Family in Colorado Springs (chapter 9). He concludes: "Despite a mixed record of successes and disappointments, the Christian Right has become influential in Colorado." The signal success of the movement was the passage in 1992 of a ballot initiative to ban gay rights laws within the state, eventually declared unconstitutional by the U.S. Supreme Court. A mix of confrontation and consolidation characterized movement politics.

Soper and Fetzer consider the impact of the Christian Right in California (chapter 10; also see Soper 1995; Fetzer and Soper 1997; Soper and Fetzer 2000). Many years of confrontation have given the movement great influence within the state Republican Party, but in the late 1990s, it suffered as GOP fortunes plummeted. It has also been adept at sponsoring ballot issues, but most have failed. The state's cultural liberalism and increasing ethnic diversity put limits on the Christian Right, suggesting the need for consolidation. Indeed, the inability of the Christian Right to recruit Latinos and Asians, many of whom are traditionally religious, is one reason for the movement's "dimming fortunes" in the nation's most populous state.

Lunch describes the Christian Right's efforts in Oregon and Washington as "two decades of frustration" (chapter 11; also see Lunch 1995, 1997; Appleton and Francis 1997; Appleton and Buckley 2000). As these northwestern states converged politically, they shared the development of indigenous movement organizations, the Oregon and Washington Citizen Alliances. Reacting to rapid social and cultural change, movement activists became engaged in Republican politics and especially in a host of ballot initiatives. Given to confrontation rather than consolidation, the Christian Right has experienced only a few successes under unusual circumstances, such as in the 1994 election. The author concludes: "[T]he Christian Right will continue to have influence in the Republican Party in the Northwest . . . , but it will continue to be frustrated in its efforts to achieve its ultimate ends."

Outpost in New England

In the final chapter, Moen and Palmer consider the Christian Right's opposition to gay rights in New England, with a special emphasis on Maine (chapter 12; also see Moen and Palmer 1997, 2000). The authors note: "Maine presents a curious situation: the Christian Right's influence within the state is real but circumscribed in many ways, and yet it continues winning on the salient issue of gay rights." Unlike the western states, where strong movement organizations repeatedly lost ballot initiatives, the marginal Maine movement enjoyed unexpected success due to a "tactical transformation."

DIVERSE ROUTES OF MARCH

These case studies show that the Christian Right's long political march has been characterized by diversity—in several senses of the word. Not only has the movement marched along diverse routes in different states, but its structure and activities can be understood as responding to social diversity and change. The impact of diversity can be seen in these case studies in the movement's sources of support, varieties of political opportunities, and range of opposition (Green, Guth, and Hill 1993). This complexity helps account for the observer's persistent misjudgment of the Christian Right's status and trajectory.

The Sources of Movement Support

It is almost a truism that the principal source of support for organizing the Christian Right was conservative religious communities (Wilcox 2000; Green and Guth 1988), but as the case studies reveal, such communities were quite diverse. One of the most important factors in the development of the movement was the presence of white evangelical Protestants within the state. South Carolina had the largest contingent of evangelicals, and the movement has been especially well organized, while Colorado and California had fewer evangelicals, and the movement was less so. In all states, evangelicals were central to all the major Christian Right organizations.

Yet the presence or absence of large numbers of white evangelicals does not determine the fate of the movement. Some states had relatively small evangelical populations and yet a fairly well-organized movement, including Florida, Michigan, and Iowa. Other states, such as Oregon, Washington, and Maine, had fairly sizable evangelical populations but weaker movement organizations. These patterns point to the importance of the broader religious environment of the state. For instance, high levels of religious commitment and the presence of conservatives in other religious traditions, especially mainline Protestants and Catholics, also aided in the organization of the movement. Thus, the traditional religious ethos of South Carolina, Virginia, and Texas also supported the movement, and helped it draw some support beyond the evangelical community. Likewise, conservative mainline Protestants and traditionalist Catholics provided crucial support for the movement in the Midwest. The Christian Right organizations faced special hurdles in more secular places, such as in the West and New England.

Ethnic diversity presented both a challenge and a largely untapped opportunity for the movement: in most states, black Protestants and Hispanic Catholics shared many of the religious values of the movement's core supporters but rarely backed movement organizations. This situation was especially problematic in California and Colorado and may become pressing in Texas and Florida in the near future. Although ethnic religious communities sometimes supported ballot initiatives backed by the Christian Right, few joined the movement in backing Republican candidates (see the Colorado case).

Indeed, religious diversity in the state as a whole was both an impediment and an encouragement for the development of movement organizations. And diversity within the evangelical community mattered as well. Several of the case studies note the importance of evangelical subgroups in developing the movement: fundamentalists, Pentecostals and charismatics, Southern Baptists, and nondenominational evangelicals were all critical sources of support in one place or another (see the South Carolina and Iowa cases for good examples). "Religious particularism" within the evangelical tradition characterized the Christian Right in some states, and especially in the early stages of its development (Rozell and Wilcox 1996; Wilcox, Rozell, and Gunn 1996).

The consequences of this religious diversity can be seen in the rich set of movement organizations mentioned in the case studies. Several regularities are worth noting. First, in many states the Christian Right was preceded by a series of social issue protests, focusing on abortion (Iowa and Kansas), gay rights (Florida and California), and the equal rights amendment (Iowa and Maine). Some of these protests developed into social movements in their own right, such as the right-to-life and antifeminist organizations. In most of these states, these movements became closely allied with the Christian Right, sometimes essentially merging with them and sometimes becoming the senior partners on the right. Indeed, right-to-life committees were very prominent in many of the case studies, especially in the Midwest (Michigan, Minnesota, Kansas), and the Eagle Forum appears in a number of the accounts (Iowa, Florida, and Texas).

Second, fundamentalists were the first group of evangelicals to become mobilized. Fittingly, these initial efforts were largely independent of one another; in some cases, the origins of such efforts reached back into the 1960s. Some of these efforts were very successful, such as the Bob Jones contingent in South Carolina and the Oregon Citizens Alliance. However, the best example of this fundamentalist mobilization was the founding of the Moral Majority in the late 1970s (Liebman 1983; Bruce 1988), which is mentioned in seven of the case studies. The mobilization of other evangelical subtraditions followed shortly, and some of their organizations, including Christian Voice and the Religious Roundtable, are mentioned in the case studies. In some states, movement activists operated through existing organizations left over from previous conservative crusades; examples include the Maine Christian Civic League (founded in 1897 to promote prohibition) and the California Republican Assembly (founded in 1934 as a caucus of right-wing Republicans). Most of this initial wave of Christian Right organizations, including the Moral Majority, was in decline by the late 1980s.

Third, Pat Robertson's 1988 presidential campaign was a catalyst for a second wave of movement organizations, headlined by the Christian Coalition (Hertzke 1993). Although the Robertson campaign itself best fits the earlier pattern of religious particularism (i.e., its reliance on Pentecostal and charismatic support), the Christian Coalition drew support from across the evangelical spectrum (Wilcox, Sigelman, and DeBell 1999). The Coalition is mentioned in all the case studies. However, the strength and longevity varied enormously. For example, in Texas and Iowa, the organizations were strong and apparently remain so despite the decline of the Coalition elsewhere. In Minnesota and Oregon, state affiliates of the Coalition were never strong, while in Michigan and Washington, the 1988 Robertson campaign spawned independent organizations, precluding the development of "official" affiliates. South Carolina, Virginia, and Florida represent the most typical pattern: the Coalition appeared in the early 1990s, peaked in the mid-1990s, and was in serious decay by 2000.

Fourth, a series of more specialized organizations is also mentioned. Although many were founded in the late 1970s, roughly contemporary with the Moral Majority, their importance increased in the 1990s. One set of groups was linked to Focus on the Family and the Family Research Council. This network is mentioned in six of the case studies, and in some states, like Michigan, it was judged to be among the most important movement groups. The American Family Association, Concerned Women for America, the Traditional Values Coalition, and a host of state-specific organizations are also mentioned in a number of the studies.

The Varieties of Political Opportunity

It is well established that the Christian Right has been most active where the political system is the most open to outside interests, but these case studies reveal the complexity of such openness (see Shafer 1998, chap. 3). One important feature of these states is political culture: more than two-thirds of the cases involve a strong element of "moralistic" political culture. Most of these states have a purely moralistic culture (from Maine to Minnesota to Oregon), although some have an individualist element as well (from Iowa to California). In Elazar's (1972, 96–99) classic formulation, moralistic political culture understands politics as a quest for the public interest, with a heavy emphasis on citizen participation. While the Christian Right's desire to restore traditional moral values to public policy differs in content from the liberalism for which these states are best known, it easily conforms to the same logic of serving the common good.

The exceptions to this regularity are the four southern states. South Carolina and Virginia are characterized by a "traditionalistic" political culture, while Florida and Texas combine individualistic elements with tradition. For Elazar, traditionalistic political culture understands politics as the maintenance of the existing social order, with a heavy emphasis on hierarchy and elites (1972, 99–102). Although grassroots political activity appears to violate these norms at least in part, the traditional moral values were always part of the social order in the South, and thus the Christian Right can be thought of as a defense of the status quo. Thus, there is a powerful "moralistic" element to traditionalistic political culture as well, although in terms more of content than of the logic of politics. The movement was markedly less active in states with individualistic political culture.

All but one of the case studies finds that the Christian Right has gained considerable influence in the state Republican parties. In most, the movement's influence is judged to be or have been "strong," and in the remaining cases, "moderate." Although the level of influence has hardly been static (for example, it rose and fell dramatically in Kansas), there is little doubt that the Christian Right has far more sway in these state Republican parties than in 1980. In fact, one of the initial goals of the movement was to gain influence in the major political parties, and after a brief flirtation with a bipartisan strategy, movement leaders made the GOP their target. This effort is best symbolized by the presidential nomination campaigns of Pat Robertson in 1988 and Gary Bauer in 2000.

The major American political parties are notoriously "permeable" to outside interests, and the parties in our case studies were particularly so (Green, Guth, and Wilcox 1998). For example, all but two of the states scored a "1" on Mayhew's (1986, 19–21, 199) five-point scale of "traditional party organizations" (where 5 is the strongest organization). The two exceptions are Virginia and Texas, which scored a 2. In contrast, the six states where the Christian Right was judged to be "weak" in 2000 (Conger and Green 2002) scored an average of 3.7. Many of the case studies describe the ease with which Christian Rightists—and any other group of dedicated activists—could participate in local and state party organizations.

Some of these states, such as Iowa, Colorado, and Minnesota, have a long tradition of open party caucuses, which regularize the entrance of new participants. In other states, the GOP organizations were simply weak. In the "progressive" states of the west coast, party organizations were weak by design and thus easy to take over because they were of limited value in elections. Interestingly, the movement clearly has harmed Republican prospects in these states. In the South, the lingering effects of one-party Democratic rule produced skeletal Republican organizations, where almost any interest could put flesh on the bones. Indeed, the Christian Right was one component in the rise of robust Republican organizations in Virginia, Florida, South Carolina, and Texas after 1980. The movement probably improved the fortunes of the "Independent Republican" Party in Minnesota, and on balance bolstered the GOP in Iowa, Kansas, Michigan, and Colorado. Some of the case studies report that this influence extended to the national GOP as well.

Influence in state Republican organizations has given the Christian Right entrée into the political process: the movement has had some influence on party platforms (see the Iowa case) and been in a position to influence nominations. The latter point should not be overstated, however, because most nominations in these states are determined by primary. Important exceptions were Virginia, where for much of the period under study nominations occurred by convention, and Minnesota, where conventions engage in preprimary endorsements. The movement was active in both these venues, engendering bitter intraparty fights that ultimately produced defeats for the movement. The type of primary matters as well. Washington's "blanket" primary, where all candidates from both parties run on the same ballot, and open primaries, such as in California, have encouraged Christian Right activity.

However, one must be careful not to overstate the impact of open rules on movement activity since political opportunities are affected by temporal factors, such as open seats, term limits, entrepreneurial candidates, and the issue agenda. Indeed, the same set of party and election rules encouraged movement activity under one set of circumstances—and discouraged it under another. A good example is the convention and blanket primary in Washington. In 1994, these rules encouraged an unusual degree of unity among GOP factions that resulted in an extraordinary victory. However, in 1996 and 1998, the same rules provided incentives for a destructive factionalism that resulted in defeat at the polls (Green, Rozell, and Wilcox 2001; see Washington case study). One such temporal element is presidential politics: the case studies point to various examples of how the vagaries of presidential primaries have "spillover" effects on the movement and the party (see Rozell and Wilcox 1997, chap. 16).

As with movement organizations, the case studies report on a wide range of candidates supported and opposed by the Christian Right, and these cases reveal a wide range of strategies and outcomes. However, three kinds of candidacies stood out across these cases. From time to time, the movement fought hard to nominate one of its own, usually provoking a bitter confrontation with other Republicans. Allen Quist in Minnesota, David Miller in Kansas, and Michael Farris in Virginia are good examples. Sometimes movement favorites—such as Oliver North in Virginia, Dan Lundgren in California, and Ellen Craswell in Washington—win nominations, only to lose in the general election. And sometimes movement candidates—like David Beasley in South Carolina and Rod Grams in Minnesota—actually obtain office but are defeated in subsequent elections. The Christian Right has had much more success with candidates who are sympathetic to the movement's goals but are not from the movement itself. Chuck Grassley in Iowa, Sam Brownback in Kansas, and George Allen in Virginia are all good examples. Finally, some more moderate Republicans are able to include the Christian Right in a broad conservative coalition with some success. The brothers Bush, George in Texas and Jeb in Florida, are good examples.

One other aspect of political opportunity is worthy of mention: ballot initiatives. Ballot issues appear in most of the case studies, but particularly in the progressive states, where it is relatively easy to gain ballot access. California, Washington, Oregon, Colorado, and Maine have had numerous examples since 1980, many placed on the ballot by movement activists. Few situations inspire greater movement activity than the chance to enact morals legislation directly. However, such efforts also mobilize the opposition. Indeed, most of the movement-based initiatives failed, often by large margins, although a few passed, such as the anti-gay-rights issues in Colorado and Maine. The Christian Right has proved somewhat more adept at opposing ballot issues it disagrees with, such as the state Equal Rights Amendment in Iowa, but often fails as well, such as in its opposition to the state lottery in South Carolina.

The Range of Opposition

The Christian Right has faced considerable opposition, but this has varied considerably by state and over time. It is worth noting that all the case studies comment on social diversity, often in the form of rapid social and economic change. The four southern states and four western states are characterized by migration, cultural liberalization, and economic modernization, all of which challenge traditional values in one way or another. The Midwestern and New England states were already diverse places, with attendant pressures for cultural liberalization. Christian Rightists and other conservatives have sometimes gained from these kinds of changes (as illustrated by the migration into Colorado and the referenda in Maine), and, in any event, they provided a strong impetus for movement mobilization.

Among the strongest opponents of the Christian Right are proponents of liberal social policy: feminists, advocates of gay rights, environmentalists, civil libertarians, and critics of organized religion. These interests are diverse in their own right, and overlap in complex ways with other kinds of liberals, including advocates of civil rights, proponents of gun control, social welfare advocates, and organized labor. There is often a broad portion of the public that holds liberal to moderate views on these issues, without necessarily identifying with the liberal groups themselves. Such groups are common in some of the states covered here, and their presence helps explain the lack of success of the Christian Right—but also its relentless activity. The West Coast states of Oregon, Washington, and California are the best examples here, followed by Colorado, where environmentalists are particularly important. Minnesota and Maine have such opposition to a lesser extent, and matters are more balanced in Michigan, Iowa, and Florida. This kind of opposition appears to be less important in the remaining states.

Social policy liberals are strongly associated with the secular (nonreligious) population, which is highest in Washington and Oregon and lowest in South Carolina and Texas. Secularists have become a potent constituency in the Democratic Party, reflecting the rise of Christian conservatives in the GOP. Seculars often make common cause with liberal religious groups to oppose the movement. Jews and other religious minorities are often central to such religious opposition (see the Florida case), and various organizations of religious liberals and mainline churches are important as well. The Texas case contains a good example of the "religious left" in traditionally conservative context, while the

Minnesota case reveals the activities of mainline church groups. Religious liberals and moderates frequently make common cause with seculars and religious minorities in the Democratic Party. Black Protestants and Hispanic Catholics are especially important groups in several of the case studies, where the Christian Right has been unable to take advantage of their traditional religiosity. But not all religious liberals, moderates, and secularists are Democrats: many are Republicans, and they often fiercely oppose the Christian Right from within the GOP.

Opposition to the Christian Right from Republican constituencies is mentioned in all the case studies in one form or another. Indeed, these intraparty battles are often especially bitter. Governor Graves in Kansas, Governor Carlson in Minnesota, and Senator Warner in Virginia were good examples of politicians embroiled in these conflicts, and the fight over evolution in Kansas and the ongoing partisan warfare in Washington and Oregon are good examples of the process. This kind of opposition appeared in three guises. Many Republican activists held more moderate or liberal religious views, reflecting mainline Protestant backgrounds and high levels of education. Other Republicans were libertarian, opposing government regulation in both economic and social realms. And important elements of the business community are opposed to the Christian Right. Perhaps the most dramatic example was the fight over gambling in South Carolina, where the numerous business interests rallied against the Christian Right, defeating one of their prominent supporters, Governor Beasley. The cases also contain examples of successful coalition building among these disparate Republican coalitions, but this usually requires concessions on the part of the Christian Right.

A final source of opposition comes from within the movement itself. Many of the case studies note the natural rivalries among Christian Right groups that have often resulted in bitter feuding. These disputes have arisen in part from the religious particularism within the evangelical community but in part from the conflicting ambitions of their leaders. Indeed, even when these organizations maintain amicable relations, it is quite common for them to disagree on candidates, policies, strategy, and tactics. Overall, the impact of the movement has often been reduced because of such divisions (for example, see the Iowa case study). There is still considerable skepticism about the efficacy of political action among the core religious constituencies of the Christian Right, and this, too, acts as a form of opposition.

With this framework in mind, we now examine the diverse routes of the Christian Right's long political march toward the millennium.

These analyses demonstrate the different strategies, successes, and failures of the movement in key states. What emerges is a portrait of a social movement that has evolved and matured over time but also continues to struggle with its identity and place in American politics.

NOTE

1. Other state case studies covered in our previous volumes include Georgia, Oklahoma, North Carolina, West Virginia, Alabama, Illinois, and New York (see Rozell and Wilcox 1995a, 1997; and Green, Rozell, and Wilcox 2000).

REFERENCES

Appleton, Andrew M., and Daniel Francis. 1997. "Washington: Mobilizing for Victory." Pp. 169–86 in *God at the Grassroots, 1996*, ed. Mark J. Rozell and Clyde Wilcox. Lanham, Md.: Rowman & Littlefield.

Appleton, Andrew M., and Michael Buckley. 2000. "Washington: Christian Right Setbacks Abound." Pp. 187–206 in *Prayers in the Precincts: The Christian Right in the 1998 Elections*, ed. John C. Green, Mark J. Rozell, and Clyde Wilcox. Washington, D.C.: Georgetown University Press.

Bruce, John M. 1995. "Texas: The Emergence of the Christian." Pp. 67–90 in *God at the Grassroots: The Christian Right in the 1994 Elections*, ed. Mark J. Rozell and Clyde Wilcox. Lanham.: Md: Rowman & Littlefield.

———. 1997. "Texas: A Success Story, at Least for Now." Pp. 33–50 in *God at the Grassroots, 1996*, ed. Mark J. Rozell and Clyde Wilcox. Lanham, Md.: Rowman & Littlefield.

Bruce, Steve. 1988. *The Rise and Fall of the New Christian Right*. New York: Oxford University Press.

Cigler, Allan J., and Burdett A. Loomis. 1997. "Kansas: The Christian Right and the New Mainstream of the Republican Party." Pp. 207–22 in *God at the Grassroots, 1996*, ed. Mark J. Rozell and Clyde Wilcox. Lanham, Md.: Rowman & Littlefield.

———. 2000. "After the Flood: The Kansas Christian Right in Retreat." Pp. 227–42 in *God at the Grassroots, 1996*, ed. Mark J. Rozell and Clyde Wilcox. Lanham, Md.: Rowman & Littlefield.

Conger, Kimberly H., and John C. Green. 2002. "Spreading Out and Digging In: Christian Conservatives and State Republican Parties." *Campaigns & Elections* 23:58–60, 64–65.

Elazar, Daniel J. 1972. *American Federalism*. 2d ed. New York: Thomas Y. Crowell.

Fetzer, Joel, and J. Christopher Soper. 1997. "California: Between a Rock and a Hard Place." Pp. 135–52 in *God at the Grassroots, 1996*, ed. Mark J. Rozell and Clyde Wilcox. Lanham, Md.: Rowman & Littlefield.

Gilbert, Christopher P., and David A. M. Peterson. 1995. "Minnesota: Christians and Quistians in the GOP." Pp. 169–90 in *God at the Grassroots: The Christian Right in the 1994 Elections*, ed. Mark J. Rozell and Clyde Wilcox. Lanham, Md.: Rowman & Littlefield.

———. 1997. "Minnesota: Onward Quistian Soldiers? Christian Conservatives Confront Their Limitations." Pp. 187–207 in *God at the Grassroots, 1996*, ed. Mark J. Rozell and Clyde Wilcox. Lanham, Md.: Rowman & Littlefield.

———. 2000. "Minnesota 1998: Christian Conservatives and the Body Politic." Pp. 227–42 in *Prayers in the Precincts: The Christian Right in the 1998 Elections*, ed. John C. Green, Mark J. Rozell, and Clyde Wilcox. Washington, D.C.: Georgetown University Press.

Green, John C. 1995. "The Christian Right and the 1994 Election: An Overview." Pp. 1–18 in *God at the Grassroots: The Christian Right in the 1994 Elections*, ed. Mark J. Rozell and Clyde Wilcox. Lanham, Md.: Rowman & Littlefield.

———. 1997. "The Christian Right and the 1996 Elections: An Overview." Pp. 1–14 in *God at the Grassroots 1996*, ed. Mark J. Rozell and Clyde Wilcox. Lanham, Md.: Rowman & Littlefield.

———. 2000. "The Christian Right and the 1998 Elections: An Overview." Pp. 1–20 in *Prayers in the Precincts: The Christian Right in the 1998 Elections*, ed. John C. Green, Mark J. Rozell, and Clyde Wilcox. Washington, D.C.: Georgetown University Press.

Green, John C., and James L. Guth. 1988. "The Christian Right in the Republican Party: The Case of Pat Robertson's Supporters." *Journal of Politics* 50:150–65.

Green, John C., James L. Guth, and Kevin Hill. 1993. "Faith and Election: The Christian Right in Congressional Campaigns 1978–1988." *Journal of Politics* 55:80–91.

Green, John C., James L. Guth, Corwin E. Smidt, and Lyman A. Kellstedt. 1996. *Religion and the Culture Wars: Dispatches from the Front*. Lanham, Md: Rowman & Littlefield.

Green, John C., James L. Guth, and Clyde Wilcox. 1998. "Less Than Conquerors: The Christian Right in State Republican Parties." Pp. 117–35 in *Social Movements and American Political Institutions*, ed. Anne N. Costain and Andrew S. McFarland. Lanham, Md.: Rowman & Littlefield.

Green, John C., Mark J. Rozell, and Clyde Wilcox. 1998. "Religious Constituencies and Support for the Christian Right in the 1990s." *Social Science Quarterly* 79:815–27.

———. 2000. *Prayers in the Precincts: The Christian Right in the 1998 Elections*. Washington, D.C.: Georgetown University Press.

————. 2001. "Social Movements and Party Politics: The Case of the Christian Right." *Journal for Scientific Study of Religion* 40:413–26.

Guth, James L. 1995. "South Carolina: The Christian Right Wins One." Pp. 133–46 in *God at the Grassroots: The Christian Right in the 1994 Elections*, ed. Mark J. Rozell and Clyde Wilcox. Lanham, Md.: Rowman & Littlefield.

————. 2000. "South Carolina: Even in Zion the Heathen Rage." Pp. 21–40 in *Prayers in the Precincts: The Christian Right in the 1998 Elections*, ed. Mark C. Green, Mark J. Rozell, and Clyde Wilcox. Washington, D.C.: Georgetown University Press.

Guth, James L., John C. Green, Corwin E. Smidt, and Lyman A. Kellstedt. 1997. *The Bully Pulpit: The Politics of Protestant Clergy*. Lawrence: University Press of Kansas.

Guth, James L., Lyman A. Kellstedt, John C. Green, and Corwin E. Smidt. 2002. "A Distant Thunder? Religious Mobilization in the 2000 Elections." Pp. 161–84 in *Interest Group Politics*. 6th ed., ed. Allan J. Cigler and Burgett A. Loomis. Washington, D.C.: Congressional Quarterly Press.

Guth, James L., and Oran P. Smith. 1997. "South Carolina Christian Right: Just Part of the Family Now?" Pp. 15–32 in *God at the Grassroots, 1996*, ed. Mark J. Rozell and Clyde Wilcox. Lanham, Md.: Rowman & Littlefield.

Hertzke, Allen D. 1993. *Echoes of Discontent*. Washington, D.C.: Congressional Quarterly Press.

Jelen, Ted G. 1991. *The Political Mobilization of Religious Beliefs*. Westport, Conn.: Praeger Press.

Kohut, Andrew, John C. Green, Scott Keeter, and Rober Toth. 2000. *The Diminishing Divide: Religion's Changing Role in American Politics*. Washington, D.C.: Brookings Institution.

Lamare, James, J. L. Polinard, and Robert D. Wrinkle. 2000. "The Christian Right in God's Country: Texas Politics." Pp. 41–58 in *Prayers in the Precincts: The Christian Right in the 1998 Elections*, ed. John C. Green, Mark J. Rozell, and Clyde Wilcox. Washington, D.C.: Georgetown University Press.

Layman, Geoffrey. 2001. *The Great Divide: Religious and Cultural Conflict in American Politics*. New York: Columbia University Press.

Leege, David C., and Lyman A. Kellstedt, eds. 1993. Pp. 53–71 in *Rediscovering the Impact of Religion on Political Behavior*. Armonk, N.Y.: M.E. Sharpe.

Liebman, Robert C. 1983. "Mobilizing the Moral Majority." Pp. 49–73 in *The New Christian Right*, ed. Robert C. Liebman and Robert Wuthnow. New York: Aldine Press.

Lunch, William M. 1995. "Oregon: Identity and Politics in the Northwest." Pp. 227–52 in *God at the Grassroots: The Christian Right in the 1994 Elections*, ed. Mark J. Rozell and Clyde Wilcox. Lanham, Md.: Rowman & Littlefield.

————. 1997. "Oregon: The Flood Tide Recedes." Pp. 153–68 in *God at the Grassroots, 1996*, ed. Mark J. Rozell and Clyde Wilcox. Lanham, Md.: Rowman & Littlefield.

Mayer, Jeremy D. and Bruce Nesmith. 1995. "Iowa: Everything Comes up Rosy." Pp. 191–210 in *God at the Grassroots: The Christian Right in the 1994 Elections*, ed. Mark J. Rozell and Clyde Wilcox. Lanham, Md.: Rowman & Littlefield.

Mayhew, David R. 1986. *Placing Parties in American Politics*. Princeton, N.J.: Princeton University Press.

Moen, Matthew C., and Kenneth T. Palmer. 1997. "Maine: Slow Growth in the Pine Tree State." Pp. 223–38 in *God at the Grassroots, 1996*, ed. Mark J. Rozell and Clyde Wilcox. Lanham, Md.: Rowman & Littlefield.

———. 2000. "Maine: Which Way Should Life Be?" Pp. 271–86 in *Prayers in the Precincts: The Christian Right in the 1998 Elections*, ed. John C. Green, Mark J. Rozell, and Clyde Wilcox. Washington, D.C.: Georgetown University Press.

Oldfield, Duane. 1996. *The Right and the Righteous: The Christian Right Confronts the Republican Party*. Lanham, Md.: Rowman & Littlefield.

Penning, James M., and Corwin E. Smidt. 2000. "Michigan 1998: The 'Right Stuff.'" Pp. 163–86 in *Prayers in the Precincts: The Christian Right in the 1998 Elections*, ed. John C. Green, Mark J. Rozell, and Clyde Wilcox. Washington, D.C.: Georgetown University Press.

Rausch, John David, and Mary S. Rausch. 1997. "West Virginia: In Search of the Christian Right." Pp. 239–54 in *God at the Grassroots, 1996*, ed. Mark J. Rozell and Clyde Wilcox. Lanham, Md.: Rowman & Littlefield.

Rozell, Mark J., and Clyde Wilcox, eds. 1995a. *God at the Grass Roots: The Christian Right in the 1994 Elections*. Lanham, Md.: Rowman & Littlefield.

———. 1995b. "Virginia: God, Guns, and Oliver North." Pp. 109–132 in *God at the Grassroots: The Christian Right in the 1994 Elections*, ed. Mark J. Rozell and Clyde Wilcox. Lanham, Md.: Rowman & Littlefield.

———. 1996. *Second Coming: The New Christian Right in Virginia Politics*. Baltimore: Johns Hopkins University Press.

———. eds. 1997. *God at the Grassroots, 1966*. Lanham, Md.: Rowman & Littlefield.

———. 2000. "Virginia: Prophet in Waiting?" Pp. 77–92 in *Prayers in the Precincts: The Christian Right in the 1998 Elections*, ed. John C. Green, Mark J. Rozell, and Clyde Wilcox. Washington, D.C.: Georgetown University Press.

Shafer, Bryon E., ed. 1998. *Partisan Approaches to Postwar American Politics*. New York: Chatham House.

Smidt, Corwin E., and James M. Penning. 1995. "Michigan: Veering to the Right." Pp. 147–268 in *God at the Grassroots: The Christian Right in the 1994 Elections*, ed. Mark J. Rozell and Clyde Wilcox. Lanham, Md.: Rowman & Littlefield.

———. 1997. "Michigan: Veering to the Left?" Pp. 115–34 in *God at the Grassroots, 1996*, ed. Mark J. Rozell and Clyde Wilcox. Lanham, Md.: Rowman & Littlefield.

Soper, J. Christopher. 1995. "California: Christian Conservative Influence in a Liberal State." Pp. 211–26 in *God at the Grassroots: The Christian Right in the 1994 Elections*, ed. Mark J. Rozell and Clyde Wilcox. Lanham, Md.: Rowman & Littlefield.

Soper, J. Christopher, and Joel Fetzer. 2000. "The Christian Right and the Republican Party in California: Necessarily Yoked." Pp. 93–114 in *Prayers in the Precincts: The Christian Right in the 1998 Elections*, ed. John C. Green, Mark J. Rozell, and Clyde Wilcox. Washington, D.C.: Georgetown University Press.

Spitzer, Robert J. 2000. "New York, New York: Start Spreadin' the News." Pp. 257–70 in *Prayers in the Precincts: The Christian Right in the 1998 Elections*, ed. John C. Green, Mark J. Rozell, and Clyde Wilcox. Washington, D.C.: Georgetown University Press.

Wald, Kenneth D. 1995. "Florida: Running Globally and Winning Locally." Pp. 19–46 in *God at the Grassroots: The Christian Right in the 1994 Elections*, ed. Mark J. Rozell and Clyde Wilcox. Lanham, Md.: Rowman & Littlefield.

Wald, Kenneth D., and Richard K. Scher. 1997. "Florida: Losing by Winning? The Odyssey of the Religious Right." Pp. 79–98 in *God at the Grassroots, 1996*, ed. Mark J. Rozell and Clyde Wilcox. Lanham, Md.: Rowman & Littlefield.

Wald, Kenneth D., Maureen Tartaglione, and Richard K. Scher. 2000. "Answered Prayers and Mixed Blessings: The Christian Right in Florida." Pp. 115–44 in *Prayers in the Precincts: The Christian Right in the 1998 Elections*, ed. John C. Green, Mark J. Rozell, and Clyde Wilcox.. Washington, D.C.: Georgetown University Press.

Wilcox, Clyde. 1992. *God's Warriors: The Christian Right in 20th Century America*. Baltimore: Johns Hopkins University Press.

———. 1999. "The Christian Right in Virginia: A Mixed Blessing for Civil Society." Paper Presented at conference on Democracy and Civil Society, Georgetown University, Washington, D.C., 15–17 June.

———. 2000. *Onward Christian Soldiers: The Christian Right in American Politics*. 2d ed. Boulder, Colo.: Westview.

Wilcox, Clyde, Mark J. Rozell, and Roland Gunn. 1996. "Religious Coalitions in the New Christian Right." *Social Science Quarterly* 77:543–59.

Wilcox, Clyde, Lee Sigelman, and Matthew DeBell. 1999. "The Second Coming of the New Christian Right: Patterns of Popular Support in 1984 and 1996." *Social Science Quarterly* 80:181–92.

ONE

Advance and Retreat in the Palmetto State: Assessing the Christian Right in South Carolina

C. Danielle Vinson and James L. Guth

For three decades, South Carolina has provided a marvel-ous case study of the Christian Right's evolution within the Republican Party. The movement appeared earlier, manifested more variation, and sustained greater influence in the state than almost anywhere else. As a result, the Christian Right has established a strong beachhead in the GOP and, perhaps, has had greater electoral impact than in other states (Smith 1997). Indeed, the South Carolina GOP is often characterized as "dominated" or at least "strongly influenced" by the Christian Right (Conger and Green 2002).

Such influence, however, is complex. As demographic changes grad-ually erode the religious dominance of conservative Protestants, Chris-tian Right forces clash frequently with other Republicans, especially the business wing, and often quarrel among themselves. The Christian Right has often been constrained by external events or countermobilization by political opponents. After a brief review of the state's religious composi-tion, we consider several critical episodes that reveal (1) the Christian Right's composition and its impact on the state GOP, (2) the nature of Christian Right activism, and (3) the resulting political influence.

RELIGION IN SOUTH CAROLINA

South Carolina, with its traditionalistic political culture modified by upstate moralism (Elazar 1966), would seem to be fertile ground for the Christian

Right. Although economic growth and inmigration have diversified the urban population, religion is still dominated by evangelical Protestants, especially Southern Baptists, the state's (and nation's) largest Protestant body, claiming over 40 percent of all South Carolina church members in 1990. There are also numerous (and mostly uncounted) independent fundamentalist congregations, usually Baptist, and large new nondenominational megachurches in the burgeoning suburbs. Other evangelical groups, such as the Presbyterian Church in America (PCA), have also benefited from suburbanization and have come to play a noticeable political role.

South Carolina also claims many mainline Protestants, especially members of the United Methodist Church (14 percent) and the Presbyterian Church in the U.S.A. (4 percent), as well as Evangelical Lutherans and Episcopalians (3 percent and 2 percent, respectively). The African American community is served by several Baptist denominations (16 percent of all church members) and others such as the African Methodist Episcopal Church, Zion (Bradley et al. 1992, 31), and African American clergy retain their historic political role. The Catholic community, both Anglo and Hispanic, has grown steadily, although these have not yet become distinct political forces.

ORGANIZATION OF THE CHRISTIAN RIGHT

For most of the twentieth century, the centrality of race in South Carolina politics precluded any large role for religion. But this changed in the 1960s and 1970s, as Republicans challenged the historic Democratic monopoly of public office. At first, the revitalized GOP reflected the religious coloration of its new urban, often "immigrant," leadership: upperstatus mainliners such as Episcopalians, Presbyterians, Methodists, and some "First Church" Southern Baptists. But more conservative religious forces soon crashed the party (Guth 1995), taking advantage of the openness of the skeletal Republican Party to any organized group. As we shall see, many Christian activists ultimately came to terms with the GOP's other constituencies and became a less distinctive, but still important, element of the party.

The Bob Jones Contingent

The Christian Right first surfaced in the 1960s as the Goldwater movement activated religious conservatives, especially at Greenville's Bob

Jones University (BJU), a mecca for the strictest wing of historic fundamentalism. By 1976, BJU loyalists had infiltrated precinct committees and captured the county GOP, the state's staunchest Republican stronghold. Some of these activists supported the candidacy of presidential challenger Ronald Reagan, others sought to push the GOP platform to the right, and many hoped to thwart federal interference with the burgeoning Christian school network (Smith 1997). The BJU encroachment met strong resistance from GOP regulars, accustomed to running their own show, but the party's 1976 electoral defeat soon forced the two factions together.

The eventual assimilation of the BJU crowd into the GOP reflected several factors. First, BJU activists were too few to control many local party committees statewide, although numerous enough to establish a presence. Even where they dominated local committees, their candidates for office usually lost. Second, Republican leaders such as Congressman (later Governor) Carroll Campbell and Governor James Edwards astutely cultivated BJU activists, patiently mediating intraparty disputes and rewarding cooperative behavior. Finally, BJU's militant separatism prevented alumni from joining other religious conservatives in a broader Christian Right organization, in effect encouraging individual activism in the GOP.

As a result, BJU leadership was soon dominated by savvy politicians, rather than by religious amateurs, permitting easier accommodation with the regulars, who gladly traded platform concessions for loyal support. Although the fundamentalists were more preoccupied with moral issues than most regulars were, the routine governmental implications of this difference were often hard to detect, and some BJU politicos soon gained the respect of even their staunchest opponents. One such GOP leader in the legislature, the late Terry Haskins, observed that the fundamentalists and the regulars soon "agreed on everything except where to go to church" (Ehrenhalt 1991, 98). BJU provided a large cadre of skilled activists, who usually backed the most conservative entrant in the GOP primaries—unless that candidate had unacceptable religious traits, such as Pentecostal beliefs. Then they behaved as loyal pragmatists, supporting the GOP winner in the general election (Smith 1997). By the mid-1980s, then, BJU Republicans were a distinct, but fairly well-integrated, GOP faction.

Ironically, the presence of BJU fundamentalists preempted Jerry Falwell's Moral Majority, heavily dependent on the very independent Baptists monopolized by the BJU network in South Carolina. As a result, the Moral Majority had virtually no grassroots organization in the state, aside from a few pastors in Falwell's Baptist Bible Fellowship. The few candidates with Falwell connections failed at the polls, especially in BJU precincts, as religious, organizational, and personal competition between the Joneses and Falwell precluded any merger of forces.

The Christian Coalition

Just as the GOP was assimilating the BJU folks, a more challenging religious insurgency emerged, when the charismatic forces of religious broadcaster Marion G. "Pat" Robertson infiltrated 1987 precinct meetings. They almost captured the state convention but were narrowly repelled by GOP regulars (with BJU help) through astute legal maneuvering. Robertson's organizational successes were not matched by his performance in the 1988 presidential primary, however, where he finished a poor third, with only a fifth of the vote. Robertson had failed to expand his religious base much beyond its original charismatic and Pentecostal core, quite small in South Carolina. A large majority of conservative Christians, including most Southern Baptist clergy and their parishioners, voted for primary winner George Bush. To keep peace, Governor Campbell, acting at Bush's behest, gave Robertson supporters some party offices, including several delegate slots to the 1988 GOP convention.

Nevertheless, the merger did not go smoothly. In 1991 Robertson loyalists reorganized as the South Carolina Christian Coalition, led by Roberta Combs. Although the Coalition's national executive, Ralph Reed, was often criticized by rivals as being far too accommodating to Republican leaders, Combs was often more belligerent. Buoyed by some apparent successes in its first electoral outing in 1992, in organizing the state's three major metropolitan areas, and in attracting some Southern Baptists and other conservative Protestants—especially those in local antiabortion groups—the Christian Coalition struck hard. Activists flooded the 1993 GOP precinct meetings, narrowly controlled the state convention, and helped elect Henry McMaster as state chairman over Greenvillian Knox White, a Campbell protégé and moderate conservative, who nevertheless had strong ties with BJU (Graham, Moore, and Petrusak 1994). Although McMaster added Coalition activists to his staff, he subsequently proved rather independent, staving off persistent Coalition efforts to gain operational control of the state executive committee while propitiating disgruntled GOP regulars.

In 1996 tension between Coalition forces and regulars reappeared at the state convention in May, where nineteen of the thirty-seven national convention delegates were to be selected. Governor David Beasley and Roberta Combs negotiated furiously over a "gubernatorial/ Coalition" slate, including many elected officials but favoring Christian conservatives. At the convention, however, the agreement fell apart. The consensus slate was distributed to all delegates, but to Beasley's surprise, each county Coalition leader provided followers with a list composed only of Coalition activists and "friends" (including some BJU activists). There were slots for Beasley and Senator Strom Thurmond, but not for former Governor Campbell or Southern Baptist conservative activist Cyndi Mosteller, a Beasley appointee to the state Health Board, chair of the platform committee, and leader of the state antiabortion movement (Guth and Smith 1997).

The subsequent vote revealed the Coalition's clout. Several Coalition unknowns outpolled both Campbell (twelfth in the balloting) and GOP Congressman Floyd Spence. Another GOP congressman had to settle for an alternate slot, and both the incumbent national committeewoman and committeeman were excluded altogether. The resulting delegation was staunchly conservative, lukewarm toward presidential primary winner Bob Dole, and very Christian Right.

Over the next four years, the Coalition forces continued their sporadic skirmishes with the state GOP leadership but gradually lost ground. The waning organizational effectiveness of the state Coalition reflected in part the decline in the national organization after Ralph Reed's departure after the 1996 election. The move of state organizational guru Roberta Combs to take Reed's place did little to reverse the declining fortunes of the national Coalition, and probably accelerated that of the state unit. While the Coalition mustered some activity in both the 1998 and 2000 elections, by 2002 it had virtually disintegrated, although its partisans continued to seek advantage in the state Republican committee, usually without success. And when GOP chairman Henry McMaster resigned in 2002 to run for attorney general, the Coalition produced no candidate to replace him in a contest won overwhelmingly by a party regular.

The Southern Baptists

The third major Christian Right element, the vote-rich Southern Baptist contingent, is more difficult to assess. The powerful state Baptist convention has clearly moved to the right politically, and like their brethren elsewhere, South Carolina Baptist clergy have become increasingly active.

Surveys reveal that an overwhelming majority of clergy consider themselves Republicans and feel close to most national Christian Right groups—but usually not to the Christian Coalition. Both clergy and laity have been prominent in the antiabortion movement, antigambling campaigns, and other social issues, but they still lack any central organizing forum. Efforts by prominent conservative Baptist activists to politicize the convention's Christian Life Committee structure have been only partially successful. Several conservative Baptist activists have become prominent politicos, especially in the state legislature, but other Baptist laity are leading business and professional people with closer ties to the old party establishment. The same could be said for Presbyterian Church in America (PCA) activists, who are much less numerous but comprise a major element in GOP organizations, especially in the upstate region.

Other Christian Right Organizations

The BJU, Christian Coalition, and state Baptist forces have been complemented by many smaller and sometimes overlapping organizations. The Palmetto Family Council, affiliated with James Dobson's Focus on the Family, has maintained a modest presence on moral issues in the legislature. The American Family Association, Eagle Forum, and the National Right to Life Committee have had small local units that have also contributed at times to Christian Right activism.

Thus, as the new millennium dawned, the South Carolina GOP remained a hybrid organization, part BJU, part Christian Coalition, and part conservative Southern Baptist, with minor strains of other conservative Christians—all grafted on the basic stock of business Republicans.

ACTIVISM OF THE RELIGIOUS RIGHT

If the Christian Right became an organizational force in the 1980s, in the 1990s it became more visible in campaigning: distributing voter guides, mobilizing voters through phone banks and direct mail, and providing activists in primary and general election campaigns.

Campaign Activism

As one might expect, the trajectory of such involvement parallels the rise of the Christian Coalition, created for just such activities. In 1992 the new Coalition began distributing hundreds of thousands of voter guides outlining candidates' positions on important issues, such as abortion, gay rights, and school prayer. The Coalition probably hit its peak in the 1994 GOP gubernatorial primaries, vigorously backing David Beasley by mailing out 100,000 voting guides and distributing 400,000 more through friendly churches. Although only about a third of evangelical churches cooperated, even this involvement was a striking departure from their traditional apolitical stance. In the fall campaign, the Coalition was a major force behind Beasley, distributing voter guides and running extensive phone banks. The broader Christian Right effort was less visible but no less extensive. BJU activists worked hard for Beasley, while smaller groups, such as the Palmetto Family Council and the American Family Association, campaigned in state, county, and school board contests (Guth 1995).

Christian conservatives also mobilized in the 1996 GOP presidential primary but not in one phalanx. The Christian Coalition seemed determined to have a foot in each candidate's tent—or perhaps recognized that members were hopelessly divided. Roberta Combs favored Bob Dole, the choice of national Coalition leader Ralph Reed, as did Governor Beasley, the Coalition's hero. But other members joined the campaigns of Pat Buchanan and Texas senator Phil Gramm. Christian conservatives at a rally in Columbia gave Buchanan's stump speech a rousing ovation, but Dole's emotional defense of his "100 percent" Christian Coalition voting record, antiabortion stance, and heroic life story was a turning point in his appeal for Coalition support (Guth and Smith 1997).

The BJU forces were also divided, but even more frustrated by the campaign's trajectory. BJU leaders initially backed Senator Gramm. Although he antagonized some conservatives by refusing to feature moral issues, he found a warm reception on the BJU campus and among other Christian activists, campaigning with Christian financial adviser and radio celebrity Larry Burkett. The BJU Republicans were left without a candidate, however, when Gramm withdrew after losses in Iowa and New Hampshire. Most then gravitated to Buchanan, whom some had previously supported in his quixotic 1992 primary challenge to President George Bush. Indeed, the "BJU precincts" in Greenville had actually given Buchanan a majority (Guth and Smith 1997).

This fundamentalist enthusiasm for a Catholic was a major development in Christian Right politics. Similar support from Pentecostals created an ironic situation in which activists in each evangelical subtradition backed a Catholic candidate without ever exhibiting similar tolerance for each other. Eventually, Buchanan stitched together a fairly strong religious coalition. His state committee included BJU activists—most notably state representative Terry Haskins, who initially headed the Gramm campaign—as well as some Christian Coalition county leaders, who rejected Combs's dalliance with Dole. Henry Jordan, a veteran of Pat Robertson's 1988 campaign, was a vice-chair of the Buchanan committee, joined by leading antiabortion activists.

Despite the resulting disarray in the primary, the Christian Right united behind Dole in the general election. Several groups distributed voter guides, religious radio stations carried discussions of the campaign, and many conservative clergy quietly backed the Republican ticket (Guth and Smith 1997).

In 1998 Christian Right activists were much involved but, once again, often supported different candidates. This is best illustrated by the race for the fourth congressional district seat being vacated by Representative Bob Inglis. The media-chosen front runner, state senator Mike Fair, was known not only for his heroics as a high school and college quarterback but also for adamant social conservatism. Ralph Reed, in his new guise as independent political consultant, had quickly signed Fair as one of his first clients. Fair also gained the support of the Greenville County Republican convention, many Christian Coalition and Bob Jones activists (he belonged to a BJU-affiliated independent Baptist church), and many conservative Southern Baptists. But Fair's connection with Reed, endorsement by upstate conservative politicians, and plugs from national Christian Right figures such as Gary Bauer failed to enhance his appeal to more moderate voters (Guth 2000).

Several other Republicans challenged Fair, each building his own "religious" constituency. While BJU alumnus Frank Raddish threatened to pull some prolife votes away from Fair on the right, others aligned themselves at varying (but small) distances to his left. The eventual victor, Jim DeMint, a public relations entrepreneur, inherited much of Representative Inglis's organization and implicit endorsement. Although he stressed economic issues attractive to small business, he was acceptable to social conservatives. Like Inglis, he belonged to the evangelical Presbyterian Church in America and drew on PCA activists, but also like his mentor, he was not personally close to the Christian Coalition or BJU. Nevertheless, for many Christian conservatives DeMint was an acceptable second choice, a fact that facilitated his surprise runoff victory against Fair and an easy win in the fall, when he enjoyed unified Christian conservative support.

The Christian Right was just as active in other 1998 races but had less success. The Christian Coalition again provided voter guides and scorecards for state offices and congressional races and mailed an abbreviated postcard voter guide on the gubernatorial and U.S. Senate races, supporting Republican candidates Beasley and Inglis. Social conservative Gary Bauer also weighed in on the Senate race with a radio ad paid for by his Campaign for Working Families, praising Inglis's profamily record (Moore and Vinson 2000). The National Right to Life Committee spent $8,000 on radio spots, newspaper ads, and mailings to stress the prolife records of Beasley and Inglis, an effort bolstered by local prolife groups' phone banks. Nevertheless, the GOP lost both contests. Governor Beasley suffered from perpetual miscues and the infusion of millions of dollars of video poker money into his opponent's campaign, and Inglis fell to a tough incumbent, Senator Fritz Hollings, who reassembled his own personal machine and also benefited from the gambling industry mobilization (Guth 2000).

Despite the electoral failures of 1998 and atrophy of the Christian Coalition, Christian conservatives were still central to the 2000 presidential primary. Knowing the importance of religious conservatives in this critical primary state, George W. Bush carefully cultivated all the major factions. He opened his campaign with a speech at BJU (the reader will recall the furor following his appearance), consulted the Christian Coalition, and used his Texas Baptist confidants to woo Southern Baptists. The Coalition sent out two mailings to 140,000 households, the first encouraging people to vote and the second noting "10 disturbing facts about John McCain," including his positions on fetal tissue research, abortion, and campaign finance reform (Moore and Vinson 2001). Coalition activists also posted signs for Bush and manned phone banks. Indeed, even Pat Robertson got involved, attacking McCain on a Sunday talk show and recording a phone message supporting Bush. Prolife groups also took a very visible role by endorsing Bush, despite the presence of prolife enthusiast Alan Keyes in the race, a decision that rankled some Christian Right leaders, including Cyndi Mosteller, head of the Citizens for Life in Charleston (Moore and Vinson 2001). Nevertheless, the prolife groups spent more than $47,000 on radio ads, aired mostly on Christian stations, and also sent out mailings and made phone calls on Bush's behalf, reinforcing the efforts of the Christian Coalition and his own organization.

Issue Activism

Christian Right activism was visible not only in the electoral battles of the 1990s but also on legislative issues. Governor David Beasley put two such issues on the legislative agenda. The first was his 1996 proposal to remove the Confederate flag from the state capitol dome. Preceded, the governor said, by "much prayer," his action divided the religious community but not entirely along expected lines. For several weeks, hundreds of clergy faced off, expressing themselves through marches, full-page newspaper advertisements, lengthy position papers, and well-scripted news conferences. Predictably, most mainline Protestant, Catholic, and Jewish religious leaders joined African American clergy in supporting Beasley's plan. More surprisingly, many conservative Southern Baptists, Pentecostals, and charismatics also stood behind Beasley, organized by Dick Lincoln, the governor's own pastor and a leader of the conservative wing of the state Baptist Convention (Guth 2000).

Other conservative clergy rejected the governor's proposal, however, warning that he was threatening religious support for his reelection in 1998 and wasting precious political capital that could be used on vital moral issues. Indeed, the state Baptist Convention was hopelessly divided, merely publishing opposing views in the Baptist Courier. Although polls showed a slight plurality of citizens favoring his plan, the governor's campaign failed. After protracted legislative maneuvering, Beasley despaired of finding an acceptable solution and gave up, promising not to raise the flag issue again (Guth 2000).

The second issue was Beasley's proposal in 1998 to ban video poker, soon transformed into a larger debate over gambling. Legislators reported strong pressure from antigambling activists, drawn from both mainline and evangelical Protestant communions, as well as from social service groups alarmed by the social ills wrought by video poker "addiction." Christian Right activists supplemented legislative lobbying by litigation, harassing local proprietors with suits alleging violations of various state laws or local ordinances. When in 1999 it appeared that video poker would finally be put to a vote in a November referendum, pastors and churches across the state began to mobilize their congregations, providing yard signs and buttons with the slogan "Vote No" and registering parishioners to vote. According to the polls, antigambling forces were gaining momentum until a state court ruling against both the referendum and video poker rendered the issue moot (Guth 2000).

Christian conservatives barely had time to celebrate this unexpected victory when they had to shift their attention to another gambling issue, a state-sponsored lottery. Democrat Jim Hodges had upset Beasley in the 1998 gubernatorial race by promising to raise new funds for education through a state lottery, but this required a state constitutional amendment. Despite resistance from religious groups, the legislature scheduled the required referendum to coincide with the 2000 general election. Every Christian Right organization mobilized behind the "Vote No" campaign, joined not only by the state Baptist Convention but also by virtually every African American and mainline Protestant group. Despite this apparent united front, the Christian Right groups and Baptists provided the bulk of the labor, funds, and organization in a losing cause.

INFLUENCE OF THE CHRISTIAN RIGHT

As the reader should surmise by this point, the Christian Right in South Carolina has become a significant force within the GOP. In addition, Christian Right groups have often been engaged in both electoral and legislative activities, although the clear emphasis has been on the former. In this section, we consider critical episodes that reveal both the extent and the limits of Christian Right influence over Republican nominations, electoral outcomes, and important social issues.

Influence on Nominations

First, the Christian conservatives have become important players in state and national GOP nomination contests. The 1994 gubernatorial primary—a three-way race among David Beasley, Arthur Ravenel, and Tommy Hartnett—shows that support from religious conservatives is critical for Republican candidates. Like Beasley, both Ravenel and Hartnett were Democratic converts and had earlier enjoyed Christian Right support, but in this race religion itself became a major dividing line. Beasley carefully cultivated all Christian Right factions, including the Coalition's Pentecostals and charismatics, the BJU crowd, and his own Southern Baptists, while soliciting support from GOP regulars. The folksy Ravenel, of aristocratic French Huguenot heritage, positioned himself as the anti-Christian Right candidate; meanwhile, Hartnett complained that his Catholicism was an electoral disadvantage in this overwhelmingly Protestant state. In the first primary, Beasley garnered 47 percent of the vote to Ravenel's 32 percent and Hartnett's 21 percent. And although Ravenel appealed to regular Republicans in the runoff by attacking Beasley's religious allies, this proved unsuccessful as Beasley took 58 percent of the vote (Guth 1995). Beasley's totals were highest in strong Southern Baptist and Pentecostal counties, while Ravenel retained his mainline constituency from the first primary.

Candidates' "religious strategies" were critical in both the 1996 and 2000 presidential primaries. Although in 1996 Pat Buchanan won 44 percent to Bob Dole's 40 percent among the religious right in the Voter News Service (VNS) exit poll in South Carolina, Dole's strong showing among these voters, his bigger margin among other conservative Christians, and a huge majority among regulars produced a decisive 45 percent to 29 percent victory (Guth and Smith 1997). And if any doubt remained about the electoral clout of conservative Christians, the 2000 Republican presidential primary erased them. Although both George W. Bush and John McCain initially wooed religious conservatives, the Bush campaign quickly sought to divide McCain and the Christian Right (Moore and Vinson 2001). The tactic worked well: Bush won 68 percent of voters calling themselves part of the religious right. Combined with support from other Republicans, that showing was more than enough to overcome McCain's huge margin among crossover independents and Democrats.

Let's be clear: the Christian Right does not "control" GOP nominations. A conservative religious appeal is a major advantage to candidates, but too strong an identification with the hard-core Christian Right is a liability, as self-conscious religious conservatives make up only 35 percent to 40 percent of GOP voters. Thus, while Beasley won the 1994 gubernatorial primary with conservative Christian assistance, "pure" Christian Right candidates lost other GOP contests for lieutenant governor, superintendent of education, and a congressional seat. Still, pure "business" Republicans usually fare no better than Christian Right types. Winning GOP nominations now requires both "economic" Republicans and social issue conservatives (Guth 1995).

Unity in November

In addition to their influence over Republican nominations, religious conservatives' willingness to unite behind GOP candidates has certainly enhanced Republican strength in most general election contests. Soon after its formation, Christian Coalition activists helped George Bush carry the state in the 1992 presidential race and assisted challenger Bob Inglis in his stunning upset of incumbent Congresswoman Liz Patterson, a Methodist. Although some observers (including Patterson) emphasized the Coalition's role, Inglis's impressive grassroots campaign owed more to activists from local PCA churches and the rock-solid support (if not affection) of the large BJU constituency.

In 1994 David Beasley won the governorship with 51 percent of the vote to Democrat Nick Theodore's 48 percent, benefiting from a united Christian conservative effort. Although the BJU fundamentalists, the Christian Coalition, and Southern Baptists might not worship together, they certainly combined behind the Republican ticket. Of the 20 percent of white voters who said they were part of the religious right in the VNS exit poll, 80 percent voted for Beasley (and other Republican candidates). He won equally strong support from "family values" voters and those who said that religion influenced their vote. Overall, Beasley won 70 percent of white born-again Christians, still a majority of the state's population. Although he fared slightly less well among mainliners, he still drew solid support from establishment Republicans. Like other successful Republicans, Beasley carried the high-income Greenville-Spartanburg, Columbia, and Charleston areas, but after one controls for that "economic vote," he did best in areas replete with Southern Baptists and Pentecostals (Guth 1995).

The Christian Right also helped to give the GOP a majority in the state house of representatives (after several conservative Democrats converted), and left the party in a workable position in the senate, still in Democratic hands. This solid Christian Right support coalesced again in the 1996 and 2000 statewide races, allowing presidential candidates Dole and Bush to carry the state comfortably, returning Senator Strom Thurmond to Washington, and keeping the state's four Republican House members safely ensconced. In both years, exit polls showed that at least 75 percent of white evangelical Protestants voted Republican for statewide contests and in U.S. House races. Christian Right activists no doubt played at least some role in making the GOP the state's leading party.

Influencing the Political Agenda

The critical role played by Christian conservatives in GOP nominating contests and in general elections has influenced the political agenda: in the new regime, Republican candidates invariably woo religious activists and voters. In 1994, for example, Beasley emphasized family values and crime, advocated tax cuts, opposed a state lottery (a hot-button issue for religious conservatives), supported educational vouchers, and took a cautiously prolife stance. His Democratic opponent took the other side on each issue and condemned Beasley's ties to the "extremist" Coalition. Thus, most issues dominating the campaign had strong religious overtones. The Christian Right's influence persisted through the early days of the new administration as Beasley moved quickly to shore up his religious base. He used religious rhetoric in public pronouncements, put some moral issues on the agenda, and appointed several outspoken Christian activists, including BJU, Christian Coalition, and Southern Baptist adherents.

Trying to build on these inroads, conservative Christian activists sought to put several new issues on the political agenda. Gay rights became prominent as never before when the Greenville County Council condemned gay lifestyles in 1996, eliciting an outpouring of protest from liberals and a boycott of the area by the committee organizing the transit of the Olympic torch to the Atlanta games. The legislature also passed the Defense of Marriage Act, signed by Governor Beasley, a legislative priority of the Christian Right groups, especially the American Family Association and Palmetto Family Council. In addition, other state and local policies, ranging from the Beasley administration's new regulations on abortion clinics to ending of free condom distribution by the state department of health to local ordinances and state laws regulating adult entertainment, reflected the influence of the Christian Right. In addition, in February 1997, the state house overwhelmingly passed Governor Beasley's "partial-birth abortion" prohibition, ensuring a confrontation with the federal courts. Although not all of these measures had much real impact on public policy, they represented considerable symbolic change (Guth and Smith 1997).

Even the agendas of presidential candidates have been shaped by the importance of Christian conservatives, given the repeated make-or-break impact of the South Carolina GOP primary. In 1996 Pat Buchanan's challenge to front-runner Bob Dole was based largely on "family issues," along with protectionist trade policy. To counter, Dole employed phone banks targeting Christian conservatives with his conservative voting record on abortion and other moral issues. Henry Hyde, the Illinois Republican congressman whose name is synonymous with antiabortion legislation, lobbied prolife groups on Dole's behalf. Elizabeth Dole, herself an evangelical Christian from neighboring North Carolina, canvassed the state addressing religious issues in explicit ways her husband usually avoided.

Four years later, candidates George W. Bush, John McCain, and Alan Keyes all emphasized issues of character and morality. Meanwhile, the Christian Coalition and right-to-life groups joined Bush and Keyes in emphasizing prolife issues. Taking a cue from Dole's 1996 campaign, Bush used a recorded phone message from Representative Hyde reminding people that Bush was prolife and that "defenseless lives" depended on their vote. In his campaign literature, Bush also took education stances favored by the Christian Right, proclaiming support for charter schools and school vouchers. Even McCain initially sought Christian Right support but soon decided that the effort was futile. Instead he attacked Bush for being too close to "intolerant" and "anti-Catholic" religious conservatives, especially at BJU (Moore and Vinson 2001).

In addition to candidates taking up the Christian Right's agenda, state officeholders have generally supported movement goals. Among Republicans in the state's congressional delegation, for example, Christian Coalition roll-call vote scores in 2000 ranged from 87 percent to 100 percent (Barone and Cohen 2001). And though the Coalition did not score them very high (23 percent to 40 percent), two of the state's three Democrats in Congress did vote for the ban on partial-birth abortions.

Limits on the Christian Right's Influence

Despite some electoral victories and successes in agenda setting, the Christian Right is by no means invincible. Its influence has been limited by two factors. On occasion, foes with more resources and more effective mobilization have posed challenges. Most such groups have worked through the framework of the Democratic Party as demonstrated below by the progambling forces in 1998. At other times, Christian Right activists have been their own worst enemies, fighting among themselves. Recent elections have illustrated both weaknesses—which sometimes appear simultaneously.

While the Christian Right enjoyed some success in the 1996 election, not all of its candidates and issues were triumphant, as mixed results came in from local races. One of the most closely watched involved the school board in Greenville County, which had been dominated by a coalition of conservative Christian activists since the high point of the 1994 Christian Right sweep. Countermobilization by opponents was successful, however, and three conservative board members were unseated, along with one of their board opponents, moving the board back to the right-center. Similar patterns appeared in school board elections in other metropolitan areas. Since 1996 Christian conservatives have been unable to stage a comeback. Once local elections became high-visibility affairs, the tight organization and high mobilization of Christian Right activists were offset by larger turnouts of more centrist voters.

In the same vein, superior funding and mobilization by opponents in the 1998 general election stymied both the GOP and the Christian Right. Incumbent governor David Beasley, as well as the Republican candidates for U.S. Senate and state superintendent of education, all lost, while Democrats reduced the GOP margin in the state house of representatives and added slightly to their own narrow edge in the senate. Because the gubernatorial candidates had made the election a referendum on video poker and a state lottery, video poker interests expended much money and manpower on defeating Beasley. On election day, thousands of convenience store owners and employees whose establishments benefited from business brought in by poker machines worked phones and neighborhoods to get people to the polls to vote Democratic. In addition, despite the often tense relations between Democratic leaders and black voters, both Hodges and Hollings sought to activate black religious leaders, with frequent campaign stops in black churches and assiduous attention to clergy. Even African American pastors strongly opposed to gambling—a significant number—regarded education, civil rights, and welfare programs as more important. Seldom in recent campaigns have African American churches been as visible as in 1998 (Guth 2000).

In addition to the obstacles posed by the mobilization and resources of its opponents, the Christian Right faces internal divisions that often weaken its influence. As we have seen, religious conservatives have often been unable to reach a consensus on the candidates in GOP primaries for statewide and congressional races. Sometimes these disagreements have reflected the distinct religious elements in the Christian Right, with fundamentalists, Pentecostals, and Southern Baptists preferring different candidates. At other times the split support has probably been consciously designed to assure access to the winner. Of course, some disagreements reflect differing assessments of the candidates' character, stances on important issues, and electability, while others may stem from the natural intractability of Christian activists, nurtured by the individualistic milieu of independent fundamentalist, Pentecostal, or charismatic churches.

Beyond such fractures, the movement is still split between hard-line and more moderate elements, exemplified by the 1998 Republican primary for superintendent of education. Christian Coalition factions backed different candidates. Moderate activists, led by state chair Roberta Combs, supported Governor Beasley's chosen candidate, David Eckstrom, while the "purist" wing supported businessman Jim White. Eckstrom defeated White handily in the primary, 53 percent to 21 percent, with still another conservative candidate drawing 14 percent. Despite the solid victory, the campaign left divisions within both the GOP and the Christian Right (Guth 2000). Such differences appeared again in the 2000 Republican primaries; indeed, both Christian Coalition and BJU activists seemed to be scattered all over the political landscape, as were more mainstream Southern Baptist and PCA politicos.

These internal divisions have sometimes carried over into general elections, diminishing Christian Right enthusiasm for GOP nominees and reducing the movement's electoral impact. Again, 1998 is instructive. Christian Right activists seem to have been dispirited by the internal factionalism described above. In addition, few responded favorably to their national leadership's effort to make Clinton's immoral behavior the focus of the campaign, instead of the core items on the Christian Right agenda. In addition, dissatisfaction with Republican Governor David Beasley's policies on abortion, law enforcement, and education (he had not pushed vouchers and school prayer with enough zeal) had also increased the sniping by hard-liners. Such dynamics within the movement, combined with the extraordinary Democratic mobilization in 1998, ensured a GOP defeat (Guth 2000).

Even the "unifying" moral issues have divided religious conservatives on occasion. The centrality of gambling and the debate over video poker in the 1998 election illustrate this problem. While Christian Right forces universally opposed gambling, they often fought over the best way to oppose it. First, the issue became so enmeshed in the partisan campaign that some conservative pastors felt uncomfortable attacking gambling because that was tantamount to endorsing the GOP. Even the strongest Republican clergy tried to separate their opposition to gambling from partisan choices. One widely publicized election-eve statement issued by 200 South Carolina Baptist ministers cautioned that they "did not intend to lift up or put down any political candidates" (Guth 2000). In addition, many Christian Right pastors refrained from action because some working-class members were also video poker aficionados. Finally, some Christian Right leaders saw gambling as a mere distraction from vital questions such as abortion. Thus, the potential impact of religious activism was blunted.

In the end, despite ubiquitous church signs deprecating gambling, the customary Christian Coalition voter guide distribution, and some use of phone banks, the modest religious counterorganization failed to bolster the GOP in 1998. Ironically, *after* the election both church bodies and pastors were more outspoken about gambling, preparing for the legislative lobbying and referendum contests soon to follow (Guth 2000), and polls suggest they would have succeeded had the state supreme court not settled the issue. When gambling was given a different rationale, however—to fund public education through a state lottery—another massive mobilization of religious conservatives was not enough. Confronting a coalition of small businesses, advertising agencies, education groups, and the Democratic Party, they lost the 2000 statewide referendum by a 54 percent to 46 percent margin (Olson, Guth, and Guth 2001).

CONCLUSIONS

The Christian Right's three-decade history in South Carolina has revealed some clear patterns. Though they do not dominate party functions, Christian activists are a major force within the GOP, especially in nominating contests, and are an essential part of a winning coalition, both for GOP nominations and for Republican victory in general elections. Christian conservatives have given moral and family values issues a higher visibility; no Republican candidate (and probably few Democrats) can avoid these issues entirely. Still, concrete policy changes resulting from these agenda victories have been modest, and sometimes temporary. Nevertheless, the Christian Right remains a force to be reckoned with. Although the Christian Coalition now seems moribund, conservative Christian activists of many stripes are firmly embedded in the state's politics, holding both GOP leadership posts and public office.

The successful institutionalization of the Christian Right within the state GOP was epitomized by the spring 2002 Republican gubernatorial primary. Although no Christian Right group explicitly endorsed any of the seven candidates, all the candidates vigorously sought conservative Christian support. They *all* emphasized the role that faith plays in their lives, their faithful church attendance, and their leadership roles as Sunday school teachers or elders—or, in one case, as minister in training. Even the Episcopalian candidate ran TV ads highlighting his Christian values and discussed his faith in press interviews. And all the candidates scrambled to pick up the endorsements of prominent Christian conservatives.

Despite success within the GOP, Christian conservatives still confront limitations on their influence. Although the state's economic modernization continually fosters the growth that often produces Christian Right sentiments among first-generation suburbanites, that process has also led to much religious diversification. Growing numbers of Catholics, Jews, and other religious minorities, as well as secular citizens, have bolstered the ranks of potential opponents, who naturally gravitate toward the Democrats. The recent adoption of a state lottery and the ending of various blue law restrictions in metropolitan areas are just two harbingers of the declining conservative Protestant cultural dominance. Even within the GOP, Christian Right politicos will have to build new kinds of alliances. How well Christian Right activists adapt to this changing religious environment will determine the future of Christian Right politics in South Carolina.

ACKNOWLEDGMENTS

Although this analysis derives in part from "participant observation," many observers have supplied us with essential information and perspectives. Dan Hoover and Jim Hammond of the *Greenville News* and Lee Bandy of the *Columbia State* are cited in much detail in our earlier analyses, which we draw on here (Guth 1995, 2000; Guth and Smith 1997). Congressmen Bob Inglis and Jim DeMint, Lieutenant Governor Nick Theodore, state representative Sara Manly, and former secretary of education Dick Riley have also been especially helpful. Guth also thanks several former students: Greenville County Democratic chair Johnnie Fulton, Beasley cabinet member Lewis Gossett, and former state Democratic chair Frank Holloman. Our colleague Brent Nelsen has provided the useful insights of a Republican activist and academic. Vinson thanks the many anonymous informants who assisted her research on the 1998 and 2000 campaigns, part of David Magleby's national study of campaign dynamics. Both authors also express gratitude to the Pew Charitable Trusts, who have supported this work both directly and indirectly.

REFERENCES

Barone, Michael, and Richard E. Cohen. 2001. *The Almanac of American Politics 2002*. Washington, D.C.: The National Journal.

Bradley, Martin, Norman M. Green, Jr., Dale E. Jones, Mac Lynn, and Lou McNeil. 1992. *Churches and Church Membership in the United States, 1990.* Atlanta, Ga.: Glenmary Research Center.

Conger, Kimberly H., and John C. Green. 2002. "Spreading Out and Digging In: Christian Conservatives and State Republican Parties." *Campaigns and Elections* (February):58–64.

Ehrenhalt, Alan. 1991. *The United States of Ambition.* New York: Random House.

Elazar, Daniel J. 1966. *American Federalism: A View from the States.* New York: Thomas Y. Crowell.

Graham, Cole Blease, Jr., William V. Moore, and Frank T. Petrusak. 1994. "Praise the Lord and Join the Republicans." Paper presented at the annual meeting of the Western Political Science Association, Albuquerque, N. M., March.

Guth, James L. 1995. "South Carolina: The Christian Right Wins One." Pp. 133–45 in *God at the Grass Roots: The Christian Right in the 1994 Elections,* ed. Mark J. Rozell and Clyde Wilcox. Lanham, Md.: Rowman and Little-field.

———. 2000. "South Carolina: Even in Zion the Heathen Rage." Pp. 21–40 in *Prayers in the Precincts: The Christian Right in the 1998 Elections,* ed. John C. Green, Mark J. Rozell, and Clyde Wilcox. Washington, D.C.: Georgetown University Press.

Guth, James L., and Oran P. Smith. 1997. "South Carolina Christian Right: Just Part of the Family Now?" Pp. 15–31 in *God at the Grass Roots, 1996: The Christian Right in the 1996 Elections,* ed. Mark J. Rozell and Clyde Wilcox. Lanham, Md.: Rowman and Littlefield.

Moore, William V., and C. Danielle Vinson. 2000. "South Carolina Senate Race." Pp. 93–109 in *Outside Money,* ed. David Magleby. Lanham, Md.: Rowman and Littlefield.

———. 2001. "Issue Advocacy Groups and Money in the South Carolina Presidential Primary." *Journal of Political Science* 29:49–69.

Olson, Laura R., Karen V. Guth, and James L. Guth. 2001. "The Lotto and the Lord." Paper presented at the annual meeting of the Association for the Sociology of Religion, Anaheim, Calif., 17–19 August.

Smith, Oran P. 1997. *The Rise of Baptist Republicanism.* New York: New York University Press.

TWO

Virginia: Birthplace
of the Christian Right

Mark J. Rozell and Clyde Wilcox

IN VIRGINIA, THE CHRISTIAN RIGHT HAS EVOLVED FROM A MAR-
ginal player in the state's once small Republican party to a major faction
in a party that now has firm control of the state legislature and has
largely dominated statewide elections since the 1990s. The movement
has developed from a small cadre of uncompromising activists into a
strong but deeply divisive faction in the Republican ranks, and finally
into a skilled and successful partner in the GOP coalition. The Christian Right played an important, though not necessarily decisive, role in
the rapid growth of the party in the state.

In many ways Virginia is the birthplace of the Christian Right. In
the late 1970s Jerry Falwell built the Moral Majority on the foundation
of a successful evangelical mobilization against pari-mutuel betting, and
Pat Robertson's Christian Coalition was initially headquartered in Virginia as well. Other prominent figures in and around the movement live
in Virginia, including fund-raiser Richard Vigurie, Morton Blackwell,
Paul Weyrich, Michael Farris, Cal Thomas, and Ralph Reed made the
state his home during his years at the Christian Coalition. Yet despite
the movement's long history in the state and the large pool of leaders
and supporters, the policy successes of the Christian Right in Virginia
remain modest.

THE CONTEXT

In his seminal *Southern Politics in State and Nation* in 1949, V. O. Key,
Jr., described Virginia as a "political museum piece." He wrote: "Of all

the American states, Virginia can lay claim to the most thorough control by an oligarchy" (Key 1949, 19). Daniel J. Elazar later echoed this sentiment when he described Virginia's political culture as "traditionalistic," in the sense that there was a strong impetus toward hierarchy, tradition, and authority. Elazar described the Northern Virginia suburbs as more "individualist" and less moralistic than other parts of the state, and that sentiment would certainly be even more true today than when he penned his classic study of federalism (Elazar 1972, 1178).

For decades, the Democratic political machine of Harry F. Byrd dominated Virginia politics. Byrd served as governor from 1926 to 1930 and as U.S. senator from 1933 until he retired in 1965. He assembled his machine from the county courthouse organizations of the landed gentry, who preferred stability to economic growth and were fiercely committed to racial segregation. This elite sought to limit political participation by holding its gubernatorial and other statewide elections in odd-numbered years, a practice that continues to this day. This fact has allowed the Christian Right (and other highly mobilized groups) to play a disproportionate role in elections.

Another remnant of the Byrd machine is the system of no formal party registration. This restriction suited the Byrd machine's objectives during the era of single-party dominance of state politics. Today it means that in those rare cases in which Republicans nominate their candidates by political primaries, all registered voters may participate. The Republicans have more frequently nominated their statewide ticket at large statewide conventions that allowed any citizen to participate who was willing to pledge to support the party nominees. Although these conventions were often huge events—in 2001 more than 10,000 delegates attended the convention—this system made it especially easy for the Christian Right to exert intraparty influence, since a few thousand delegates could easily tip the balance. Ralph Reed said "the caucus-convention nominating process in the [Virginia] Republican Party is unusual in that it does tend to give [our] grassroots activists a greater voice than they have in primaries" (Reed 1994).

Yet the Christian Right has also sometimes prevailed in party primaries. In 1989, the GOP gubernatorial primary favored the most conservative candidate, who won with less than 37 percent of the low-turnout vote in a three-way race. In 1996 the primary for U.S. Senate heavily favored the more moderate candidate in a two-way contest that featured a candidate backed by the Christian Right. In 1997, a Christian conservative candidate won nomination for attorney general in a very low-turnout, multicandidate primary race.

The evidence is nonetheless clear that Christian Right influence on Republican nomination politics has often hurt the party in general elections. The urban corridor that includes the D.C. suburbs has a majority of the state's population, and the Northern Virginia suburbs in particular are distinctive in their affluence, their high levels of education, their relatively low levels of religious involvement, their social liberalism, and their many Republican voters. Many of these Republican voters are unwilling to support candidates strongly identified with the Christian Right and have defected in large numbers to moderate Democrats and even an independent candidate in some recent elections.

Virginia is a heavily Protestant state, full of Baptist and Methodist churches, and in much of Virginia these churches are theologically conservative, regardless of denomination. Surveys show that nearly half the state's residents profess an affiliation with an evangelical denomination and that more than 10 percent identify as fundamentalists. More than 40 percent of likely voters indicate that they believe that the Bible is literally true. The Northern Virginia area has a sizable number of Catholics in what is perhaps the most conservative diocese in the country, and a growing number of non–Judeo-Christian immigrants. Overall, white evangelical Protestants, the core constituency of the Christian Right, comprise about 25 percent of the Virginia population. White mainline Protestants comprise 18 percent; black Protestants, 18 percent; seculars, 17 percent; and Catholics, 14 percent. Various other religious affiliations, including Jews and Muslims, comprise the remaining 8 percent of the Virginia population.[1] In the 2000 election, 17 percent of Virginia voters identified as part of the "white religious right," and 82 percent of them supported George W. Bush for president. Not surprisingly, these voters also heavily identified with the Republican Party (62 percent).[2]

During the 1970s and early 1980s, Virginia was home to the Moral Majority, a Christian Right organization based in the Bible Baptist Fellowship, which was centered mainly in the fundamentalist right. Reverend Jerry Falwell, former head of the Moral Majority, lives in Lynchburg, and his huge congregation is a major institution in that region of the state. The Moral Majority was more active in Virginia than in most other states, and its presence was visible at state nominating conventions. The group was also somewhat involved in policy advocacy, although its statewide lobbying effort was never very sophisticated, and it faced a large Democratic majority in the legislature.

In 1989, Marion G. (Pat) Robertson built the Christian Coalition from his failed presidential campaign. Robertson and Falwell were longtime rivals in religion and in politics, and many of the fundamentalists of the former Moral Majority did not become involved in the Pentecostal- and charismatic-oriented Coalition. The Christian Coalition focused its efforts primarily on electoral politics, where it could count on the votes if not the membership of Falwell's fundamentalist supporters. As is true elsewhere, the Christian Coalition in Virginia declined rapidly in the latter half of the 1990s. Where once there were active county chapters throughout the state, in recent years the group has struggled to retain a state chair, a position that has turned over frequently. But as elsewhere, the organization continues to distribute voter guides through its network of activists, albeit in reduced numbers.

The most active and effective group in policy advocacy has been the Family Foundation, which affiliated itself with Focus on the Family. The organization has retained at least one statewide lobbyist for more than fifteen years, and several of its leaders have served in Republican gubernatorial administrations. The organization is involved in elections and has produced both voter guides and incumbent scorecards, but its distinctive niche has been its statewide lobbying.

Among the other social conservative groups that have been active in the state are Concerned Women for America, the Virginia Society for Human Life, and the Madison Project. Home schooling advocacy groups have also been active parts of coalitions of conservative groups on a variety of social issues. Leaders of the various social conservative organizations in the state confer frequently and have effective means for reaching their many group members on matters of policy interest or to help mobilize potential voters.

These groups operate in an ecology that includes few strong opposition groups. Unions are weak in Virginia: many of the state's coal miners, unlike those in neighboring West Virginia, work in nonunion mines, and those who do belong to the union are generally socially conservative. Although the high level of education in the Northern Virginia suburbs creates support for gender equality and abortion rights, feminist groups also are not strong in the state. The state has a sizable African American population, though not as large as that in other southern states, which reliably supports Democratic candidates. In general, liberal interest groups have very little presence or influence in Virginia politics. By contrast, Virginia is one of the states defined in *Campaigns and Elections* as having a "strong" Christian Right influence (Conger and Green 2002).

The state is also a stronghold of the National Rifle Association (NRA). Many Virginians are hunters, and even in the state's northern suburbs many citizens have lined up to apply for permits to carry concealed weapons. The power of the NRA is evidenced both in the policy debates that sometimes occur (whether concealed weapons can be carried into bars and public recreation centers), and in the policy itself (the state's law banning carrying guns near school property allows for an exception for hunters). In most but not all cases the NRA and the Christian Right have worked in tandem to help GOP candidates—indeed, Chuck Cunningham was first an NRA electoral activist, then headed the Christian Coalition voter guide efforts, and is now back at the NRA working on legislative affairs. Yet the libertarian bent of some NRA members produces some policy divisions with conservative Christians, especially on abortion (Rozell and Wilcox 1996).

MODERN VIRGINIA ELECTIONS AND THE CHRISTIAN RIGHT

The Christian Right has been active in Virginia elections since the late 1970s, with increasing sophistication over time. In 1978, conservative Christians attended the state Democratic nominating convention to support G. Conoly Phillips, a Virginia Beach car dealer who said that God had called him to run for the U.S. Senate. Phillips expressed surprise that the call had even specified the Democratic Party, for he would have preferred to run as an independent. Campaign mentor Pat Robertson, the son of a former Democratic U.S. senator, also urged that choice. Phillips called his campaign "a ministry unto the Lord" and his campaign headquarters a "prayer room" (Rozell and Wilcox 1996). His strength in a losing cause surprised many observers and presumably helped alert elites to the potential power of evangelical voters. A smaller number of Christian conservatives participated in the GOP nominating convention, backing the eventual nominee, former state party chair Richard Obenshain. Conservative Christians rallied to Obenshain's campaign until he died in a plane crash. The party selected John Warner as a replacement candidate, and he won and remains in the Senate today.

The Republican realignment took on metaphysical overtones in the 1980s, as the Christian Right moved into the GOP. In 1981 the Moral Majority helped to mobilize some seven hundred delegates to the state GOP nominating convention, primarily to support lieutenant governor candidate Guy Farley, a former Byrd Democrat turned born-again Republican. Farley lost a bitter nomination fight in which opponents characterized him as a Christian Right extremist. But Falwell openly endorsed the Republican ticket, headed by Attorney General J. Marshall Coleman, and this endorsement became the centerpiece of the Democratic campaign. In what was to become the standard Democratic tactic for many years, moderate Democratic candidate Charles S. Robb attacked the GOP ticket as being too closely linked with the unpopular Falwell. The Democrats swept all three statewide races.

In 1985, Christian conservatives mobilized behind the gubernatorial candidacy of Wyatt B. Durette, a prolife leader who advocated a constitutional amendment to ban abortion, even in cases of rape and incest, and an amendment to allow spoken nondenominational prayers in the classroom. Christian Right supporters pressed Durette even further to the right, and he eventually advocated the mandatory teaching of creationism in public schools. Falwell again endorsed the GOP ticket, the Democrats again made this a central issue in the campaign, and the Democrats again swept all three statewide offices.

In 1988, Pat Robertson's presidential campaign did poorly in the state primary but well in the local and congressional caucuses that selected delegates to the national convention. Because the state party central committee is selected out of those caucuses and the resultant state convention, Christian conservatives gained a strong foothold in the party apparatus and helped select a Christian conservative as party chair.

In 1989, the GOP experimented with a party primary, its first since 1949. Former attorney general Coleman ran as the most conservative candidate on abortion and won the gubernatorial nomination in a close three-way contest. After the primary the U.S. Supreme Court handed down the controversial *Webster* decision, which allowed states to impose some limits on abortion. That decision rallied prochoice voters, and Coleman scrambled toward the middle on abortion in a general election race that centered on that issue (Cook, Jelen, and Wilcox 1994). Large numbers of moderate Republicans defected to support Democratic nominee L. Douglas Wilder, who became the nation's first elected black governor.

By 1993 Christian conservatives had a strong foothold in the party. The state GOP chair, Patrick McSweeney, had won office by appealing to the Christian Right, and our survey of the state central committee showed that about one-third of its members were strong supporters of Christian Right organizations and issues (Rozell and Wilcox 1996). The statewide nominating convention selected Michael Farris, a former Washington state Moral Majority executive director, a former attorney for Concerned

Women for America, and then head of a legal defense organization for home-schooling families, to be the GOP candidate for lieutenant governor. At the top of the ticket was former U.S. Representative George Allen, who appealed to Christian Right activists with promises to push hard for parental notification on abortion, support for charter schools, and rollbacks in the state's Family Life Education program.

Yet unlike Republican nominees in earlier contests, Allen did not stress his socially conservative views in the general election campaign. Rather, his campaign centered on traditional GOP issues such as tax cuts and crime, and he sought to portray himself as a moderate on abortion. By 1993, more pragmatic activists such as Ralph Reed of the Christian Coalition and Walter Barbee of the Family Foundation were leading the movement, and they worked hard to keep their followers from demanding that Allen move right on abortion. Farris's controversial pronouncements on public schools, public inoculation programs, and other topics dominated the statewide media, allowing Allen to appear quite moderate compared with his running mate. Allen won in a landslide, as did the GOP attorney general candidate James Gilmore, but Farris lost, running an extraordinary twelve percentage points behind the top of his ticket.

In a major switch in movement tactics, the Christian Right (especially the Christian Coalition) was more supportive of Allen and Gilmore than of Farris. The movement was self-consciously focusing on working for candidates who could actually win an election and who would appear nonthreatening. The 1993 elections marked another departure, for although the Democratic candidates again campaigned by linking the GOP ticket to Falwell and Robertson, this tactic was successful only against Farris because of his past record of Christian Right leadership and some controversial writings and statements in speeches.

In what was to signal a bitter intraparty feud, incumbent GOP Senator John Warner refused to endorse Farris, although he campaigned for the rest of the GOP ticket. In 1994, this split widened as Warner not only refused to endorse GOP nominee Oliver North but also recruited former GOP candidate Marshall Coleman (now running as a social moderate) to run against North as an independent. North had long been a popular speaker and effective fund-raiser for the Christian Right in Virginia, and he had the enthusiastic support of the Christian Coalition, which reportedly coordinated its voter guide with the campaign and allowed the campaign to use its membership and activist lists. North defeated conservative Jim Miller for the nomination in a convention

with strong Christian Right participation. Despite this strong movement support, and despite a nationwide tidal wave for the GOP, North
lost to a weak incumbent who was tainted with a sex scandal. As before,
the Democratic candidate linked North to Falwell and Robertson, but
many Republicans also opposed North because of his role in the Iran-
Contra scandal.

By now the state GOP was deeply divided. Our surveys of delegates
to GOP statewide nominating conventions showed moderates rating
North and Farris quite poorly, and Christian conservatives equally negative toward Warner—indeed, many found that a score of o degrees on
a feeling thermometer was insufficiently low, and penciled in negative
numbers. The state party chair, a Christian conservative, unsuccessfully
lobbied Senate GOP party leaders to strip Warner of his membership
on the defense committee, a major source of jobs and pork for Virginia.
Jim Miller, who in 1994 had been the candidate of the moderates
against North, decided to run in 1996 as the candidate of the Christian
Right against Warner in the primary. Had Warner been forced to run
in a party convention, he would clearly have lost, but state law allowed
him to choose a primary. The Virginia GOP challenged the constitu-
tionality of the state law in federal court, but a federal judge tossed the
case out.

Ten days before the primary, the state GOP held its convention,
endorsing Miller by a three-to-one margin in a straw poll and electing a
Christian conservative as state party chair. The most dramatic moment
of the convention came when Oliver North addressed the delegates and
urged them to get behind the candidacy of his former opponent. He
asked that each delegate pledge twenty dollars to Miller's campaign and
actively work to identify and urge similar help from every 1994 North
supporter. North mailed a plea to 16,500 supporters asking for their
assistance for Miller's campaign. Despite these efforts, Warner won the
primary handily with 66 percent of the vote, in part because of crossover
voting from Democrats and Independents. Perhaps the most apt comment after the primary came from former state GOP spokesman Mike
Salster, who said that the Christian Right had been "spoiling for this fight
for three years. . . . Now they have found their base, and it is 34 percent,
not 50.1 percent" (Rozell and Wilcox 1997).

In a remarkable display of pragmatism, Christian conservatives then
rallied behind Warner in a tough general election fight against Democrat Mark Warner (no relation). The 1996 exit polls showed that the
Christian Right turned out, that they overwhelmingly voted for John

Warner, and that they contributed 30 percent of his overall vote. The clearest example of this pragmatism was the activity of the Christian Coalition. Although a January 1996 Christian Coalition scorecard gave the senator a 100 percent voting record for 1995, in June 1996 during the GOP primary the group's voter guide gave him a 20 percent rating (Miller received 100 percent). After the primary, however, a new Coalition guide gave the senator an 83 percent rating. The organization used different issues for its primary election and general election voter guides for the senate race, allowing it to portray Warner first negatively and then positively. In the statewide congressional races, the Coalition used the same issues for both elections.

An Associated Press survey of the Virginia delegates to the Republican National Convention in 1996 showed the continued strength of the Christian Right in the state party. Of the fifty-two delegates, forty-eight responded to the survey. Among those, twenty-one responded that they considered themselves a part of the Christian social conservative movement, nineteen said "no," and eight chose "no answer." Among those who chose "no answer" were delegates Pat Robertson and Ralph Reed (Rozell and Wilcox 1997). The delegation also included Farris, former National Right to Life spokesperson Kay Coles James, antiabortion leader Anne Kincaid, and Family Foundation head Walter Barbee.

By the latter half of the 1990s, the division between the Christian conservatives and moderates began to heal, primarily because the Christian Right worked to support conservative candidates who took more moderate stances on social issues. In 1997, the movement supported the nomination and election of Jim Gilmore, then attorney general, to the governorship. Gilmore was clearly more conservative than his Democratic rival, but his campaign centered on a promise to end the personal property tax (commonly called the car tax), not on abortion or other social issues. Democratic candidate Don Beyer, who had defeated Michael Farris for lieutenant governor in 1993, sought to link Gilmore with Falwell and Robertson, but this worked even less well than it had against Allen in 1993.[3] The lieutenant governor candidate, John Hager, also won election, despite his pugnacious character, his penchant for embarrassing remarks, and his strong protobacco position.

The only contested race for the Republicans was for attorney general, and a Christian conservative who had support from many labor and African American leaders won. Mark Earley, a state legislator who had promoted Christian Right positions and was an able politician, defeated three candidates in a primary that attracted only 6 percent of eligible

Republican voters because the other two statewide offices were uncontested. Prolife activist and former Family Foundation head Anne Kincaid managed Earley's primary campaign. Earley focused his resources on Christian radio and targeted mailings. While the other three candidates attacked each other in mass media ads, the Earley campaign sought to stay below the radar and mobilize its base.

Although Earley ran as the social conservative candidate in the party primary, he did a masterly job at presenting himself to the general electorate as a mainstream conservative. In truth, his views on the social issues were not easily distinguishable from the views of Michael Farris and Oliver North. Earley opposed abortion, even in cases of rape and incest, a position to the right of the vast majority of Virginia voters. Yet Democrats found the electorate reluctant to accept a depiction of Earley as a pawn of Robertson and Falwell. Unlike Farris, Earley had not been active in a Christian Right organization, and, unlike North, he lacked any elements of public scandal. Whereas Farris had been the Christian Right attorney in a trial known as *Scopes II*, in which he advocated restricting a school textbook on religious grounds, Earley had served as a missionary in Manila. And unlike either Farris or North, he had a record as a successful state legislator who was clearly willing to compromise on issues. Earley's pragmatism even earned him the general election endorsement of the *Washington Post*.

Although Earley opposed most abortions, his campaign focused on parental notification and consent, a ban on partial-birth abortions, and denying public funding for abortions. Although Virginia is a prochoice state, these positions were popular. By contrast with the 1989 election, when prochoice moderates were frightened that the GOP candidate might take away their abortion rights, Earley could point to his ten years of activity in the state legislature, where he was one of the most active supporters of parental notification but had never introduced legislation to ban abortions. When asked about his views on the procedure generally, Earley merely responded that he respected current constitutional interpretation and had no plan as attorney general to challenge federal law in that area.

The failure of Democratic candidate Bill Dolan to successfully link Earley to the Christian Right is telling, for on the merits it was an easy case. In part, Dolan's attacks on Earley—for making a speech at a "Field of Blood" prolife rally that featured hundreds of crosses displayed on a hillside to mourn fetal deaths, and for accepting $35,000 from Pat Robertson—seemed too negative. In endorsing Earley, the *Washington*

Post criticized the tone of the Dolan campaign. Perhaps a more subtle campaign would have gained some traction, but it seems likely that after nearly twenty years, this campaign theme had gone stale. Ultimately Earley won in a landslide and even carried 40 percent of prochoice voters.

Earley's success suggests that Christian Right candidates need not moderate their social views so long as they focus on popular issues and have a record of public service that is seen by voters as evidence of an ability to compromise. A Christian Right nominee also is electable statewide if he or she can credibly campaign as a broad-based coalitional candidate with appeal beyond more typical ideological boundaries. Earley was the most unusual Christian Right candidate we have encountered in our studies of the movement in Virginia Republican politics. He joined the NAACP in 1982, supported a state bill to mandate multicultural education in the public schools, and supported a bill to require nonunion employees to pay union dues or be fired. He attracted the endorsements of the state firefighters' union and of the immediate past president of the NAACP (Rozell and Wilcox 2000).

However, Earley lost his bid for the governorship in 2001. The GOP nomination was a contest between Earley and Lieutenant Governor John Hager, and although Hager had little chance of victory, he contested the nomination to the end. Hager focused his campaign on the contrast between his package of economic conservatism and social moderation and Earley's economic moderation and social conservatism. Although Earley won the convention easily, the charge of social extremism from a very conservative Republican damaged his public image of moderation. He faced a Democratic Party desperate to win the governorship and a multimillionaire opponent, Mark Warner, who had run a credible campaign for the U.S. Senate in 1996 against incumbent John Warner. Mark Warner also positioned himself as a social moderate and vigorously (but unsuccessfully) sought the endorsement of the NRA.

Earley tried to convince Republican donors to try to match Warner's millions, and this task was made far more difficult by the terrorist attacks of September 11, 2001, which essentially froze the campaign for weeks and made fund-raising events seem divisive. George W. Bush canceled planned appearances for Earley as he sought to maintain bipartisan support for his foreign policy. Republican squabbling, including disputes over state budget issues, also hurt Earley. With a big lead to start the campaign, Warner did not attack Earley on the social issues or for his ties to Pat Robertson or Jerry Falwell. Interestingly, it was Earley who raised the issue, in a last desperate effort to mobilize his base. Earley ran a radio ad that quoted Warner out of context criticizing the Christian Right in the GOP, and charged that Warner was hostile to "people of faith." This echoed a theme of the Farris campaign in 1993, but it was widely seen as an unfair and negative attack. Warner won easily.

Earley's defeat was a disappointment to the Christian Right and a relief to critics who saw him as the movement's Trojan horse. Yet in defeat, the movement and the GOP as well had much to celebrate. In 1999 the GOP achieved control of both houses of the state legislature, making Virginia the first state of the old confederacy to have Republican control of all statewide elected state offices and both houses of the legislature. In 2000, former governor George Allen defeated incumbent Senator Chuck Robb, also giving the party both U.S. Senate seats. And in 2001, despite losing the governorship, the GOP won the attorney general race and picked up a remarkable twelve seats in the house of delegates, giving the party control of two-thirds of the seats of the lower house.[4]

Perhaps one of the best examples of the movement's electoral success in recent years was in the 2000 GOP presidential primary in Virginia. The Christian Right was largely united in its opposition to the candidacy of Arizona senator John McCain and supported Texas governor George W. Bush. McCain made a controversial speech in Pat Robertson's hometown of Virginia Beach to denounce the Christian Right leader and Jerry Falwell for what McCain considered their deceitful electoral activities. McCain's speech emphasized what he saw as the negative impact of various Christian Right leaders' activities on the Republican Party. Although many party moderates applauded McCain's speech, Christian Right activists turned out in large numbers against him. Exit polls revealed that McCain had won the votes of moderate Republicans and non-Republicans voting in the open GOP primary, but Christian Right opposition to him was intense and united. McCain's defeat in Virginia marked the practical end of his presidential aspirations (Rozell 2002).

THE EVOLUTION OF THE CHRISTIAN RIGHT IN VIRGINIA

In the 1980s the Christian Right in Virginia was primarily a cadre of intolerant political novices that helped nominate politically extreme candidates and pushed them to take unpopular stands on social issues. In the 1990s the movement entered the political mainstream of Virginia, a major influence not only on GOP nominations and platforms but on general elections as well. In the new century, now twenty-five years after the movement first emerged on the scene in state politics, Christian Right organizations are less visible, but activists are firmly ensconced in the Republican Party, and its supporters are habitual voters.

The Christian Right in Virginia learned the art of electoral politics. In part this was a result of new leadership in the 1990s, which stressed the importance of pragmatism and winning over ideological purism and likely defeat (Rozell and Wilcox 1998). It could also be attributed to the fact that certain longtime leaders had learned from past mistakes. These arguments for movement pragmatism were bolstered by data from exit and tracking polls showing that moderate Northern Virginia voters would reject any candidate who took socially extreme positions and would mobilize against any highly visible movement efforts. They were also aided by the taste of political victory in 1993, when moderate rhetoric helped elect a social conservative as governor. The Christian Right may have learned the art of electoral politics partially by necessity as well. By the 1990s, the GOP became a competitive party, thereby attracting better candidates and more diverse coalition elements. In 2002 the GOP is a far bigger tent than before, and thus it is harder for the Christian Right to fully dominate party nominations.

Virginia has experienced successive waves of Christian Right mobilization, which have brought different types of activists into politics. Falwell's Moral Majority brought Baptist fundamentalists into politics, and Robertson's Christian Coalition mobilized Pentecostals. Farris brought in home-school advocates, and North drew strong support from charismatics. The fundamentalists of Falwell and the home-schoolers for Farris were often unsophisticated political ideologues, and many of them are no longer active in politics. Those that remain are more pragmatic, both because they learned the value of compromise and because those who were unwilling to compromise dropped out. Many activists in the movement, however, have been around for twenty years or more, and they have learned valuable lessons.

As a result, the Christian Right no longer arouses so much fear in the electorate, at least so long as it supports pragmatic candidates. Although Robertson and Falwell are unpopular in the state, the intensity of this opposition has declined.[5] As the movement has become more strategic in its use of campaign appeals and issue positions, the public perceives less of a threat from GOP candidates who have some association with the Christian Right. It is telling that in 2001, the Virginia Democratic gubernatorial candidate determined that a key to election was to avoid talking about the GOP candidate's social issue positions. He correctly understood that the days of being able to run Democratic campaigns by simply declaring the GOP nominees social extremists were over—assuming, of course, that the GOP does not again someday nominate a Farris or a North for statewide office. If the Christian Right continues to back mainstream conservatives with broad-based electoral appeal, it will remain an important part of the successful GOP coalition in Virginia.

The Christian Right also has succeeded in state politics by more closely aligning its policy positions with the preferences of significant portions of the public. Earlier appeals to outlaw abortion rights frightened the electorate, but parental notification is as popular in Virginia as elsewhere, and it does not mobilize prochoice opposition. Today the movement is much more likely to be involved in a debate over allowing public school students to say prayers during a moment of silence than in advocating the mandatory teaching of creationism.

The evolution of the state electorate has had some advantages for the movement as well. In recent years the suburbs have experienced phenomenal population growth. Given the tendency of suburbia to vote Republican, this change has helped the movement increase its fortunes, as the state has become GOP dominated. In the 2001 elections, most of the newly elected state legislators hailed from GOP-leaning suburban districts on the farther outskirts of the central urban areas. Although in the past suburbia led the way in Virginia in defeating Christian Right candidates for state office, today the growing suburbs are leading the way toward a Republican-dominated state. As long as the Christian Right works within the GOP and avoids the mistakes of the past—pushing for the nominations of extreme candidates and taking extreme issue positions—the movement appears poised to continue to be part of winning GOP coalitions.

THE PAYOFFS OF CHRISTIAN RIGHT ACTIVISM

For many Christian Right activists, elections are now exciting enterprises that are worthwhile in their own right. For others, voting has become a habit, and even without a strong Christian Right get-out-the-vote drive evangelicals are likely to be a major element of the electorate.

Yet after nearly twenty-five years of electoral activity, the policy achievements of the movement remain modest. It is possible that this will soon change, for the large GOP legislative majority, if coupled with a Republican governor in 2006, could enact policy with little input from Democrats.

Yet it is also instructive to consider the policy victories of the movement by 2002, after some twenty-five years of activity. Although most Christian Right activists would prefer to ban most abortions, the only victory to date has been a legislative mandate for parental notification and a ban on certain late-term abortions. Although these are highly symbolic victories, some activists privately complain that it is not evident that these policies have prevented *any* abortions in Virginia. Most Christian Right activists would like to see prayer in schools, religion as a natural part of the curriculum, and evolution replaced by (or at least supplemented by) creationism in the classroom. The most visible victory to date is a mandatory moment of silence, in which very few public schoolchildren pray. The Christian Right has also succeeded in limiting the scope of sex education in the classroom to a certain extent, although most social conservative activists want it eliminated altogether.

Most movement activists prefer that mothers remain in the home with their children and oppose policies that make it easier for them to work outside the home. In this area the movement has clearly lost ground, for localities increasingly offer after-school care with public subsidies to meet the demands by two-income families. Indeed, a majority of evangelical mothers of school-aged children work outside the home. The movement is divided in its preferences on gay rights, but at a minimum activists would like to see all discussion of homosexuality taken out of the classroom, and no laws providing benefits or protections to gays and lesbians. Here the movement has succeeded in stopping various policies that might expand gay rights, but public attitudes are clearly changing rapidly on this issue, even in Virginia.

The Allen administration, from 1994 to 1998, was the most favorable to the Christian Right of any in contemporary history, so it is worthwhile to consider what payoffs Allen provided to one of his most loyal constituency groups. Christian Right leaders lobbied hard for the state to refuse public funding for the Goals 2000 program, which they feared would mandate weak national learning standards and incorporate values they opposed into the curriculum. Allen refused federal funds from 1994 through 1996 and then bowed to public pressure to accept the funds after negotiating some exceptions for Virginia. The governor launched a

$300,000 "traditional values"–based series of advertisements to extol the importance of fatherhood. Called the "Virginia Fatherhood Campaign," the initiative was an outgrowth of the gubernatorial Commission on Citizen Empowerment. The governor supported initiatives in the state legislature to mandate parental notification on abortion for underage girls and to establish a new criminal category of "feticide" to declare the act of killing a fetus a murder. The former eventually gained approval during the Gilmore administration. The latter failed. Allen made other gestures in the area of charter schools that were also unsuccessful.

These efforts represented partial victories for the movement and provided activists with some evidence that winning elections actually mattered. But the movement's gains remain limited to secondary issues. In 2002 the effort to build on the parental notification legislation with a new parental consent bill stalled in the state legislature. Legislative initiatives to post the Ten Commandments in public schoolrooms and to incorporate values-based teaching in the curriculum also failed. The legislature did pass a bill to post the motto "In God We Trust" in the public schools, and at this writing the governor has not signaled his intention to sign it. Even if the governor consents, the major policy victory of the latest legislative session is a largely symbolic measure, even though the GOP has considerable strength in the two chambers. The movement has had some successes defending against initiatives supported by social libertarians. In one case, the movement lobbied successfully against a bill that would have allowed emergency contraceptives to be available to women over the counter at pharmacies.

It is likely that the movement will have more policy successes in the future as long as it is focused on defensive actions and on promoting secondary policy gains. But over a quarter-century of activism has not yielded a major change in the state public's attitudes toward social issues, and policy gains of the movement have been limited in character. Even in this GOP-dominated, conservative Southern state, the Christian Right is limited in the degree to which it can achieve its foremost policy goals.

NOTES

1. These percentages are figured from studies by the Ray Bliss Center of Applied Politics at the University of Akron as well as Kosmin, Meyer, and Keyser (2001).

2. From 2000 exit polling data.

3. In 1993, although Allen won the election easily, his momentum was slowed temporarily when his opponent ran ads linking him with the Christian Right.

4. This remarkable contrast—between losing the top two statewide races and picking up a huge number of state legislative seats—is a credit to the masterful redistricting efforts of the GOP.

5. This unpopularity increased sharply in fall of 2001 following some highly publicized comments by Falwell on Robertson's 700 Club television program, blaming feminists and gays for evoking God's punishment in the September 11 terrorist attacks on the United States.

REFERENCES

Conger, Kimberly, and John C. Green. 2002. "Spreading Out and Digging In: Christian Conservatives and State Republican Parties." *Campaigns & Elections* (2 February):58–65.

Cook, Elizabeth Adell, Ted G. Jelen, and Clyde Wilcox. 1994. "Issue Voting in Gubernatorial Elections: Abortion in Post-*Webster* Politics." *Journal of Politics* 56:187–99.

Elazar, Daniel J. 1972. *American Federalism: A View from the States*. New York: Thomas Y. Crowell.

Key, V. O. 1949. *Southern Politics in State and Nation*. New York: Knopf.

Kosmin, Barry A., Egon Meyer, and Ariela Keyser. 2001. *American Religious Identification Survey*. New York: Graduate Center of the City University of New York.

Reed, Ralph. 1994. Interview with author. Washington, D.C., 29 September.

Rozell, Mark J. 2002. "The Christian Right in the 2000 GOP Presidential Campaign." Pp. 57–74 in *Piety, Politics, and Pluralism: Religion, the Courts, and the 2000 Election*, ed. Mary Segers. Lanham, Md.: Rowman & Littlefield.

Rozell, Mark J., and Clyde Wilcox. 1996. *Second Coming: The New Christian Right in Virginia Politics*. Baltimore: Johns Hopkins University Press.

———. 1997. "Virginia: When the Music Stops, Choose Your Faction." Pp. 99–114 in *God at the Grass Roots, 1996: The Christian Right in American Elections*, ed. Mark J. Rozell and Clyde Wilcox. Lanham, Md.: Rowman & Littlefield.

———. 1998. "Pragmatism and Its Discontents: The Evolution of the Christian Right in the United States." Pp. 193–202 in *Religion in a Changing World: Comparative Studies in Sociology*, ed. Madeleine Cousineau. Westport, Conn.: Praeger.

———. 2000. "Virginia: Prophet in Waiting?" Pp. 77–91 in *Prayers in the Precincts: The Christian Right in the 1998 Elections*, ed. John C. Green, Mark J. Rozell, and Clyde Wilcox. Washington, D.C.: Georgetown University Press.

THREE

Texas: Religion and Politics in God's Country

James W. Lamare, Jerry L. Polinard,
and Robert D. Wrinkle

IT SURPRISES NO ONE FROM A LESSER STATE WHEN THEY HEAR A
Texan refer to Texas as "God's country." It does surprise them when
they realize the Texan is serious. Texas has always been fertile ground
for a mixture of religion and politics. Virtually every one of the apparently limitless number of textbooks on Texas government and politics
identifies Texas as falling within the individualistic and traditionalistic
political cultures described by Daniel Elazar (1972). A strong commitment to religion fits comfortably in this core culture and provides an
environment that is very friendly to religious movements—particularly,
but not exclusively, to those associated with the religious right.

In this chapter, we comment on the general social characteristics of
Texas, paying close attention to the pervasiveness of traditional, Christian religious beliefs and the extent to which these orientations have
given shape and form to the state's politics and its policy commitments.
Political organizations extolling the social, economic, moral, and political views of the Christian Right arose easily and quickly out of this cultural milieu. They have achieved their greatest political success in taking
over the state's Republican Party, a goal that was accomplished through
gaining control of the party organization at its grassroots level. They
have been less successful in securing electoral victories and in influencing policy outcomes, although their adventures into these areas have
almost always generated publicity and controversy. The religious left
has also made its presence felt in Texas. Working mostly in Texas's predominately Hispanic communities, religious left organizations have had

some success in elections and in affecting policy decisions, albeit usually at the local level of government.

THE SOCIAL AND POLITICAL CHARACTERISTICS OF TEXAS

Texas, in some ways, is a dynamic, rapidly changing state. Its population, for starters, has grown dramatically, from 212,000 hearty souls
counted in 1850 to more than 20 million, surpassing New York as the
second most populated state, as registered by the 2000 census. It is estimated that there will be nearly 34 million Texans in 2030 (Texas State
Library and Archives Commission 2002). Over the last century, Texas
has changed from a predominately rural, agricultural state to a heavily
urbanized state featuring a fairly diversified economy based mostly on
petroleum and mineral production, manufacturing, and an expanding
electronics and technology sector.

Ethnic and racial diversity characterizes Texas's population. Racial
and ethnic minorities constitute almost 45 percent of the state's residents, with Hispanics accounting for 31 percent, African Americans
11.3 percent, and Asian Americans (mostly Vietnamese or Chinese) 2
percent. Much of the recent population growth in the state is the result
of the expansion of its Hispanic population. Texans from "minority"
groups will make up a majority of the state's overall population by 2008.
This pattern is already evident in some areas, with 56 percent of Houston and 50 percent of Dallas currently composed of African Americans
and Hispanics. Hispanics alone constitute 56 percent of San Antonio
and 69 percent of El Paso (Lamare 2001, 15).

Texas is a land of contrast in terms of economic status. Wealth is
abundant—and highly concentrated. About 250,000 Texans control
nearly 40 percent of the state's assets. On average, each member of this
elite group was worth more than $1 million; ninety-nine had fortunes
in excess of $50 million a piece. Conversely, almost half of the state's
population has an annual income below $25,000. Indeed, 3.3 million
Texans, 16.5 percent of the population, live below the poverty line
(Lamare 2001, 17).

One constant in Texas is support for religion (Lamare 2001, 16).
Most Texans (60 percent) are Protestant, with more than one-third
being Baptist. Twenty-five percent are Roman Catholic, the predomi-
nant religion of choice among the state's Hispanic population. Regardless of specific denominational preference, more than 90 percent of

Texans consistently profess some form of religious commitment and identify religion as "important" in their lives. Only 4 percent have no religious affiliation.

Some 86 percent say that they pray at home at least once a week. Seven of every ten proclaim that they attend religious services at least once a month, a figure that doubles the national average and is a 12 percent increase over patterns of religious attendance evident in Texas fifteen years ago. A majority express a traditionalist view of religion, with an additional 19 percent characterizing their faith as fundamentalist, evangelical, or charismatic: only 4 percent consider their beliefs to be "New Age." Most (54 percent) are God-fearing Christians who "say that they have been born again or have had a born-again experience." Nearly two-thirds claim that at some time in their lives they had "tried to encourage someone to believe in Jesus Christ or accept Him as . . . [his] savior." About 72 percent hold that the Bible is the literal word of God and that each of the prophecies is bound to occur. Sizable majorities want prayers in public schools (87 percent) and at sporting events (62 percent). Almost two-thirds contend that creationism belongs in the curriculum alongside evolution.[1]

Given this religious tradition, and the overall presence of a conservative outlook in the state, it is not surprising that the Christian Right found Texas ripe for recruitment, mobilization, and organization. In addition, within the last three decades Texas has moved from being a one-party state, dominated by the Democrats, to a two-party state, and, in recent years, the Republican Party has prevailed in many electoral contests, especially in statewide races. During its ascent, the GOP was very open to attracting new members, and the Christian Right took full advantage of this situation.

ORGANIZATION OF THE CHRISTIAN RIGHT

Precursors to the organization of today's Christian Right are rife in Texas history, for religion has often been at the foundation of the state's politics. Even the Texas Constitution's protection of religious freedom comes with a twist. Article I, section 4, of the Texas Constitution prohibits any religious test as a qualification for office *as long as the candidate acknowledges "the existence of a Supreme Being"* (emphasis ours). A U.S. Supreme Court decision nullified this provision several decades ago, but in the minds of most Texans, what God has put together, no court can put asunder.

At the same time there is some irony to the wedding between religion and politics in the Lone Star state. The state's historical conservatism, a rule proved by only a few exceptions in which a populist candidate squeaked out an electoral victory here and there, has so subsumed the goals of the Christian Right, both old and new, as to mask their influence (for a look at the early role of the Christian Right in Texas politics, see Green 1979, chap. 5 and Davidson 1990, chap. 10).

Although the cultural wars of the 1960s that stimulated the emergence of the new Christian Right were not unknown in Texas, in point of fact, these wars were fought on battlegrounds removed from the South in general and Texas in particular. Indeed, when Pat Buchanan aroused a nation and convention delegates, albeit in different directions, with his claims of a cultural war at the 1992 GOP convention, it was no trick of the political gods that he was speaking in Houston.

The emergence of the new Christian Right in Texas followed a pattern common to the national emergence of the movement. The earlier convergence of religion and politics in Texas politics was mostly evident in the policy rather than electoral arena. The state's prohibitions on various forms of gambling (for instance, at racetracks), drinking alcohol in establishments open to the public, and the retail sale of items on Sunday exemplify the religious cast to policy decisions reached over the course of the state's history. Perhaps the best-known example of this suffusion of policy outcome with religious conviction was the role that fundamentalists, most notably Mel and Norma Gabler, played in textbook selection for Texas public schools.

Texas was the nation's largest purchaser of textbooks in the 1960s; a statewide adoption would virtually guarantee a publisher's profit (Martin 1996, 120–21). The Gablers exerted tremendous influence over textbook selection, offering detailed critiques of textbooks that strayed from what they considered traditional Judeo-Christian values. Their support for, or opposition to, a particular textbook often spelled the difference between adoption and rejection.

Both the visibility and the intensity of religious involvement in Texas politics began to change in the 1970s. In part this was a response to the changing nature of national and state society. The 1960s challenges to traditional authority, the impact of Watergate and various social movements—including the women's movement and the gay-rights movement—and the emergence of abortion as a national issue after *Roe v. Wade* served to stimulate a response from what would become known as the new Christian Right. The "new" was often a reference to the activities of the evangelicals, who traditionally had remained more in the background or focused on single-issue campaigns. Although the rise of the new Christian Right paralleled that of the new political right, James Guth's research identified the major source of mobilization as a wellspring of the religious institutions (1983, 31–45). In addition, the movement was also "new" in terms of scope, scale, and size (Liebman 1983, 229). Moreover, the movement differed from its predecessors by merging the issues above into a broader program.

In the late 1970s, organizations such as the Moral Majority and the Religious Roundtable were formed to represent the ideological outlook of the Christian Right. Their indirect influence in electoral politics was felt strongly in Texas and fostered the legitimacy of this type of activity by other religious groups. However, there is little evidence that these organizations played a direct role in the party or electoral system of the state. To be sure, one small but interesting incident involving then presidential candidate Ronald Reagan and the Religious Roundtable occurred in 1980 in Dallas. Reagan had a thirty-minute conversation with members of the Roundtable during which he assured the group that once elected, he would consider qualified Christians for government appointments. In exchange, this evangelical organization pledged its support to the Reagan candidacy (*Washington Post* 1980). Overall, however, the direct impact on Texas politics by these groups was negligible.

This was about to change. In the late 1980s and early 1990s, the intense public reaction to the cultural wars and the simmering social issues, such as abortion, launched the growth of organizations in Texas formed specifically to fight politically against the perceived moral decay of the United States. Feeding from the ideological menu of Christian principles, beliefs, and tenets, these groups easily mixed religious precepts with political action. The foremost social conservative or Christian Right organizations formed in the Lone Star state were the Texas Eagle Forum (an affiliate of Phyllis Schlafly's Eagle Forum), Concerned Women for America of Texas, two major antiabortion groups (American Family Association of Texas and Texans United for Life), and the Texas Christian Coalition (TCC), the largest—and the politically most potent—of these organizations. Each of these organizations had some presence in the state and they all usually saw eye to eye on the critical Christian Right agenda in the state. The TCC, as we will discuss in the next section, can usually count on their support in rallying voters to cast a ballot for a social conservative candidate and in lobbying decision-makers to enact policy promoting the Christian Right agenda.

The TCC was established in 1991 through the organizational efforts of Dick Weinhold, the chief fund-raiser for Pat Robertson's unsuccessful run for the presidency in 1988. Weinhold became the TCC's first chairman and also held a seat on the four-person national board of the Christian Coalition. Initially, the TCC had 10,000 members and chapters in 38 of Texas's 254 counties. By the late 1990s, its membership base had expanded to 200,000 and chapters could be found in 100 counties (see Texas Christian Coalition 2002 and Evans 2001). Today, it is difficult to pinpoint the exact number of people in the TCC, but it claims to have a 175,000-person mailing list, with estimates of 26,000 hard-core activists among its supporters.

There have been some changes within the TCC's leadership ranks. In 2001, after serving as chairman for ten years, Dick Weinhold stepped down and was replaced by Norm Mason of Sugar Land, a suburb of Houston and also the home of Tom DeLay, House Majority Whip (and a personal friend of Mason). At the same time, Mike Hannesschlager replaced Chuck Anderson as executive director.

Even though the TCC has not expanded greatly in recent years and has experienced change in its leadership, it remains an important political force in the state, at a time when the national Christian Coalition has suffered a loss of political strength elsewhere. As noted by John Green, director of the Ray C. Bliss Institute of Applied Politics at the University of Akron, "there are six to eight Southern and Western states where the [Christian] coalition is still viable, and Texas might well be the strongest" (Kirsch 2001, 1; also see Conger and Green 2002). Or, in the words of Charlotte Coffelt, president of the Houston chapter of Americans United for Separation of Church and State: "Those who predicted the Christian Coalition would no longer be a power don't live in Texas. This is ground zero" (Kirsch 2001, 1).

In 1999 the national headquarters of the Christian Coalition was moved from Chesapeake, Virginia, to Bedford, Texas, the home of the Texas affiliate of the Coalition. This switch of addresses was a direct response to a ruling by the Internal Revenue Service that the national Christian Coalition was not entitled to tax exemptions enjoyed by nonpartisan religious organizations, owing to the fact that the group overtly engaged in widespread political activities. The tax-exempt status of the TCC was a major attraction for shifting the home base of the more politically active wing of the national organization to the Lone Star State.

The bedrock of TCC's beliefs is found in the Book of Genesis, according to which man must repent from turning against the word of

God, his creator. Redemption is possible only through atoning the sacrifice of Jesus Christ: "[T]hose that accept Christ's sacrifice and resurrection and make Jesus their Lord will be reconciled with God and, while still being sinners, will not have their sins counted against them and will live in heaven forever after their physical death" (Texas Christian Coalition 2002). The organizational purpose of the TCC is fivefold: (1) to represent Christians and traditional values before governing bodies; (2) to speak out for these Christian values in the media and in the public arena; (3) to train Christian leaders for effective social and political action; (4) to inform Christians about issues and legislative proposals; and (5) to protest anti-Christian bias and defend the legal rights of Christians.

Translated into a policy stand, TCC's comprehensive conservative platform contains a wide array of economic, political, social, cultural, and moral issues, constituting "a political philosophy that starts and ends with Christ" (Texas Christian Coalition 2002). The current tax system, including the marriage tax penalty, is opposed because of its harmful effect on families. In its place the TCC recommends a flat tax or a sales tax. Fiscal responsibility would be ensured if the budget were balanced and if a two-thirds vote in Congress were required before taxes could be raised. A concern for family values also guides the TCC's opposition to performing abortions (unless the life of the mother is at stake), using tax dollars to fund abortions, and permitting abortions on minors without the consent of their parents.

Along the educational front, parents, according to the TCC, should not only know what their children are being taught but should also be given the right to shape school curriculum. The curriculum should be grounded in the basics of math, science, history, and, most emphatically, reading and writing. Parents should have the right to send their children to any school, and to teach them at home if they so choose. Educational policy should be left in the hands of local schools, without the intrusive influence of federal bureaucrats. Voluntary school prayer should become a normal part of the school day. Governmental prosecution of religions is particularly abhorred.

The TCC's strong commitment to traditional family values translates into its opposition to divorce and homosexuality, which is characterized as "a sin." The TCC advocates a strong health care system for families—one, however, that is not predicated upon a government-based system but rather on tax-free medical savings accounts established by families themselves.

The TCC favors capital punishment, victims' rights, requiring criminals to serve their full sentences, prosecuting to the fullest extent drivers who operate their vehicles under the influence of alcohol, and the right to keep and bear arms. In rendering decisions, judges, according to the TCC, should be guided by the Constitution and "the will of the people."

Funding for social conservative organizations in Texas comes from a variety of sources, including membership contributions, outside benefactors, and financial assistance from parent national organizations. It is difficult to discern precisely the funding base for these groups, since they are not required to report their finances. Reportedly, in 2000 the TCC raised $180,000 in revenue, presumably from its members (Kirsch 2001).

One clearly identifiable major benefactor of Christian Right groups in Texas has been Dr. James Leininger of San Antonio. Over the decade of the 1990s, Leininger contributed heavily to political candidates, to various groups and organizations, and to efforts aimed at swaying public opinion. Indeed, his largess has earned him the nickname of "God's Sugar Daddy" (Ivins 1998). Social conservative organizations, such as the American Family Association, the Christian Pro-Life Foundation, the Family Research Council, Focus on the Family, the Heidi Group, and the Republican National Coalition for Life PAC, have, it is estimated, received $5.6 million of Leininger's money. Another $3.2 million has been spent attempting to move public opinion toward the views of the religious right (Ivins 1998). A study of the top 100 donors to political campaigns in Texas between 1996 and 1999 conducted by the *Houston Chronicle* named Leininger the top contributor in the state. He gave various candidates, mostly Republicans, a total of $1.9 million. Christian Right candidates seeking a seat on the Texas State Board of Education have received more than $60,000 from Leininger (Castillo 1998; Nathan 1999; Stutz 1998a). Furthermore, he cosigned a $1 million loan that greatly assisted Rick Perry, now governor of the state, in his 1998 quest to be elected lieutenant governor (Ratcliffe and Bernstein 1999).

Dr. Leininger, who is worth an estimated $340 million, is listed among the 100 richest Texans and the 400 wealthiest Americans. He initially earned his fortune by manufacturing high-tech hospital beds designed for the comfort of patients who must endure lengthy stays in hospitals. Leininger's Kinetic Concepts International (KCI) grew rapidly in the 1980s as a result of its dominant position in the sales of these beds. He sold KCI in 1998 for $875 million but still maintained a 31 percent ownership share in the company. He also has a variety of other business interests, including a 10 percent interest in the San Antonio Spurs. Several of his businesses directly produce and promote Christian messages and material. His Promised Land Dairy, for instance, distributes milk, which is readily available at the leading super-markets in Texas, encased in containers printed not only with nutritional facts but also with verses from the Bible (Nathan 1999).

POLITICAL STRATEGIES OF THE CHRISTIAN RIGHT

Social conservatives have deployed several successful strategies to achieve prominence in the Texas political scene. In particular, they have secured a commanding position in the state's Republican Party, fared well in securing some political offices, and effectively influenced the outcome of a few political decisions.

The Republican Party

Unlike many other social movements in Texas—for example, the Chicano movement, the George Wallace movement, and the Ross Perot movement— the Christian Right did not attempt to form a third party to field candidates in opposition to the Republicans and the Democrats. Rather, it developed a strategy designed to gain a substantial foothold in the existing major political parties, especially the Republicans. This was a shrewd decision for a couple of reasons.

First, third parties have rarely obtained significant political clout in Texas. To be sure, they often start with a flourish and have, on occasion, attracted reasonably impressive voter support. However, they rarely win any political offices and, as a consequence, fade from the scene without much fanfare. The road to success for third parties in Texas is strewn with formidable obstacles, including difficulty securing access to the ballot, the enduring psychological ties between voters and the established major parties, and the disincentive inherent in electoral systems based on the principle of winner take all.

Second, the Christian Right was, as mentioned earlier, in position to take advantage of the emergence of the GOP as the dominant party. The ranks of the party began to swell as Republicans migrated from other states to Texas and conservative Texans who once identified with the Democrats abandoned that party as it was perceived to be drifting to the left. During the 1980s and 1990s, the Texas GOP gradually, but inexorably, began winning statewide elections as the Christian Right became the central core of the party, and a tight symbiotic relationship was formed between the two.

Prior to the 1970s, the Texas GOP was somewhat typical of the national party. That is, one part of the party identified with the eastern "Rockefeller" wing, focusing mostly on economic issues (there is some irony, of course, in that the Bush family was most comfortable in this wing). Another segment identified with those who ranked various social issues, such as abortion and prayer in public schools, as the most important issues to be addressed. As was the case with the national party, by the 1980s this internal debate had largely been resolved in favor of the latter group.

By the 1990s, the social wing of the party, indistinct now from the Christian Right, was firmly in control. Perhaps the strongest evidence of this control is seen in the selection of the state party chair. In 1994, Tom Pauken, with the support of the Christian activists, replaced the more moderate Fred Meyer. This was done even though Pauken was not the choice of the party's gubernatorial candidate, George W. Bush. In 1996, Pauken, not Governor Bush, was selected by the state convention delegates to lead the Texas delegation to the GOP national convention. In 1997, Susan Weddington, an active participant in the Christian Right, who teaches Bible study and Sunday school, succeeded Pauken. Weddington placed other members of the Christian Right on the State Republican Executive Committee.

The presence of Pauken and, then, Weddington at the top of the state GOP is a tribute to the work done lower down the totem pole. That is, the Christian Right has gained its influence the old-fashioned way: it outorganized the opposition. The Christian Right involvement is a textbook example of how to obtain control over a party organization. The Texas GOP is organized on a traditional pyramid basis. At the base are the precincts, which elect delegates to the county conventions, which, in turn, select the delegates for the state conventions.

The starting point for this takeover was at the grassroots level of the party precinct. Immediately after the closing of the polls on primary day, each major political party in Texas conducts a precinct convention, admission to which is gained simply by voting in the party's primary. To be sure, very few people vote in Texas's primaries—an average of less than 10 percent of eligible voters—and even fewer (around 2 percent) of these voters actually attend the precinct convention. However, this presents a ripe opportunity for a dedicated group of fervent believers to capture the structural organization of a party.

The Texas Christian Coalition has taken great advantage of this opening by training and mobilizing its members to vote in the Republican Party primary and to participate in the subsequent precinct convention. In 1994, the TCC distributed to its members a forty-five-page handbook, called "1996 Operation Precinct Workbook," that clearly delineated the functions and importance of the precinct convention. As noted by Dick Weinhold, then chairman of the TCC, each precinct "is the building block of the political process. For those who want to get involved for the first time, it's the logical place to start" (quoted in Gonzalez 1996, 18).

Participants at the more than 8,700 precinct conventions adopt resolutions and select election judges, the party's precinct chair, and delegates to the county convention. Each precinct is entitled to one delegate vote at the county or district convention for every twenty-five votes the Republican candidate received in the precinct in the previous gubernatorial election.[2] The total delegate votes at the county convention for a precinct are assigned to a delegate, regardless of the actual number of people selected at the precinct convention to attend the county or district convention. For example, one typical precinct in Tom Green County had an allotment of eighteen delegate votes at the Republican Party's 1996 county convention. Only four voters attended the precinct convention. Although only two of these people served as delegates at the Tom Green County Republican convention, they commanded all of the precinct's eighteen delegate votes (Hooker 1998).

County or district conventions select the state convention delegates. Given the ability of the Christian Right to control county or district conventions, the result was predictable. By 1994, more than 60 percent of the 6,000 delegates and 6,000 alternates attending the Republican Party state convention were affiliated with the social conservative movement (Bruce 1997, 35). Their strength increased two years later, and the hold of the Christian Right over the GOP has not been relinquished since.

This control was unambiguously manifested in the Texas delegations to the GOP national conventions in 1996 and 2000. Well over half of the state's delegates to these two conventions were linked to the Christian Right. It was widely agreed that the 124 delegates and 124 alternates sent to the national GOP convention in Philadelphia in 2000 were, in the words of Chuck Anderson, the former executive director of the Texas Christian Coalition, "definitely going to be very conservative" (Brooks 2000, B-3).

According to a firsthand observer of the 2000 Republican state convention, national delegate wannabes were given sixty seconds to address the district caucuses that selected the two delegates and two alternates to the national convention from each congressional district. "Of course, politicking already had gone on and compromises had been reached, but, if you didn't mention your opposition to abortion, you weren't going to go." The TCC circulated its slate of candidates each day, a slate that would change depending on positions on various issues and compromises reached with other groups. The result was that, while the Christian Right could not always name a specific delegate to the national convention, it had a virtual veto over the selections (Anonymous Interview 2001).[3]

Electoral Politics

The importance of social conservatives in the electoral process is no secret; their votes have at times been crucial to the election of GOP candidates in Texas. The most visible role of Christian Right organizations has been at the grassroots level. In every state election held over the course of the last decade, the Texas Christian Coalition has, for example, distributed millions of voter guides and instructed its members to make get-out-the-vote phone calls.

The Christian Right has also attempted to win political office in Texas, but, in so doing, it has met with limited success. Particularly targeted in this quest has been the fifteen-person State Board of Education (SBOE). For purposes of selection to the SBOE, Texas is divided into fifteen geographical districts. One board member is selected from each of these districts. The Christian Right has attempted over the last decade to achieve majority status on the SBOE. The board is responsible for establishing overall policy for the state's primary, secondary, and vocational schools. Among other tasks, it assists in budget preparation, textbook approval, assessing whether schools are reaching their goals, administering the multibillion-dollar Texas Permanent Fund, and overseeing the financial performance of schools.

After expending a great deal of time and effort, the best the Christian Right could manage was winning six seats on the board, two short of majority status. Nonetheless, social conservatives made their presence on the board known. They often engaged in open hostile exchanges with other board members, especially moderate Republican colleagues. Indeed, the infighting has been so intense that the board has been described as "the most divided, the most embattled, and the most uproarious political body in Texas" (Burka 1998, 140).

The Christian Right has also fielded candidates for office at the local level in Texas, again meeting with mixed results. It has been able to gain control over city government in a few Texas municipalities such as Friendswood and League City. In each of these places, the city council has officially adopted "Godly principles," which "propose that there is a Creator who makes all things and governs by his Providence. There is an afterlife, and 'in the next life, individuals are judged by the Creator for the conduct in this one'" (Long 2000, 1). League City, along with several other communities in Texas, routinely inscribes moral messages on bills for municipal services such as water bills sent to its customers.

Social conservatives have also exerted some influence over electoral activities in less obvious ways. For example, in the late 1990s, as Governor Bush prepared his run for the GOP presidential nomination, he brought Ralph Reed on board as an adviser. This was done to alleviate some of the reservations the Christian Right had about the governor, reservations that also had been manifest with respect to his father. In a similar action, David Dewhurst, a candidate for the 2002 GOP nomination for lieutenant governor, a position widely considered the most powerful in the state, hired Chuck Anderson, the former executive director of the Texas Christian Coalition, to assist in his campaign and to fix some of the problems that Dewhurst has had with social conservatives. According to a member of a prominent Christian Right organization, "Anderson had more pull at the last [GOP] state convention than anyone there" (Anonymous Interview 2001).

Another example of the Christian Right's behind-the-scenes electoral clout occurred after rumors surfaced that Senator Kay Bailey Hutchison, who is not a favorite among social conservatives, was thinking of challenging incumbent Rick Perry for the GOP's gubernatorial nomination in 2002. Enter David Barton, described as "the 400-pound gorilla of the religious right in Texas." Barton is the current vice-chair of the state Republican Party and considered the "next Ralph Reed, the intellectual leader of the [Christian Right] movement." In addition to his credentials, Barton is well known in the Christian media, "talks to President Bush once a week," and was "very influential" in the appointment of John Ashcroft to the attorney general's post. He assured Christian activists not to fret over Senator Hutchison's potential challenge, noting that he would meet with the senator, and that afterwards she would call a joint press conference with Governor Perry to announce her support for his candidacy. The press conference took place shortly thereafter (Anonymous Interview 2001).

Lobbying and Policy Outcomes

Social conservatives have also experienced mixed success in reaching statewide policy goals. In saying this, it should be borne in mind that Texas is predominately a tradition-bound, conservative state, and therefore there is little output from the state decisionmakers that could be described as "liberal" policies. However, the Christian Right has targeted some policy areas for special attention. Moreover, it does actively attempt to influence policy outcomes. According to one insider, members of these organizations are often called to come to Austin to lobby for particular policies endorsed by social conservatives. "We [are] an informal network with different coalition groups." These groups include the Texas Christian Coalition, the Texas Eagle Forum, the American Family Association of Texas, and other groups not so well known (e.g., Christian Fellowship International, an organization of several churches in Texas, New Mexico, and northern Mexico). The process is described as "structured, but ad hoc" (Anonymous Interview 2001).

The most notable social conservative policy success occurred in 1998 when the SBOE, at the insistence of its six Christian Right members, voted to sell the Texas public school system's stock in the Walt Disney Company. The case against Disney was led by the American Family Association of Texas, which claimed that the "world's largest family entertainment company has extended company insurance benefits to the live-in partners of homosexual employees, but not unmarried partners of heterosexual employees; allowed homosexual celebrations in its objectionable films; allowed a convicted child molester to direct a Disney movie; published a book aimed at homosexuals; and promoted numerous other anti-family policies and activities" (American Family Association of Texas 2002). AFA/Texas lobbied a wide variety of state officials, including members of the legislature, to cease doing any business with Disney. The only governing body that acquiesced was the SBOE, which voted eight to four to discontinue the Texas Permanent School Fund investment in Disney. It is estimated that this decision translated into a divestiture of $45 million in Disney stock.

The Christian Right has not fared as well in persuading the legislature to adopt its policy proposals. The policy agenda most sought includes a state-funded voucher program that would provide tax money to parents who wish to send their children to private schools, a prohibition on performing abortions on minor children without prior parental consent, and never legalizing same-sex marriages. In reviewing the recent failure of passing the Defense of Marriage Act (DOMA), one social conservative observer noted: "We [thought] we had the votes, but [the Speaker] put the bill in a committee where it couldn't come out." Several members of the religious right met with Governor Rick Perry, but were unable to get him to call a special session to address the issue. "The issue will return to the forefront in the 2003 session" (Anonymous Interview 2001).

At the national level, the Christian Right appears to have some support, especially among Republicans, in affecting the formulation of public policy. The Christian Coalition's ratings of key votes registered by Republicans in the 105th Congress were very positive, with Texas's two Republican Senators (Phil Gramm and Kay Bailey Hutchison) rated on average 95.5 and with its thirteen-member Republican congressional delegation receiving an average rating of 98.7. Democrats, conversely, were accorded an average rating of 20.4 (Barone and Ujifusa 1999).

CONSTRAINTS ON THE CHRISTIAN RIGHT

The rise of the Christian Right in Texas has been dramatic and, on some fronts, impressive. However, the movement has encountered some bumps along the road. First, there has been internal division among social conservative groups. For example, although most Christian Right organizations favor a state-funded school voucher program, political activist Cathy Adams, who is president of the Texas Eagle Forum, has decried the program because it would require mandatory testing of the academic skills of students attending these private schools. According to Adams, the voucher program "is a back door approach to control every private school in Texas. Vouchers are coupons for control. Whoever holds the purse string is the one who will call the shots" (Stutz 1998b, 8A).

In addition, as a result of their success, Christian Right organizations have generated oppositional groups that attempt to counter the work and activities of social conservatives. At various times, the state's environmentalists, feminists, and gay and lesbian rights activists have decried the policy substance and assertive style of the Christian Right movement. However, the foremost counterpoints to the Christian Right have been the Texas Faith Network and the Texas Freedom Network, founded in 1996 by Cecile Richards (daughter of former Texas governor Ann Richards). They have, for example, continuously and strongly challenged the propriety of Christian Right organizations' distributing voter guides in churches. They also closely monitor the activities of the Christian Right and report on its actions and supporters. Interestingly, these two organizations joined forces with Cathy Adams's Texas Eagle Forum to help defeat the school voucher program in 1999.

Moreover, George W. Bush has been an enigma for the Christian Right. Though they have often denounced him as "too liberal," social conservatives nonetheless were drawn to Bush's winning fortunes, at both the state and national levels. In the 2000 presidential race, Bush received 80 percent of the ballots cast in Texas by voters describing themselves as "religious right" (Associated Press 2000).

Finally, it is hard to estimate the fallout in Texas from the troubles that the Christian Coalition is experiencing at the national level. Thus far, the Texas Christian Coalition, as mentioned earlier, is still strong, although it is not growing at the same pace as before. Whether the TCC can sustain its position without a strong national parent remains to be seen.

THE RELIGIOUS LEFT IN TEXAS

In opposition to the religious right, the religious left in Texas finds its voice most consistently in a group of Saul Alinsky Industrial Areas Foundation organizations that have had major impacts on the local policies of such cities as San Antonio, Austin, Dallas, Fort Worth, Houston, El Paso, and the region of the Rio Grande Valley. Foremost among these groups are Community Organized for Public Service (COPS) in San Antonio, Austin Interfaith Sponsoring Committee, Dallas Interfaith Sponsoring Committee, Allied Communities of Tarrant County (Fort Worth), The Metropolitan Organization (Houston), the El Paso Interreligious Sponsoring Organization (EPISO), and Valley Interfaith (Rio Grande Valley).

These groups organize at the local level in areas that are predominantly Mexican American. Local Catholic churches form the organizational backbone of these organizations, providing them with facilities, financial support, leadership, and spiritual inspiration and guidance. Influencing political decision making in order to improve the lot of impoverished Hispanics is clearly a primary goal of religious left organizations. At times, they have been quite successful.

COPS, for example, racked up a series of victories in Alamo City in the 1970s that resulted in better city services (drainage, sidewalks, streetlights, etc.) for the poor and replacing at-large elections with the districtwide election of city council members. COPS emerged in San Antonio "as a major political force—some would say the major political force" (Burka 1978, 245). The Metropolitan Organization has succeeded in improving city services for the poor of Houston and establishing a trust fund to help the impoverished purchase homes (Lamare 2001, 232). Valley Interfaith recently organized the winning campaign to change the electoral structure of McAllen from an at-large system to a single-member-district system. The latter was considered more likely to recognize and represent the interests of the lower-income population in the city, which is 80 percent Hispanic. These organizations routinely hold "accountability sessions" with elected officials, eliciting promises of financial support in return for their campaign support. In part as a result of the growing political influence of the Mexican American population, increasingly these accountability sessions attract not just local politicians but statewide officeholders as well.

Indeed, the religious left has achieved some noteworthy statewide victories. It successfully challenged the method by which Texas funded its public school system, creating, in so doing, a system of school finance that provides more revenue to impoverished school districts. Valley Interfaith was able to spearhead the passage of a constitutional amendment that improved the infrastructure of the *colonias* in south Texas, a group of unincorporated communities inhabited largely by migrant workers.

CONCLUSION

Although courts, usually federal ones, can force the separation of church and state in Texas, nothing can disentangle the symbiotic relationship that exists between religion and politics in the Lone Star State. Throughout the state's history, and deeply embedded in its core culture, religion seamlessly fits into the political milieu of Texas.

The natural connection between religion and politics means that the structural foundation of the state rests squarely on tenets and principles rooted in Christianity. The foundation thus is already composed of material from which any edifice built will be reflective of traditional—indeed, socially conservative—values. This foundation also serves as a solid platform on which groups and organizations can form, mobilize, and articulate Christian messages directly to political decisionmakers without raising too much of an eyebrow about the proper role of church and state.

For more than a decade, the Christian Right has developed organizations well grounded in the literal interpretation of the Bible that attempt to affect the shape of the political system in Texas. They have been very successful in taking over the state Republican Party through capturing the party organization at its grassroots level. Indeed, since 1994, the Christian Right, led by the efforts of the Texas Christian Coalition, has exerted a great amount of influence over the Republican Party, more than in most of the other states (see Conger and Green 2002 and Persinos 1994). The Christian Right has been somewhat less effective in winning elections and controlling policy outcomes in the state, although social conservatives have stirred up a substantial amount of controversy in some elections and over some policy issues.

The religious left has been well entrenched in many of Texas's Hispanic communities for more than a quarter of a century. Although these organizations have had limited success at the party and electoral levels, they have influenced several important policy decisions, decisions that have improved the lot of impoverished Hispanics living in Texas.

The future of specific organizations founded upon religious tenets is always uncertain, dependent upon several factors including achieving success in their efforts, the mobilization of opposition to their activities, and the ability to sustain, if not increase, their resources, including members and financial support. However, there is little doubt that religion will continue to suffuse Texas politics. Texas, after all, is God's country.

NOTES

1. The data are found in a series of surveys conducted by the Texas Poll, which is currently run by the Scripps Howard Data Center in Abilene.

2. The most populated counties in Texas are divided into districts for party organizational purposes. These districts coincide with the geographical boundaries of the state senatorial districts located in each of these counties.

3. The anonymous interview was conducted by one of the authors with a person who holds a high-ranking position with a Christian Right organization. The interviewee participated in the selection of delegates to the 2000 Repub-

lican Party national convention and is a lobbyist for the Christian Right on select policy issues.

References

American Family Association of Texas. 2002. www.afatexas.org/document/ boycotts.

Anonymous Interview. 2001. Conducted by J. L. Polinard, 25 July.

Associated Press. 2000. Exit Poll. 7 November.

Barone, Michael, and Grant Ujifusa. 1999. *The Almanac of American Politics 2000*. Washington, D.C.: National Journal.

Brooks, Karen. 2000. "Conservative Likely to Dominate Texas Delegation." *Fort Worth Star Telegram* (14 June).

Bruce, John M. 1997. "Texas: A Success Story, at Least for Now." Pp. 33–50 in *God at the Grass Roots, 1996: The Christian Right in the American Elections*, ed., Mark J. Rozell and Clyde Wilcox. Lanham, Md.: Rowman and Littlefield.

Burka, Paul. 1978. "The Second Battle of the Alamo." Pp. 245–56 in *Texas Monthly's Political Reader*. Austin, Tex.: Texas Monthly Press.

———. 1998. "Disloyal Opposition." *Texas Monthly* (December): 140.

Castillo, Jaime. 1998. "Anti-Voucher Group Blasts Contributions." *San Antonio Express-News* (26 March).

Conger, Kimberly H., and John C. Green. 2002. "Spreading Out and Digging In: Christian Conservatives and State Republican Parties." *Campaigns and Elections* (February):58–61.

Davidson, Chandler. 1990. *Race and Class in Texas Politics*. Princeton: Princeton University.

Elazar, Daniel J. 1972. *American Federalism: A View from the States*. 2d ed. New York: Thomas Y. Crowell.

Evans, Marjorie. 2001. "Sugar Land Man Takes Reins of the Texas Christian Coalition." *Houston Chronicle* (7 June).

Gonzalez, John. 1996. "Christian Coalition Members Urged to Be Active in Politics." *Fort Worth Star-Telegram* (1 March).

Green, George N. 1979. *The Establishment in Texas Politics, 1938–1957*. Westport, Conn.: Greenwood Press.

Guth, James L. 1983. "The New Christian Right." Pp. 31–45 in *The New Christian Right: Mobilization and Legitimation*, ed. Robert J. Liebman and Robert Wuthnow. New York: Aldine.

Hooker, Charles H. 1998. "Comment: Attend Conventions to Have Say in Party." *San Antonio Express-News* (10 March).

Ivins, Molly. 1998. "Keeping Track of 'God's Sugar Daddy.'" *Austin American Statesman* (9 December).

78 THE CHRISTIAN RIGHT IN AMERICAN POLITICS

Kirsch, John. 2001. "Texas Christian Coalition Seen as a Stronghold." *Fort Worth Star-Telegram* (15 July).

Lamare, James W. 2001. *Texas Politics: Economics, Power, and Policy*. 7th ed. Belmont, Calif.: Wadsworth.

Liebman, Robert C. 1983. "The Making of the New Christian Right." Pp. 49–73 in *The New Christian Right: Mobilization and Legitimation*, ed. Robert C. Liebman and Robert Wuthnow. New York: Aldine.

Long, Steven. 2000. "Almighty Municipality." *Houston Press* (2 March).

Martin, William. 1996. *With God on Our Side: The Rise of the Religious Right in America*. New York: Broadway Books.

Nathan, Debbie. 1999. "Saint Sickbed." *Texas Observer* (22 January).

Persinos, John. 1994. "Has the Christian Right Taken Over the Republican Party?" *Campaigns and Elections* (September):20–24.

Ratcliffe, R.G., and Alan Bernstein. 1999. "Political Donors Have the Money, and Get the Time." *Houston Chronicle* (23 May).

Stutz, Terrence. 1998a. "Religious Conservatives Aim to Win Majority on Board." *Dallas Morning News* (26 October).

———. 1998b. "School Voucher Issues Divide Conservatives." *Dallas Morning News* (20 December).

Texas Christian Coalition. 2002. www.texascc.org.

Texas State Library and Archives Commission, Archives Information Service. 2002. www.tsl.state.tx.us/lobby/ref/census.htm.

Washington Post. 1980. "Evangelicals Claim Reagan Made Job Vow" (28 September).

FOUR

"A Necessary Annoyance"? The Christian Right and the Development of Republican Party Politics in Florida

Kenneth D. Wald and Richard K. Scher

As the Florida legislature assembled for its annual session in January 2002, senators were treated to free pies from a local bakery. The sweetness of the pies was offset somewhat by the stern warning that accompanied them: "If you have never trusted the eternity of your soul to Jesus Christ," senators were told, "your vote is now with Satan and you stand condemned." On the house side, a representative sent his colleagues reprints of a patriotic painting in which the artist likened the red of Old Glory's stripes to "the cleansing blood of Christ for this newborn Christian country." These incidents occasioned a public rebuke by the American Jewish Congress, angered by efforts to transform an ostensibly secular public agency into "a bully pulpit for a majority religion" (Wasson 2002).

These events during the legislature's opening week nicely symbolize the development of the Christian Right in Florida over the past two decades. In the 1970s, Christian activists were more likely to picket the state legislature than to lobby it or work it from the inside. By the 1990s, the movement had gained a substantial presence in the halls of government. Today, Christian Right activists and fellow travelers hold senate and house seats, some rising to high positions of leadership in both the legislature and the executive branch. Using their positions to place conservative Christian priorities on the public agenda, these elites "work as insiders on outsider issues." In Santoro and McGuire's (1997, 504) characterization, the Christian Right has spawned a cadre of "social movement participants who occupy formal statuses within the government and pursue social movement goals through conventional bureaucratic channels." Over the past twenty years, then, the Christian Right has developed gradually from an outsider social movement to a conventional interest group to a durable faction within a major party.

If access to decisionmakers had been the only goal of the Christian Right in Florida, the movement would be judged a remarkable success. Yet the Christian Right has pursued a much more daunting goal, the transformation of public policy in the direction of moral traditionalism. By this standard—impact rather than access—the movement has fallen far short of its ambitions (Wald 1995; Wald and Scher 1997; Wald, Scher, and Tartaglione 2000; Wald and Corey 2002). As an outsider movement fueled by an intense religious impulse, the Christian Right has never wholeheartedly embraced legislative and political norms and, in consequence, has frequently shot itself in the foot. The triumphalist rhetoric on display during the first week of the 2002 legislative session may well promote cohesion among the legislature's more ardent advocates of Christian America, but it also stamps them with a sectarian image that undermines both public and governmental influence.

We discuss the factors that both empower and constrain the Christian Right, and we review the movement's role in the 2000 election and its aftermath. Though the names may have changed, nothing in the last two years alters our judgment about the movement's inability to shed fully its outsider orientation and exert a major influence on state-level public policy. The Christian Right remains more significant in local government and at a symbolic level. To many insiders, it remains what one well-connected Republican described as "a necessary annoyance."

A PARTISAN REVOLUTION

The major plot line of Florida politics in the last two decades was the displacement of the once hegemonic Democratic Party by the Republicans. For much of the twentieth century, the Democratic Party held a viselike grip on all aspects of state politics, and dominated local politics as well. By the end of the century, things looked very different from what V. O. Key (1949) described in *Southern Politics*. The GOP took control of the state legislature in 1996 and increased its hold steadily. By 2000, Republicans controlled both houses by margins of nearly two to one. The governorship, formerly a Democratic preserve, has rotated between the two parties over the last twenty years. The GOP has also steadily built up its profile in other statewide contests, reducing the once dominant Democrats to a single seat in the state cabinet and to just eight of twenty-three seats in the U.S. House delegation. The two parties have also split control of Florida's U.S. Senate seats for most of the period since 1980. At the presidential level, Florida's electoral votes were awarded to the Republican candidate in four of the five presidential contests between 1980 and 2000.

To explain the transformation of the state's political landscape, most scholars have emphasized the parallel transformation of Florida's social landscape. The old political system was the product of an essentially rural state dominated by native Floridians whose commitment to the Democratic Party was an anachronism. During the 1980s, the political system began to reflect a different social system. Florida had become primarily an urban and suburban state with millions of new residents, many of whom traced their political loyalties to Republican strongholds in the suburban East and Midwest. Cuban refugees became Republican for reasons having to do more with foreign policy than with domestic issues. They produced a substantial Republican electorate in South Florida. In the panhandle, the concentration of military facilities and retirement communities produced yet another center of GOP electoral support. This new Republican-oriented migration coincided with growing partisan instability among longtime Democrats in both rural and urban areas. Discontented with Democratic policies on civil rights, social issues, and the economy, many natives shifted allegiance to the GOP. Hence, the post-1980 Republican electoral surge simply synchronized the political and social systems.

What role did the Christian Right play in this changing political environment? Few would deny that it was a component of the shift to GOP dominance. The Republicans found fertile soil for their appeals among social conservatives. The movement itself became a training ground in which activists learned mobilizing skills that would enable them to compete effectively for public office. They also developed organizations that promoted the candidacies of Christian Right advocates for various levels of government. We now turn to the conditions that provided an opening for the movement and three factors that set limits on its progress.

SOCIAL CONDITIONS AND THE CHRISTIAN RIGHT

Compared with other southern states, Florida has relatively low levels of religious affiliation and high rates of religious diversity. The level of religiosity is largely explained by the transient nature of much of the state's population. With so many newcomers and "snowbirds" who reside in the state for only part of the year, many residents do not form the strong social ties that encourage affiliation with religious or other organizations. Among those who are religiously connected, however, Florida boasts a much wider religious spectrum than has been common in the South.[1] The large migration streams from the Northeast that gathered steam in the 1930s produced a strong Jewish community concentrated in Dade, Broward, and Palm Beach Counties. Florida's Roman Catholic population, dating back to the Spanish presence in the sixteenth century, has been augmented by the large immigrant waves from the Caribbean and South America. Florida's Protestant population is divided into three general categories: white mainline, white evangelical, and African American. These three tendencies capture unique combinations of religious style and social values. The African American churches, known for an exuberant style of worship and preaching, have a curious mixture of social conservatism and political liberalism. In practice, with race as the dominant factor, their social traditionalism is usually trumped by political liberalism.

If the broad nature of religious affiliation is not particularly conducive to the style of politics practiced by Christian conservatives, there is clearly a "base" for the movement in the core constituency of the Christian Right, evangelical Protestantism. The varieties of evangelicalism are clearly on display in Florida. From modest one-room sanctuaries in rural areas to massive congregations in cities and suburbs, Southern Baptists remain the single largest denomination among Protestants. With its multiplicity of new suburbs attracting migrants from around the country, Florida is also a natural home for a great many nondenominational or paradenominational "megachurches." These institutions, founded by religious entrepreneurs, appeal to "religious seekers" who have cut ties with their family traditions and do not have the same degree of denominational loyalty as their elders. Such churches have been the natural spawning ground of the Christian Right in Florida as elsewhere.

The nature of party politics in Florida facilitated both the emergence and political integration of groups affiliated with morally traditionalist religious organizations. Social movement success is often dependent on the degree to which activists can penetrate the political system by forming alliances with other groups. In the case of the Christian Right, the vehicle for such efforts has been the Republican Party. By comparison with their experiences in some other states, movement leaders have found it relatively easy to attain positions of power and authority within the GOP. In Florida, parties have a long tradition of organizational weakness that makes them relatively easy to capture. Many GOP county party organizations were weak and underdeveloped, allowing a determined minority of Christian Right activists to obtain control in relatively short order. Similarly, until quite recently, the Republican primary for many offices was a sideshow because the real contests occurred within the Democratic Party. As such, Christian Right candidates would find few barriers to seeking and obtaining nomination for public office under the Republican label. The high level of population turnover also worked in their favor. With a substantial turnover of the electorate every few years, voters did not have long memories that attached them strongly to individual officeholders. Thus candidates with relatively shallow roots in the state or district could compete on an equal footing with individuals who had much longer residence but who were not especially well known. With such high levels of permeability, it is not surprising that the Christian Right made serious inroads within the state GOP. As early as 1994, Florida was classified as a state where the Christian Right had become the dominant force within the state party (Persinos 1994). While this judgment appears to have been overstated (Conger and Green 2002), it also reflects the ease with which the social movement managed to join the political party.

If the environment encouraged political mobilization by conservative Christians, it also set limits on their impact. By the estimates of Republican elites and exit poll data compiled by Voter News Service (VNS), Christian conservatives now constitute about a third of the core Republican vote in primary elections. The level of religious right identification among Florida Republican primary voters was between 4 percent and 19 percent lower than in other southern states, ranking last among the eight states for which we have data from 2000. Whereas Protestants typically made up 80 percent–90 percent of the Republican primary electorate in southern states, they constituted only two-thirds of GOP voters in Florida. Groups that have been less hospitable to the Christian Right, Roman Catholics and Jews in particular, accounted for nearly a third of GOP primary voters in Florida. Elsewhere in the South, excepting the atypical case of Louisiana, those two groups seldom exceeded 10 percent of the GOP primary electorate.

These figures translate into a Republican electorate that is less socially conservative than in other southern states. The exit poll data

suggest that Florida Republican voters are more likely than their counterparts elsewhere in the South to identify themselves as moderate and
less likely to embrace the conservative label. Approximately 40 percent
favor keeping abortion legal in all or most cases. To some degree, this
reflects a statewide political culture that is more libertarian than Christian Right (Elazar 1984). Thus the social conservatives in the Florida
GOP face opposition in their own party from a large bloc of Republicans, described by one activist as "pragmatic" and "probusiness," who
are moderate on most social issues.[2] The chief lobbyists for the business
community counsel party leadership to give Christian conservatives
only enough to keep them in line.[3] Ethnic voters are another barrier to
Christian Right dominance. Self-described Hispanics accounted for 7
percent of the GOP primary electorate in 2000, a figure that was generally double that recorded in other southern states. The largest single
bloc, Cuban Americans, has reacted uneasily to the evangelical fervor
building within the state GOP.

The Christian Right is too big for the Republican Party to ignore
but too controversial for it to embrace wholeheartedly. Aware both of
the movement's power in the GOP and its divisiveness to the electorate
as a whole, Republican candidates for statewide office often try to avoid
taking extreme positions in the primary lest they be tarred in November by too close an association with the Christian Right. The most dramatic example was the odyssey of Jeb Bush, the Republican GOP
nominee in both 1994 and 1998. In 1994, facing strong opposition from
two centrist Republicans with extensive government experience, Bush
positioned himself well to the right. He chose a Christian Right icon as
his running mate and embraced the message of the movement in his
campaign pledges. Bush's narrow general election defeat in a banner
Republican year was widely attributed to his perceived extremism in the
primary. Having learned his lesson, Bush subsequently moved his image
to the center. In 1998, he took great pains to avoid appearing rigidly
ideological. In a year that was less favorable to Republicans, Jeb Bush
won the governorship easily.

Apart from internal competition, the Christian Right also has to
deal with a variety of interest groups outside the Republican Party.
Although organized labor has traditionally not played a substantial role
in state politics, several groups have been consistent opponents of the
Christian Right. The state's large Jewish community has monitored the
evolution of the Christian Right with a mixture of concern and alarm.
Concentrated primarily in north Dade, Broward, and Palm Beach

Counties, the state affiliates of national Jewish and interfaith organizations have raised public awareness of the Christian Right as a threat to church-state separation and the rights of minority groups in general. Though it shares the same antiabortion stance, the Florida Catholic Conference has also fought many of the policy initiatives of the Christian Right. African American legislators, teachers' organizations, and other interests have usually sided with the opponents of Christian conservatism on most legislative issues. By the same token, feminists, gay rights advocates, and environmentalists have won several victories against the movement in various localities.

CHRISTIAN RIGHT ORGANIZATIONS

In a large state that is less a cohesive political community than a collection of media markets, it is not surprising that the Christian Right developed unevenly across Florida. Most observers attribute the movement's emergence to the 1977 Dade County gay rights referendum (Crawford 1980). Responding to an ordinance banning employment and housing discrimination on the basis of sexual orientation, several evangelical and fundamentalist churches joined a petition drive to put the issue on the ballot for a public vote. Though the symbol of the repeal effort was the singer Anita Bryant, the key mobilizing force came from the national media ministry of the Reverend Jerry Falwell of Lynchburg, Virginia. Following the success of the repeal effort under the "Save Our Children" banner, Falwell created his national organization, the Moral Majority, conferring leadership largely on fellow members of the Baptist Bible Fellowship. Individual branches developed in greater or lesser degree, reflecting the energy and resources of the local leadership. In the early 1980s, the Florida movement had little organizational life apart from independent Baptist churches.

Throughout most of the 1980s, the principal action was local. No single organization emerged as paramount. In Hillsborough County, David Caton pursued his antipornography and anti–gay-rights crusade through a Florida affiliate of the American Family Association. His most notable success, "Take Back Tampa," emulated the Miami referendum by launching a successful campaign to repeal a local gay-rights ordinance. In the late 1990s, Caton's organization split from the national American Family Association and, apart from a failed effort to ban a gay student group in the public schools, largely receded from public view.

Caton eventually emerged as a leader of an unsuccessful effort to repeal the gay rights ordinance passed in Miami in 1998. In Broward County, Reverend D. James Kennedy built another center of Christian Right activity around his megachurch of 9,000 members, the Coral Ridge Ministries. In the mid-1990s, he set up two new organizations, a Center to Reclaim America and a Center for Christian Statesmanship. Neither has been much involved in Florida politics. Though he is head-quartered in Florida and intermittently involved in Broward County politics, Kennedy's focus appears primarily national.

Elsewhere, local Christian activists created ad hoc structures in response to local issues and occasionally mounted "stealth" campaigns for school districts or other local offices. As we noted in earlier studies (Wald 1995; Wald and Scher 1997; Wald, Scher, and Tartaglione 2000) these campaigns often succeeded to the extent they were local in scope, clearly nonpartisan, and based on issues that invoked moral traditionalism. When they were not, they often failed. The Christian Right managed to gain control of several school boards, but these officials were usually ousted by voters at the first available opportunity.

Things changed significantly when John Dowless of Orlando became executive director of the Florida Christian Coalition in 1991 (James 1996; Rado 1999). Formed out of the unsuccessful presidential candidacy of Pat Robertson in 1988, the Christian Coalition has a statewide organization with particular centers of strength in Jacksonville, Orlando, and Melbourne. Although we are aware of no empirical research on the structure of the Florida chapter, it appears active primarily at the state level with relatively little organizational development beyond the chapters in its primary areas. In 1995, Dowless began to lobby the Florida legislature on a nearly full-time basis and became a substantial presence in Tallahassee. The organization emulated other state chapters by distributing its highly partisan voter guides through a network of evangelical churches.

As we shall relate later, the policy achievements of the group, notable in a few cases, fell far short of aspirations. Particularly disappointed by failures on school prayer and abortion after the Republicans obtained control of both legislative chambers and the governor's office in 1998, Dowless resigned in 1999 to join the ill-fated presidential campaign of Steve Forbes. When the Forbes campaign collapsed, Dowless returned to Florida, seeking a seat in the state legislature he had previously lobbied. He barely made it into a runoff primary and was defeated handily by another Republican who went on to win the seat in

November. (In the same election, the Coalition's former field director, Bob West, was also beaten in the primary when he tried to challenge an incumbent county commissioner in Seminole County, just south of Orlando.) Dowless's departure seems to have robbed the Coalition— and the Christian Right—of much of its luster in Tallahassee. Other groups, such as the Eagle Forum, have tried to fill the void but none has come close to the access achieved by Dowless during his heyday. Indeed, many of the national organizations active elsewhere barely maintained a presence in Florida or were essentially one-man organizations. For example, the right-to-life movement had been a presence of some significance under the leadership of Tallahassee attorney Ken Connor. When Connor became national head of the Family Research Council, the antiabortion movement lost its most effective statewide leader.

THE 2000 FLORIDA ELECTIONS AND THE CHRISTIAN RIGHT

The Christian Right was active during the 2000 general elections, but its impact was uneven. At the presidential and U.S. senatorial levels there were candidates who sought and received support from Christian conservatives. But at the presidential level the presence of three significant third-party candidates, the extraordinary closeness of the vote, and the ambiguities associated with the various recounts make it difficult to assess whether Christian Right voters actually made the difference in that election.[4] Results in the U.S. Senate race were much clearer as the Christian Right candidate lost convincingly. In state legislative races, term limits kicked in for the first time in Florida history, and they had a far greater impact on the outcome of those races than did religious conservatives.

Christian conservatives strongly favored George W. Bush in the presidential contest. Bush in Florida portrayed himself as a moderate Republican, avoiding the kind of close association that might harm him but sending clear signals that he was sympathetic to the Christian Right. Beneath the surface his campaign sought the support of prominent Christian conservatives and employed Ralph Reed, former national director of the Christian Coalition. The major players in the Bush campaign in Florida, including his brother, Governor Jeb Bush, and Secretary of State Katherine Harris, have been much more closely associated with the business/economic conservative wing of the Florida GOP than with the Christian Right; they and others in their political orbit have significant ties to conservative Christian organizations at the county level throughout the state.

A complicating factor for the general support religious conservatives gave George W. Bush was the candidacy of Pat Buchanan on the Reform Party ticket. By the 2000 presidential campaign, the Reform Party was a mere shadow of what it had been in 1992 and 1996. Nonetheless, over 15 percent of registered voters in Florida—fully 1.4 million people—have no party affiliation, prompting Buchanan to court this potential mother lode of voters. Buchanan also enjoyed some support among religious conservatives, Catholics, nativists, and parts of the blue-collar white male population.[5]

Did Christian Right support for Buchanan hurt Bush? Hard data are not available, but a few points can be made. Buchanan actually hurt Gore in heavily Democratic Palm Beach County because of the infamous "butterfly ballot." Buchanan's unusually high vote total there has generally been regarded by statisticians as an outlier that can be explained only by voter error, not as a true indication of intended votes cast (Wand et al. 2001). But Buchanan hurt Bush elsewhere. One of the major political regions of Florida, the so-called I-4 Corridor, contains some fourteen counties running through central Florida from Daytona Beach on the east to St. Petersburg on the west.[6] It holds the largest concentration of Christian Right churches and voters in the state and sends some of the most assertive Christian conservatives to the Florida legislature. Thus data on Buchanan in this area give an indirect indication of the extent of his electoral strength among Christian conservatives. When the Palm Beach County votes are discounted, Buchanan found 40 percent of his total statewide vote along the I-4 Corridor, winning some 5,596 votes there. Only in two other counties where the Christian Right is strong—Escambia (Pensacola) in the western panhandle and Duval (Jacksonville) on the northeast coast—did Buchanan receive more than a handful of votes.

It cannot be concluded with certainty that Buchanan's absence would necessarily have benefited Bush. Some voters undoubtedly would have stayed home instead. Others might have found another candidate. But the conservative Christians who chose Buchanan are not likely to have found any of the other third-party nominees very attractive.[7] Thus it is a reasonable conclusion that the Buchanan showing along the I-4 Corridor damaged Bush.

Christian conservatives do not seem to have played a decisive role in the postelection fiasco. Though religious conservatives were among those Republicans outraged by what they saw as Gore's efforts to steal the election from Bush, their voice was scarcely heard, as other, more powerful, political voices and powers entered the fray on behalf of the GOP candidate (Scher 2001). Indeed, to the extent the election was ever resolved, the U.S. Supreme Court and media, not the Christian Right, played the crucial roles.

In the Senate race, religious conservatives had their ideal candidate in Representative Bill McCollum from the middle of the I-4 Corridor. McCollum achieved national visibility during the Clinton impeachment proceedings by serving as one of the House managers bringing charges against the president. McCollum was in a dogfight from the outset. Although he received endorsements from religious and other conservative groups, he was unable to exploit them. The Democratic nominee, former Congressman Bill Nelson, painted him as an ideological extremist.[8] McCollum was on the defensive from the start. His campaign never jelled, and he never found a coherent campaign message. He lost to Nelson by 51 percent to 46 perecent.

What role did Christian Right voters play in the campaign? McCollum was clearly their man, but Nelson attracted some religious conservatives.[9] Nelson never made issues of public morality a part of his campaign but his clean-cut image and obvious spiritual commitment appealed to some religious voters who might otherwise have supported the Republican candidate. In the I-4 Corridor, McCollum did not do nearly as well as did George W. Bush. While the Texas governor won the I-4 Corridor by 57,566 votes, McCollum lost it by nearly double Bush's margin of victory. McCollum won largely in underpopulated, largely agricultural counties where Christian conservatives are plentiful.[10] But in the populous urban counties that have provided bedrock Republican support in recent years, he did poorly.[11] Thus, the strong support of Christian conservatives was not sufficient to overcome the ineptitude of his campaign or the appeal that Nelson developed among voters.

Term limits produced massive change in the composition of the legislature following the 2000 election. Newcomers comprised 54 percent of the senate and 40 percent of the house. Despite this turnover, there was little partisan change. In the senate, the partisan balance stood at fifteen Democrats and twenty-five Republicans, the same as in 1998. Republicans gained a net of two house seats to raise their total to seventy-five, thirty more than the Democrats.

But perhaps what was most striking following the 2000 election was the choice of leaders for the house and senate. John Thrasher of Orange

Park (Clay County), a business conservative, was replaced as house speaker by Tom Feeney of Oviedo in Seminole County, in the center of the I-4 Corridor. Feeney has close ties to the Christian Right similar to those of the first Republican Speaker, Dan Webster (1997–98). Webster was from an Orange County district directly on I-4 and an original member of the house "God Squad."

In fact, Feeney had been then candidate Jeb Bush's running mate in 1994, chosen to position the ticket firmly on the right. As the 1994 campaign proceeded, religious conservatives became more secure with Bush, but it was Feeney who did the heavy religious-conservative lifting in the campaign. When Feeney ascended to the speakership following the 2000 state legislative elections, murmurings of concern were heard among the more secular elements of the Republican Party, and among Democrats.

The senate showed far more continuity in its choice of its new president for 2001–2002 than did the house. John McKay of Bradenton followed Toni Jennings of Orlando. Both Republicans were from the I-4 Corridor, but neither was ever identified with the Christian Right. They were secular business conservatives who showed little support for the Christian Right's agenda. Jennings conceded some issues to the Christian Right in order to preserve party harmony, but the legislation approved by the senate under her leadership was mild compared with some of the bills floated in the house.

THE FLORIDA CHRISTIAN RIGHT AND PUBLIC POLICY

Throughout the 1990s, religious conservatives focused most of their political energy and activity in two major venues—the state legislature and local government, especially school boards—and concentrated on abortion, parental rights, protection of the family, and prayer and religious curricula in public schools. Social conservatives did meet with some successes: the legislature passed a "parental consent" bill aimed at minor females seeking abortions and overrode the late Governor Lawton Chiles's veto of a partial-birth abortion ban. But they did not succeed in passing a school prayer bill, in part because new Governor Jeb Bush insisted that one not be placed on his desk. On the other hand, social conservatives realized success in electing members of the school board in some counties, finding ways to include "voluntary" prayer at school events such as football games and graduations, and establishing

Bible study groups on high school campuses and even courses that included sectarian interpretation of the Bible and religion.

We concluded in earlier studies (Wald 1995; Wald and Scher 1997; Wald, Scher, and Tartaglione 2000) that religious conservatives in Florida did not succeed in shaping statewide public policies despite the size of their constituency, energy and focus in the political arena, and access to state officials. This latter point is especially important. In the 1997–98 session, the Christian Coalition's John Dowless essentially operated directly out of the office of House Speaker Dan Webster. But Christian Coalition leaders did not have the same level of access to the subsequent speaker, John Thrasher (1999–2000).

How does the most recent period in Florida politics (2000–2002) fit into this pattern of continuity? Have religious conservatives pursued the same agenda as they did in the past, and with the same level of success?

During its 2000 session, the legislature passed and Governor Bush signed into law a bill that banned so-called partial-birth abortions. Various groups of religious conservatives, including the Christian Coalition, strongly supported it. In fact, a similar bill had been passed years before on an override of a veto by Governor Chiles but was subsequently held unconstitutional (Becker 2000a). But in 2000, Christian conservatives secured a clear-cut victory in passing the legislation, unfettered by executive vetoes or delays. The passage of a partial-birth abortion ban was not quite the victory religious conservatives trumpeted. Passage of the ban in no way interfered legally with other types of abortion procedures that are more common. In late June 2000, the U.S. Supreme Court struck down a Nebraska law similar to the Florida statute. The Court's five-to-four decision overturned the Nebraska statute on the grounds that it was too broad, could be interpreted to cover other types of procedures, and unnecessarily put women seeking a procedure at risk (Mitchell 2000). Much to the disappointment of religious conservatives, Florida officials made no effort to enforce the state ban.

The 2001 Florida legislative session saw a shift in the agenda of social conservatives. While bills were introduced on the perennial issues of school prayer and abortions, they never emerged from committees. The major issue that engaged social conservatives in the 2001 legislature focused on the Florida Supreme Court and the manner in which judges are chosen. In fact, this was not a new issue at all. When the Constitutional Revision Commission met during 1997, social conservatives put forth proposals that would have required nominees for judgeships to state their positions on certain key issues, thereby creating a sort of litmus test for applicants that religious conservatives could publicize, presumably with the goal of defeating judicial candidates who did not provide the "right" answers.

The attack on judicial independence gained steam following the involvement of the Florida Supreme Court in the aftermath of the presidential election. By allowing some recounts, the court appeared hostile to the candidacy of George W. Bush. When the 2001 legislative session convened, bills had already been prefiled to pack the supreme court by expanding its membership to nine, and by significantly changing the way the governor appointed new judges.[12] The court-packing plan died, but the legislature did give the governor vast new powers to choose judges by allowing him to stack the state's judicial nominating commissions with his own appointees, greatly reducing the role of the Florida Bar, and even allowed the governor to reject commissions' list of names forwarded to him until he received a list he liked (Wasson 2001).

The Christian Coalition and its allies strongly supported this legislation. But the Christian Right had little influence on passage of the judicial nominating bill. Republicans in the legislature, and apparently the governor as well, were incensed over the role of the Florida Supreme Court during the election aftermath. Determined to attack it but recognizing that a frontal assault would assuredly lose, they could accomplish their purposes more quietly, but just as effectively, by removing the Florida Bar from the judicial appointment process and substituting gubernatorial authority instead. Undoubtedly legislative Republicans and the governor were happy to have the support of the Christian Right as they carried out their plan, but the bill would have passed anyway.

ASSESSING THE POLITICAL IMPACT OF CHRISTIAN CONSERVATIVES IN FLORIDA STATE POLITICS

What can we conclude about the impact that Christian conservatives have had on Florida politics in recent years? The evidence is mixed and in large measure it depends on what criteria one uses in making the assessment.

If, for example, one looks solely at legislation sponsored or supported by the Christian Right in Tallahassee as the dependent variable, the evidence suggests its impact has been fairly modest. True, two important pieces of legislation social conservatives wanted were passed: the partial-birth abortion ban and increasing the role of the governor in picking judges. But in terms of substantive legislation, these were the only major successes they had, and their victory on partial-birth abortions was immediately snatched away by the U.S. Supreme Court.

No doubt, the disappointments of the Christian Right since 1998 are due in part to specific circumstances. Knowledgeable Tallahassee journalists interviewed for this chapter indicated they noticed a significant change in both the visibility and style of the Christian Coalition and its allies. The departure of John Dowless had a significant impact on the organization. Dowless was smart, articulate, politically savvy. He was respected even by his opponents as an effective spokesman for Christian conservatives. Although there was no criticism of the new director, Terry Kemple, the point was made more than once that "Kemple is not Dowless."

Moreover, Dowless had the advantage of working directly out of the office of the Speaker of the House Dan Webster. Speaker Thrasher did not provide such immediate access to Dowless or the Christian Coalition, and journalists felt the Christian Coalition's influence waned. Just as important—perhaps more important—is the fact that Governor Jeb Bush upon assuming office in 1999 did not wish to become a captive of the Christian Right's political agenda. By drawing a fence around religious conservatives, he limited what they were able to expect. Speaker Feeney, of course, represents a throwback to the strong support Webster gave religious conservatives, but there is no evidence that he provided office space to Kemple. It is not clear that they have quite the level of access to Feeney that Dowless did to Webster, or hold key slots in the Tallahassee political loop, as they did a few years earlier.

Apart from these essentially transitory phenomena, the Christian Right is also subject to structural limitations. In our judgment, the major such barriers to influence beyond the local level are (1) differences between the two houses of the Florida legislature, (2) term limits, and (3) the state judiciary.

The Legislature

Over the past two decades, the Christian Right has done best in the house of representatives but has frequently seen its house victories undone by senate indifference or conscious resistance. As if to illustrate that point, just as we were putting the final touches on this chapter, a special session of the legislature adjourned without passing a bill to revise the state's school code. The crux of the difference was a "religious freedom" code that house conservatives insisted on but the senate refused to consider. Although public commentary emphasized the personal animosity between the leaders of the two bodies, the difference goes beyond personality. The house has had two speakers who were Christian Right stalwarts and, assuming Republicans hold their large majority after the 2002 elections, will have a third in Johnny Byrd from Plant City, one of the most socially conservative members of the house. On the other side, the business-oriented moderates who have run the senate in the last two legislatures will be succeeded by another urban Republican associated with the GOP moderate wing, James King. King rather decisively defeated his rival, former house speaker and Christian Right darling Dan Webster.

Why should the senate prove less amenable to Christian Right influence than the house? The most likely suspect is size: Florida senate districts have roughly three times as many inhabitants as house districts. In three ways, this seems to make members of the senate generally more moderate than representatives in the house.

First, with larger and more heterogeneous districts, senators have to appeal to a more diverse electorate than typically characterizes a house district. Under these circumstances, state senators are likely to avoid taking positions that are identified with intense minorities lest such stands alienate significant portions of their larger constituency.

Size also moderates the Florida senate through its influence on the culture of the chamber. As political activists recounted to us, senators inhabit an environment permeated by a sense of trusteeship. Senators take both a longer and a broader view in evaluating legislative proposals than is true of house members, exhibiting a greater sense of personal responsibility for the conduct of government. On first sitting at a desk on the senate floor, one newly elected senator who had previously served in the house described feeling that "Everybody can see me!" In the house, by contrast, "I could throw a bomb and nobody would notice" amidst 119 other representatives. By increasing the visibility of every legislator, our informant concluded, the senate's intimate environment moderated the behavior of new senators who had been firebrands while serving in the house.

Size matters in yet a third way. In a summary essay about the qualities that make the U.S. Senate so different from the U.S. House, Larry Dodd (2002, 359) points to the adaptive learning environment that occurs in a body that reserves substantial power for a relatively small number of legislators. A variety of factors—institutional role, size, method of election, susceptibility to external shocks, and others—produce in the Senate a "transient, erratic, idiosyncratic and improvisational political world." The consequence is an operating style that differs substantially from the heavily structured, majoritarian, partisan U.S. House. We believe the same dynamic is at work in the Florida senate.

Term Limits

The second structural factor, term limits, was adopted by referendum in 1992 but first applied to sitting legislators in 2000. Apart from their effects on the general struggle for power, term limits provided interest groups such as the Christian Right with both an opportunity and a challenge. They have to identify, recruit, and groom favored candidates on a regular basis to assure a steady stream of legislators sympathetic to their views. This, of course, augments their role in political campaigning. But they also know that the useful shelf life of their candidates is limited, because today's ally will be gone tomorrow. Thus the process never ends. In addition, the Christian Right needs to establish close ties with the dominant party in each house and its leadership circle to influence the succession of legislative leaders in the years ahead.

The Judiciary

Finally, the Christian Right has to deal with the continuing role of the judiciary. It remains charged with responsibilities that may impede the progress of the movement. On several occasions, state judges have declared unconstitutional important legislation passed at the behest or with the support of Christian conservatives. The justices of the Florida Supreme Court retain the capacity to approve or disapprove ballot language on critical initiatives proposed by social conservatives. In instances in which judges may agree with the policy positions of religious conservatives, they nonetheless remain bound by judicial norms and the constraints of constitutionalism. Even the most sympathetic social conservative on the bench may decide that the movement's goals are incompatible with the rule of law. We should thus expect the judicial branch to continue as an obstacle in the way of some of the most cherished policy goals of the Christian Right.

The Longer View

To this point, we have stressed the limits of the Christian Right, noting both the influence of the state's religious and social diversity and the structural forces that operate to weaken the movement at the state level. If we change the dependent variable, looking at the impact of the Christian Right through another set of lenses, a different picture emerges, one that suggests social conservatives have had a significant impact on Florida politics. These lenses involve, first, the Christian Right in local government, and, second, its effect on the political culture and climate of Florida.

In earlier studies (Wald 1995; Wald and Scher 1997; Wald, Scher, and Tartaglione 2000) we showed that much of the Christian Right's political success in Florida took place in local governments, especially school boards. Whether or not they ran "stealth" campaigns to mask their true purposes or ran overtly as candidates of the Christian Right, they succeeded in capturing a number of school board seats and in some cases a majority of the board. These instances, such as in Lake County along the I-4 Corridor and in Lee County (Ft. Myers) in southwest Florida, have been well documented, including the extraordinary levels of conflict and community resentment that occurred as Christian Right school board members shoved their values and beliefs right into the school curriculum.

In both of these instances, of course, voters eventually replaced the religious conservatives with secular ones. But religious conservatives have not disappeared as candidates. Indeed, they continue to surface and in some cases succeed in winning office. For example, the chair of the Citrus County School Board, a self-professed Christian conservative, continues to open meetings with an overtly Christian prayer ending with the phrase "I pray in the name of Jesus my savior" (Behrendt 2001). Newspaper accounts detailed steps she proposed to enhance the extent of Christian religious activity in the public schools. In the nearby agricultural community of Inglis along the Citrus-Levy county border, the mayor issued a Christian proclamation banning Satan from the town (Voyles 2002).

A reasonable argument could be made that these instances are trivial and amount to nothing beyond symbolism. But in fact they can also point to a much larger matter, which is the way in which both the rhetoric and agenda of religious conservatives have become part of the very fabric of political style and culture in Florida. Indeed, wherever one now looks in Florida, religious phrasing and concerns permeate the political environment, and much of it is based in the Christian Right. The two examples cited above and the incidents that we described at the outset of the chapter are small but evocative illustrations of this point.

But matters don't stop there. Governor Bush publicly supports many of its goals, especially on abortions, parental rights, family values, judicial reform, and school vouchers. His appointee, Health Secretary Bob Brooks, attracted considerable media and public attention when he told a Christian Coalition luncheon that they help "elect godly and moral people" to public office as a way of helping good triumph over evil (Hauserman 2000). Interviews conducted for this study with even moderate Democratic public officials, including one Jewish legislator, indicated they were very conscious of the power of religious conservatives in the political atmosphere. Several indicated they voted for legislation about which they were very dubious just because they did not want to be attacked or even smeared by the Christian Right in upcoming political campaigns. One indicated that both during campaigns and once in office, he tried during public forums or presentations to sound sympathetic to some of the concerns of religious conservatives, even though their agenda was low on his list of priorities. He felt doing so was for his own political protection.

Other examples could be given, but the point should be clear. While the impact of the Christian Right on Florida politics may be limited in terms of its role in passing statewide legislation, it may have much greater effect on the political texture of the state. Indeed, it may well be that the major effect of the Christian Right in Florida has little to do with specific policies. Rather, the movement has unleashed a spirit of religiosity that has permeated the fabric of politics in the state.

NOTES

1. A comparison with the neighboring state of Georgia emphasizes the difference. Forty percent of Florida voters told the Voter News Service (VNS) exit survey that they seldom or never attended religious services, compared with just 30 percent in Georgia. Whereas Protestants constituted three-fourths of Georgia voters, they made up only 56 percent of the Florida electorate. The proportions of Roman Catholics and Jews in Florida were, respectively, two and a half times and two times the proportion in Georgia. These data can be found at www.cnn.com/Election/2000/primaries. See also Kosmin and Lachman (1993, 82).

2. The social location of the respective GOP constituencies is apparent from the voting patterns of Florida's Republican congressional representatives. The three representatives who voted for the traditionalist position on social issues at least 90 percent of the time (as defined by *National Journal*) represented districts that were predominantly military or small town in nature. By contrast, the Republicans who represented the major urban centers such as Jacksonville,

Orlando, and Palm Beach County voted conservatively on these questions three-fifths of the time. The same relatively low rate of support for the Christian Right agenda was evident among representatives from districts on the southwest coast with large numbers of midwestern retirees and among the Cuban Americans from South Florida. Were such data available for state legislators, it would probably show similar results.

3. This activist drew an analogy with the role of African Americans in the Democratic Party.

4. Gore actually won the county vote cast on Election Day 2000, by 172 votes. The 2000 VNS Florida exit poll did not include the now standard question on membership with the "religious right." However, the national exit poll found that 19.7 percent of Florida voters were white and members of the religious right. This figure must be viewed with some caution, but it is comparable to the 1996 Florida exit poll, where the comparable number was 17 percent.

5. This last group, sometimes referred to as the "Bubba" vote, probably switched to George W. Bush, whose swagger and macho style would have appealed to them.

6. These counties are Brevard, Flagler, Hardee, Hillsborough, Lake, Manatee, Marion, Orange, Osceola, Pinellas, Polk, Seminole, Sumter, and Volusia.

7. It would, for example, have been a great leap of faith for Christian conservatives to choose Harry Browne of the Libertarian Party. The Libertarian reluctance to legislate morality or invade privacy rights does not sit well with religious conservatives' agenda.

8. In truth, while Florida is a conservative state, in the main state leaders and the congressional delegation have been nondoctrinaire conservative pragmatists. The most recent exceptions are McCollum and Governor Bush.

9. There are not large numbers of these individuals, but they can be found in the more traditional, "old South" parts of the state in north central Florida north of Marion County and from west of Duval County to the central panhandle.

10. Besides the three counties mentioned, McCollum won Hardee, Lake, Seminole, and Sumter.

11. McCollum lost Brevard (Nelson's home county), Flagler, Hillsborough (Tampa), Orange (Orlando), Pinellas (St. Petersburg and Clearwater), Polk (Lakeland), and Volusia (Daytona Beach).

12. A similar bill had been introduced in the 2000 session but was subsequently killed by its own sponsor (Becker 2000b).

REFERENCES

Becker, Jo. 2000a. "Governor Signs Ban on 'Partial Birth' Abortions." *St. Petersburg Times* (26 May).

———. 2000b. "Sponsor Kills Proposal to Pack Supreme Court." *St. Petersburg Times* (9 March).

Behrendt, Barbara. 2001. "Critic Blasts School Official's Prayer." *St. Petersburg Times* (14 February).

Conger, Kimberly H., and John C. Green. 2002. "Spreading Out and Digging In: Christian Conservatives and State Republican Parties." *Campaigns & Elections* (February):58–64.

Crawford, Alan. 1980. *Thunder on the Right.* New York: Pantheon.

Dodd, Lawrence C. 2002. "Making Sense Out of Our Exceptional Senate: Perspectives and Commentary." Pp. 350–63 in *The Exceptional U.S. Senate,* ed. Bruce I. Oppenheimer. Columbus: Ohio State University Press.

Elazar, Daniel. 1984. *American Federalism: A View from the States.* 3d ed. New York: Harper and Row.

Hauserman, Judy. 2000. "Health Secretary, 'Elect Godly and Moral People.'" *St. Petersburg Times* (24 March).

James, Meg. 1996. "State's Christian Coalition Leader Gaining Influence." *Palm Beach Post* (7 July).

Key, V. O., Jr. 1949. *Southern Politics.* New York: Vintage Books.

Kosmin, Barry A., and Seymour P. Lachman. 1993. *One Nation Under God? Religion in Contemporary American Society.* New York: Harmony Books.

Mitchell, Robin. 2000. "Late-Term Abortion Ban on Hold." *St. Petersburg Times* (7 July).

Persinos, John F. 1994. "Has the Christian Right Taken Over the Republican Party?" *Campaigns & Elections* (September):20–24.

Rado, Diane. 1999. "Conservative Voice Leaves to Join Forbes." *St. Petersburg Times* (29 July).

Santoro, Wayne A., and Gail M. McGuire. 1997. "Social Movement Insiders: The Impact of Institutional Activists on Affirmative Action and Comparable Worth Policies." *Social Problems* 44:503–19.

Scher, Richard K. 2001. "Grasping at Straws, Rushing to Judgment: Election Reform in Florida, 2001." *Journal of Law and Public Policy* 13:81–102.

Voyles, Karen. 2002. "Inglis Mayor Banishes Satan." *Gainesville Sun* (5 January).

Wald, Kenneth D. 1995. "Florida: Running Globally and Winning Locally." Pp. 19–46. In Mark J. Rozell and Clyde Wilcox, eds., *God at the Grassroots.* Lanham, Md.: Rowman and Littlefield.

Wald, Kenneth D., and Jeffrey Corey. 2002. "The Christian Right and Public Policy: Social Movement Elites as Institutional Activists." *State Politics and Policy Quarterly* 2:99–125.

Wald, Kenneth D., and Richard K. Scher. 1997. "Losing by Winning? The Odyssey of the Religious Right in Florida." Pp. 77–78. In *God at the Grassroots 1996,* ed. Mark J. Rozell and Clyde Wilcox. Lanham, Md.: Rowman and Littlefield.

Wald, Kenneth D., Richard K. Scher, and Maureen Tartaglione. 2000. "Answered Prayers and Mixed Blessings: The Christian Right in Florida." Pp. 115–44 in *Prayers in the Precincts: The Christian Right in the 1998 Elections*, ed. Mark J. Rozell and Clyde Wilcox. Washington, D.C.: Georgetown University Press.

Wand, Jonathan N., Kenneth W. Shotts, Jasjeet C. Sekhon, Walter R. Mebane, Jr., Michael C. Herron, and Henry E. Brady. 2001. "The Butterfly Did It: The Aberrant Vote for Buchanan in Palm Beach County, Florida." *American Political Science Review* 95 (December):793–810.

Wasson, David. 2001. "Bush Gets More Power to Choose Judges." *Tampa Tribune* (20 June).

———. 2002. "Jewish Group Criticizes Legislature." *Tampa Tribune* (25 January):1B, 6B.

FIVE

The Christian Right's Mixed Success in Michigan

Corwin E. Smidt and James M. Penning

SINCE THE 1970S, THE CHRISTIAN RIGHT IN MICHIGAN HAS enjoyed mixed success in promoting its political agenda. While Christian conservatives can point to some notable victories, including efforts to provide state funding for charter schools, restrict access to abortions, and promote term limits for elected officials, they have been less successful in efforts to limit the spread of casino gambling and secure vouchers for students attending private and parochial schools. This chapter examines the politics of the Christian Right in Michigan over the past two decades in an effort to better understand the nature of the Christian Right in the state and to explain the reasons for its varied success. Three major topics are addressed: (1) the ecology of Michigan politics, (2) the organization of the Christian Right in Michigan, and (3) the political impact of the Christian Right in Michigan. The chapter concludes with a discussion of factors contributing to the success and failure of the Christian Right in the state.

By "Christian Right," we are referring to a wide variety of individuals and groups, rooted largely, but not exclusively, in the Protestant tradition, and committed to the promotion of culturally conservative values. It is important to recognize that, in Michigan as in other states, the Christian Right is not a static phenomenon but has changed considerably over time. Like the Christian Right in Virginia (Rozell and Wilcox 1996, 4), the Christian Right in Michigan has evolved from a disorganized social movement into a set of organized interest groups and party factions. During the 1970s, the Christian Right in Michigan was perhaps best categorized as a disorganized social movement consisting of a diverse array of individuals and groups concerned about perceived cultural drift in American society and ideologically liberal public policies. However, today's Christian Right in Michigan is best perceived either as a collection of organized interest groups or as a faction within the state's Republican Party.

THE ECOLOGY OF MICHIGAN POLITICS

Political groups, whether viewed in terms of social movements, interest group systems, or party factions, arise out of, and can be profoundly shaped by, the ecology in which they are rooted. Michigan exhibits tremendous economic diversity. Long known as the nation's leading automobile manufacturing center, the state also relies heavily on such varied industries as agriculture and tourism to bolster its economy. Michigan's economic diversity is accompanied by considerable ethnic diversity, as approximately 82 percent of Michigan's population today is white, 15 percent black, and 3 percent Hispanic, with the remaining population consisting of native Americans, Asians, and others (State of Michigan 2000).

Michigan is also religiously diverse. The state's largest religious denomination is Roman Catholic, with approximately 24 percent of Michigan residents claiming Catholic affiliation. Indeed, Catholics are exceedingly powerful politically in the state, not only because of their large numbers but because, in recent years, traditional Catholic loyalty to the Democratic Party has diminished. Today, Catholics constitute the most important group of "swing" voters in the state, and the Republican Party is making a significant effort to woo Catholic voters (Potts 2001). Other major denominations in Michigan include mainline denominations such as United Methodist, Congregational, and the Presbyterian Church (USA) as well as evangelical denominations such as Assemblies of God and American Baptists. In addition, Michigan has witnessed the growth of a number of independent "megachurches" that claim little or no relationship to specific denominations but tend to be theologically and culturally conservative.

Most studies of Michigan point to its largely "moralistic" political culture, characterized by a search for a broad public good and a suspicion of specialized interests (Elazar 1972). This "moralism," a legacy of the northern European heritage of many of Michigan's early settlers, has contributed to the state's reputation for pursuing innovative, progressive public policies (Fenton 1966). However, the moralism of Michigan's early settlers has been tempered by the individualism of white "ethnics" and African Americans who dominate some of the state's major cities and, in particular, Wayne County (Detroit). The two cultures frequently clash in the Michigan legislature as moralistic legislators from regions such as West Michigan find themselves at odds with more individualistic legislators from the southeastern region of the state.

A final component of the ecology in which the Christian Right in Michigan must operate is the institutional environment. One important element of this environment is the structure of the state's government. Michigan government is complex, rational, and professional. Top executive officials such as the governor are granted substantial formal powers (Hanley and Rozycki 2000, chap. 7), and the state legislature is among the most "professional" in the nation, as indicated by its high levels of staff support, full-time salaries of members, and unrestricted length of legislative sessions (Squire 1992).

One fairly recent development affecting both Michigan governmental institutions and the groups that seek to influence public officials has been the implementation of term limits for state officials. In 1992, Michigan voters approved a constitutional initiative that limits the maximum term length to a total of six years for state representatives and eight years for state senators and top state executives (including the governor, secretary of state, and attorney general). These term limits are among the most restrictive in the nation, and they have important implications for groups such as Christian Right organizations that seek to influence state government. One important consequence, for example, is that term limits have stimulated a continual search for new leadership to replace term-limited officials. Thus, groups are increasingly focusing on local elections (e.g., for city and county commission) as prime recruiting venues for developing future state leaders (Penning 2003).

Michigan's strong political parties are able to exercise considerable control over nominations and to provide substantial resources to candidates for elective office. The parties tend to garner distinct regional and group support. In general, Democrats receive substantial support from labor unions, trial lawyers, and minority groups, while Republicans fare better among small businesspersons, farmers, and suburban whites. Democrats find their greatest support in Wayne County (Detroit) and in the cities of the I-75 corridor, while Republicans do best in suburban areas and in the medium-sized cities of western Michigan. The two parties don't like each other very much, and they often find it difficult to work together in the state legislature.

Michigan is home to a wide variety of strong, active interest groups that seek to influence state and local officials (Hanley and Rozycki 2000, chap. 4). Some of the most active and powerful interest groups lean Democratic—e.g., the major labor unions (particularly the United Auto Workers and the Michigan Education Association), the trial lawyers associations, and the beer and wine wholesalers. Other active and powerful interest groups in the state lean Republican—e.g., the Chamber of Commerce, the Farm Bureau, and the Michigan Realtors Association. The fact that there are so many powerful interest groups in Michigan means that Christian Right groups must struggle to make their voices heard above the cacophony of competing demands placed on state government.

THE ORGANIZATION OF THE CHRISTIAN RIGHT IN MICHIGAN

The Christian Right in Michigan is organizationally fragmented; no single group or organization fully embodies the movement or speaks for all its supporters. In part, this fragmentation reflects the fact that, in an organizational sense, the Christian Right in the state is still a relatively new phenomenon. Today's Christian Right political activism in Michigan can trace its roots to the early 1960s, when U.S. Supreme Court decisions outlawing prayer in public schools and protecting abortion rights, as well as the political turmoil surrounding the Vietnam War, shocked cultural conservatives, generating widespread concern over perceived cultural drift and government hostility toward traditional values. However, it took several decades for these somewhat amorphous concerns to generate political action and organizational development.

The political success of Jimmy Carter, a born-again Christian, and the 1988 presidential campaign of Reverend Pat Robertson no doubt contributed to raising both the political consciousness and the levels of political confidence among potential Christian Right activists (Penning 1994). Nonetheless, with the exception of Right-to-Life of Michigan, the Christian Right in Michigan has only recently moved from a rather disorganized social movement, consisting of a wide variety of disparate individuals with diverse concerns, to a set of political organizations. This "institutionalization" of the Christian Right is still incomplete, and not all Christian Right organizations are healthy and politically effective.

Right-to-Life of Michigan (RTLM)

Begun in the late 1960s, RTLM is one of Michigan's most powerful interest groups—well led, well focused, well financed, and well organized. Indeed, the *Detroit News* has suggested that RTLM "now rivals organized labor as a power on the state's political landscape" (Cain 1997, 1). Its power is revealed by the considerable support it receives among the state's political leaders. Not only has RTLM enjoyed the support of Michigan's (Roman Catholic) former governor, John Engler, but it is currently supported by a majority of members of the state legislature (particularly Republicans).

A second indicator of RTLM's political clout is its success in influencing the nomination process for candidates running for top elected offices, particularly in the Republican Party. Not since Governor Milliken's 1978 campaign has a prochoice Republican been nominated for governor. And recently, RTLM has successfully blocked efforts of prochoice candidates seeking GOP endorsement at statewide conventions (Cain 1997, 1).

The political muscle of RTLM is also reflected in its ability to help elect candidates in general elections. One important race in which RTLM may have played a decisive role was the exceedingly close 1990 gubernatorial race pitting incumbent Democrat James Blanchard and (RTLM-endorsed) Republican challenger John Engler. In general, RTLM has had a very high success rate in those elections in which it has endorsed candidates, although some of this success may reflect the group's selectivity in candidate endorsement. For example, in 1998, a remarkable 83.3 percent of RTLM-endorsed candidates won, and the organization saw a gain of eleven prolife seats in the Michigan House and a gain of one seat in the senate. In the 2001–2002 legislative session, fully 66 of the 110 members of the Michigan house and 25 of the 38 members of the Michigan senate came to Lansing with RTLM's endorsement, whereas only 34 members of the house and 10 members of the senate were endorsed by Planned Parenthood, a leading prochoice group (Scott and Deiters 2001, A4).

Finally, the political effectiveness of RTLM is revealed by its ability to influence public policy. RTLM has successfully developed voter initiatives to ban tax-paid abortions for poor women (1988) and require parental consent for minors seeking abortions (1990). RTLM has been so successful in working with the Michigan legislature that *Detroit Free Press* reporter Brian Dickerson argues that "the Legislature is practically a wholly owned subsidiary of Right to Life" (Dickerson 2000). In the 1999–2000 session, members of the Michigan legislature introduced sixty-six bills, the most ever, which made the "watch list" of prochoice activists (Scott and Deiters 2001, A1), and passed twenty-three measures dealing with abortion and family planning, many of them intended to limit the numbers of abortions (Heinlein 2000).

Several factors help to explain the success of RTLM in Michigan. First, RTLM is among the best-organized interest groups in the state, carefully coordinating over 120 affiliates across the state. In addition, the group has benefited from a long period of stable, skilled leadership from its president, Barb Listing, a woman with excellent political instincts, outstanding organizational skills, and a high degree of commitment to her cause. And, finally, RTLM's political clout reflects the sheer numbers as well as the commitment of its political supporters (Scott and Deiters 2001, A4).

Michigan Family Forum

Another relatively strong Christian Right organization is the Michigan Family Forum (MFF). Headquartered in Lansing, MFF was founded in April 1990, as a nonprofit research and education organization with a 501(c)3 Internal Revenue Service status. As a 501(c)3 organization, MFF must abide by IRS regulations that prohibit it from devoting a "substantial part of its activities" to influencing legislation. Consequently, in contrast to RTLM, MFF does not hire lobbyists or sponsor a political action committee.

MFF was established to function as a "family policy council" and is associated with Focus on the Family, a national organization headed by Dr. James Dobson, whose radio program is aired on over 1,450 radio stations nationwide. However, MFF is neither legally nor financially tied to the Focus on the Family organization. Though both groups promote a similar agenda, they do not share funds or attempt to integrate their organizational structures.

MFF generally advocates efforts to limit the size and scope of government (Michigan Family Forum 2001, 2), but it does tend to favor government activity in support of a profamily legislative agenda, including support for repeal of no-fault divorce laws, abstinence-based sex education, and school choice. MFF pursues a fairly broad policy agenda, since it perceives numerous types of policies as having the potential to influence the family. Although the group's primary focus is on social issues such as divorce, education, and school choice, it also has emphasized a number of economic issues, including tax breaks for families. Pursuing such a large policy agenda has its drawbacks in that it limits the organization's ability to target its resources very effectively.

Although MFF is arguably Michigan's leading profamily organization, several other groups also claim the profamily label and pursue agendas that, to some degree, overlap with MFF's agenda. One of these is the Michigan chapter of the American Family Association (AFA), which in recent years has played an increasingly visible role in state politics, focusing its attention on opposing gay-rights initiatives across the state. In addition, AFA of Michigan opposes pornography, "radical" environmentalists, and speech codes (American Family Association of Michigan 2001, 1).

AFA's aggressive style has sparked countermobilization, particularly from the gay community and certain members of the political left. Recently, for example, a group labeling itself, "We all are Traverse City," vehemently opposed AFA's efforts to block a proposed gay rights ordinance in Traverse City, going so far as to publish an "AFA of Michigan Report Card" on its website. The Report Card suggested that, for the most part, AFA's efforts to oppose gay-rights proposals have been failures. However, other AFA of Michigan opponents give the group grudging praise. For example, the *Adult Video News* claimed that "Michigan is infested with the strongest and largest chapter of the AFA" (American Decency Association 2001, 2).

Another profamily group operating in Michigan is the American Decency Association (ADA). ADA, a 1999 offshoot of AFA, seeks to monitor "offensive" broadcasting and to persuade advertisers not to support such broadcasting. One of its chief activities is to monitor the Howard Stern radio show in nineteen cities and the Howard Stern television show in ten cities across the United States. Each month ADA sends over 1,000 letters to sponsors of the Howard Stern show. The group claims considerable success in this effort, contending that of the 14,339 advertisers who have been contacted, 12,835 have withdrawn their advertisements. ADA's activities, however, are not limited to opposing Howard Stern. In recent years its targets have been as diverse as women's magazines (*Cosmopolitan* and *Glamour*), major businesses (Disney, Abercrombie & Fitch, Victoria's Secret, Family Video), and even some public arenas that have accommodated "objectionable content" (Van Andel Arena).

Citizens for Traditional Values

Based in Lansing, Citizens for Traditional Values (CTV) traces its origins to Reverend Pat Robertson's 1988 presidential campaign. Originally organized in 1986 as the Michigan Committee for Freedom, it promptly became involved in supporting Robertson's campaign for the White House. However, shortly after Robertson's defeat, the Robertson forces largely withdrew from the state, leaving the organization in shambles— leaderless, confused, and deeply in debt. At that time, the board of directors of the Michigan Committee for Freedom decided to employ James Muffitt, former director of Pat Robertson's Vermont campaign, to head their organization. Muffitt acted quickly and decisively to eliminate the organization's $500,000 debt. In 1995, the group adopted its current name.

To a substantial degree, CTV's guiding principles parallel those endorsed by MFF, although CTV tends to take a more explicitly free-market approach to economic issues and to give higher priority to economic policy. Moreover, CTV also parallels MFF in that it has adopted a rather broad policy agenda. Indeed, CTV literature (Citizens for Traditional Values 1997, 1–2) encourages citizens to question candidates for public office on a wide variety of policy issues relating to "faith and family," the "proper role of government," and "education."

In pursuing its objectives, CTV has enjoyed at least a limited degree of success. Indeed, former Michigan Lieutenant Governor Dick Posthumus has called CTV "the most underrated political organization in Michigan in relation to the amount of impact generated." And former Michigan Speaker of the House, Paul Hillegonds, asserts that "without the help of Citizens for Traditional Values, many of the important legislative reforms that the House passed in 1993 might never have been passed" (Citizens for Traditional Values 1997, 4).

Over time CTV has institutionalized and developed a fairly complex organizational structure, though not as complex as that of RTLM or MFF. In 1993, CTV created the Foundation for Traditional Values (FTV), a tax-exempt, nonprofit organization, to serve as its educational wing. FTV publishes a newsletter that gives special attention to education issues, sponsors an annual Student Statesmanship Institute, and distributes a variety of educational books, tapes, and other materials.

CTV has also established a separate political action committee (PAC) to assist candidates running in select, targeted legislative districts. To win endorsement, a candidate must "reflect basic pro-family values, which include support for: the sanctity of life, Judeo-Christian standards of morality in public policy, educational and academic freedom for parents and schools [and] a free enterprise philosophy minimizing governmental control over families and business" (Citizens for Traditional Values 2000).

Perhaps CTV's primary electoral activity involves producing voter guides for key state legislative races. In addition, CTV has endorsed large numbers of candidates for federal office. In the 2000 election, for example, CTV's PAC endorsed 71 candidates for the 110-member state house of representatives as well as one U.S. Senate candidate, eight candidates for the U.S. House of Representatives, three state supreme court candidates, and a variety of candidates for university governing boards and the state board of education. In addition, the PAC publicized the group's positions on two ballot proposals, including a controversial proposal to provide vouchers for students attending nonpublic schools. Virtually all of the endorsed candidates are cultural conservatives, and the vast majority are Republicans (Citizens for Traditional Values 2000). Like MFF, CTV makes a special effort to mobilize church members, its natural constituency, and has produced a brochure titled "Why Should Christians Vote?"

Compared with RTLM or even MFF, CTV is exceedingly small. For example, CTV and FTV combined have a staff of approximately ten people, including clerical workers. And whereas FTV has a relatively modest annual budget of approximately $200,000, CTV spends less than half that amount each year.

Christian Coalition of Michigan

While the national Christian Coalition may be the best-known Christian Right organization, its strength and activity level vary tremendously across states and localities (Berkowitz and Green 1997). In Michigan, the Christian Coalition (CCM) is exceedingly weak across the entire state, demonstrating little ability to mobilize volunteers or influence elections. For example, when the national Christian Coalition sponsored its tenth annual Road to Victory convention in Washington (1999), only a few Michigan residents showed up. Asserts CCM Chairman, Jack Horton, a former state legislator, "For all practical purposes, the Christian Coalition in Michigan is non-existent" (Zagaroli 1999, 1).

Like CTV, CCM traces its heritage in part to the Michigan Committee for Freedom. But it wasn't until 1991 that CCM was officially established as a tax-exempt, nonprofit organization. Thus, like CTV, CCM has devoted itself to such "nonpartisan" activities as distributing voter guides for election campaigns. Indeed, over the past decade, distributing voter guides has been the single most important political activity undertaken by CCM.

To the frustration of national Christian Coalition leaders, CCM has tended to remain organizationally and politically independent of the national organization. In practice, this has meant that its president and board of directors have felt relatively free to establish and pursue their own agendas—agendas that have changed with each change in CCM leadership.

CCM autonomy has generated considerable tension both within CCM and between CCM and the national organization. In both cases, the basic source of tension has involved conflict between "purists," who have sought to hold the Christian Coalition to a conservative social agenda, and "pragmatists," more willing to compromise with political opponents. Indeed, the willingness of national-level pragmatists to compromise apparently has alienated some of the Coalition's strongest supporters in Michigan. Former CCM leaders Tom McMillin of Auburn Hills and Harry Veryser of Clinton Township report that they have withdrawn from the organization. According to McMillin, "There's a general feeling that maybe the [national] Christian Coalition is compromising too much on Christian principles" (Zagaroli 1999, 1). Moreover, CCM supporters have also resented efforts of the national headquarters to control state affairs (McDiarmid 1997, 1).

Recently, Jack Horton, former state representative and current county commissioner from the Grand Rapids area, has served as temporary CCM president. But the organization is an empty shell. In nonelection years, CCM maintains no paid staff whatsoever. The organization maintains an exceedingly small mailing list of 10,000 persons, although it claims a larger contributor list of approximately 55,000. CCM has attempted to organize on a county basis across the state, but it has had minimal success in generating broad, grassroots appeal.

THE POLITICAL IMPACT OF THE CHRISTIAN RIGHT IN MICHIGAN

Social movement organizations articulate the concerns and grievances of the movement, provide important resources and leadership within the movement, and seek to direct the movement toward particular ends. But social movements are far broader in composition than their particular organizational manifestations. It is much more difficult to determine who constitute members of a social movement within the mass public, as movements, by definition, are fairly dynamic in nature and amorphous in structure.

We seek to ascertain the relative size of the Christian Right movement in Michigan, analyze its particular sociodemographic base, and assess its relative success in the electoral arena. We begin by examining the percentage of Michigan voters in 2000 who might be classified as part of the Christian Right and their particular social and political characteristics.

It is clear from table 5.1 that the Christian Right voters constitute a sizable, though far from overwhelming, bloc of voters in the state of Michigan—as 15 percent of Michigan voters in the 2000 election can be so classified.[1] Generally speaking, it appears that Christian Right members are more likely to be found among the youngest (those under thirty years of age),[2] among the less well educated, within small towns and suburbs, among Protestants and particularly among those who choose "other Christian" as their religious preference, and among Republicans and conservatives. It is less clear whether males or females are more prone to claim membership in the Christian Right.[3]

Table 5.1   The Social Location of White Christian Right Members in Michigan: Exit Poll Data (2000)

Christian Right Voters	%
% of Michigan Voters	15
Gender	
Male	16
Female	14
Age	
18–29	17
30–44	15
45–59	15
60+	14
Education	
High school or less	19
Some college	16
College graduate	13
Some postgraduate	9
Size of residence	
City over 50,000	10
Suburbs	17
Small city/ rural	18
Religion	
Protestant	25
Catholic	7
Other Christian	23
Party identification	
Democrat	8
Independent/other	10
Republican	29
Ideology	
Liberal	7
Moderate	10
Conservative	33

To what extent has the Christian Right experienced success in the electoral arena? In terms of the nomination process, it might be remembered that Senator John McCain scored a major victory over Bush in the Michigan presidential primary in late February 2000. However, Michigan is an open primary state, so Democrats were permitted to participate in Michigan's 2000 GOP presidential primary. McCain's candidacy mobilized a considerable number of voters (Republicans, independents, and some Democrats) who traditionally had not voted in previous Republican presidential primaries. Exit poll data from the 2000 Michigan presidential primary, however, did not include a question that tapped membership in the Christian Right, only an item tapping level of church attendance. And, despite McCain's general appeal, Bush clearly won a majority of primary voters who attended church weekly (*Detroit News* 2000, 1–3).

To assess the Christian Right's success in the general election process, we once again employ data taken from the 2000 exit polls (see table 5.2). In the 1996 election, the votes of reported Christian Right members were cast decidedly for Dole, with only 28 percent recalling that they had cast their vote for President Bill Clinton. Nevertheless, Clinton easily carried the state in 1996, with nearly two-thirds (63 percent) of the non-Christian Right voters claiming that they had voted for him.

While members of the Christian Right strongly supported Dole in 1996, they were even more supportive of George Bush and incumbent Republican Senator Spencer Abraham in the election of 2000. Both Bush and Abraham garnered over three-quarters of the votes cast by

Table 5.2   The Voting Behavior of White Christian Right (CR) Members in Michigan: Exit Poll Data (2000)

Election	Non-CR (%)	CR (%)
Presidential vote in 1996		
Clinton	63	28
Dole	27	67
Perot	10	5
Presidential vote in 2000		
Gore	57	21
Bush	41	77
Nader	2	2
Senate in 2000		
Stabenow (D)	56	22
Abraham (R)	44	78

members of the Christian Right in Michigan, while their opponents attracted majority support among non-Christian Right voters (57 percent for Gore and 56 percent for Stabenow, the Democratic senatorial candidate). Given the fact that Al Gore carried the state and Debbie Stabenow narrowly defeated the GOP incumbent, Senator Spencer Abraham, it is clear that the Christian Right did not provide the margin of victory needed in the state for either George W. Bush or Spencer Abraham. Approximately 25 percent of the votes cast for Bush and Abraham in the Michigan election were delivered by Christian Right voters (data not shown). Thus, in terms of statewide races, it appears that the Christian Right in Michigan provides an important base for GOP candidates running in statewide elections, but the support of Christian Right voters is far from sufficient in terms of ensuring statewide electoral victory in the fall.

On the other hand, despite these Democratic victories at the state level, the Republican Party in Michigan won control of the state house of representatives as well as overwhelming control of the state senate. The Christian Right has been relatively successful in targeting local races in an effort to ensure GOP control of the state chambers (Penning and Smidt 2000). It has also been active in state partisan organizational activities (Smidt and Penning 1997), and it has elected state legislators who articulate and represent many of the interests advanced by the Christian Right. As a result, the Christian Right in Michigan today can be viewed as constituting a faction within the Michigan Republican Party. Indeed, recent work by Conger and Green (2002) suggests that, since 1994, the influence of the Christian Right within the Michigan GOP has increased from "moderate" to "strong." Nonetheless, while the Christian Right may find a "home" in the party, the Michigan Republican Party is far broader in terms of its composition and representation than that of the Christian Right. The Christian Right plays an important, but not determining, role within party politics.

With GOP control of the state legislative bodies, the governor's office, and the (elected) Michigan Supreme Court, the 2001 GOP reapportionment plan had clear sailing into law. Indeed, the newly drawn congressional districts, in which Michigan lost one seat following the 2000 census, helped shift the partisan balance of the state's congressional representation from its previous nine-to-seven distribution in favor of the Democrats to a nine-to-six GOP advantage following the 2002 election. This could be politically significant in that Michigan's Democratic and Republican members of Congress differ widely in their support for the Christian Right agenda. Table 5.3, for example, demonstrates that the year 2000 mean Christian Coalition Report Card scores for Michigan's Democratic senators (14.0) and Democratic representatives (21.1) were relatively low. In contrast, the mean score for Michigan's Republican representatives was a relatively high 83.1.

Finally, it should be noted that the 2000 election revealed another important dynamic at work within Michigan politics—the growing cooperation between conservative Protestants and Catholics on particular matters of public policy. The 2000 election in Michigan saw a ballot proposal that each year would have provided students attending poorly performing public school systems with about $3,300 in vouchers from tax funds to enable them to attend private schools. While the

Table 5.3   Christian Coalition Roll Call Report Card Rating: Michigan Members of Congress (2000)

Member	District	Roll Call Score
Senate Democrats		
Carl Levin	State	15
Debbie Stabenow	State	13
Mean		14
House Democrats		
Jim Barcia	5	67
David Bonior	10	27
John Conyers	14	0
John Dingell	16	20
Dale Kildee	9	33
Carolyn Kilpatrick	15	0
Sander Levin	12	0
Lynn Rivers	13	0
Bart Stupak	1	43
Mean		21.1
House Republicans		
Dave Camp	4	79
Vern Ehlers	3	87
Pete Hoekstra	2	93
Joseph Knollenberg	11	87
Mike Rogers	8	a
Nick Smith	7	73
Fred Upton	6	80
Mean		83.1

Source: Barone, Cohen, and Ujifusa 2001, 768–819.
[a]Newly elected

proposal was decisively defeated in the general election, it made the ballot through the combined efforts of conservative Protestants and Catholics, and the two groups worked throughout the campaign on behalf of the ballot measure. If the Christian Right can break out of its "conservative Protestant" base, forge alliances with additional religious groups, and attract new members outside its traditional base, it is likely to be more successful in its political efforts within the state.

CONCLUSION

Over the past two decades, a variety of Christian Right groups have formed in Michigan in an effort to promote a culturally conservative agenda. However, as we have seen, these groups differ considerably in terms of objectives, size, organization, and political effectiveness. This chapter argues that the general direction of the Christian Right has been away from a disorganized social movement toward the formation of organized interest groups or party factions. While the Christian Right has achieved some notable political victories, particularly in the area of placing restrictions on abortion rights, it has also suffered defeats in its efforts to limit pornography and achieve voter support for school vouchers.

Several factors help to account for the political success of Christian Right organizations in Michigan. First, over time, the Christian Right has found a home in the Republican Party, where it now constitutes a major party faction. It wasn't always so. In 1988, for example, supporters of the Reverend Pat Robertson threw the Michigan GOP into chaos with their aggressive efforts on his behalf, which resulted in a split between the Christian Right supporters of Robertson and the more moderate supporters of George Bush (Smidt and Penning 1997). In fact, the state Republican convention split into two groups—a regular convention dominated by Bush delegates and a rump convention dominated by Robertson's supporters (Penning 1994). Although the resulting ill will took a long time to dissipate, the Christian Right and the GOP in Michigan have, over time, developed a symbiotic relationship, with many former Christian Right firebrands becoming assimilated into the party and many Christian Right voters helping provide GOP candidates with necessary electoral support. This relationship between the Christian Right and the GOP has helped the movement to achieve some of its political objectives, particularly since both houses of the Michigan legislature, as well as the statehouse, are controlled by the Republican Party.

A second factor contributing to the growth and success of the Christian Right in Michigan involves the impact of events at the national level. As we noted above, a variety of events, including U.S. Supreme Court decisions (e.g., on prayer and Bible reading in schools) and social turmoil surrounding the Vietnam War, generated concern on the part of social conservatives and prompted them to engage more directly in political activity. In addition, the presidential campaigns of born-again presidential candidates such as Jimmy Carter and Pat Robertson helped to generate enthusiasm among the faithful and provided them with opportunities to hone their political skills. According to Ralph Reed, former national director of the Christian Coalition, it was Robertson's 1988 presidential campaign that served as "the political crucible" for the proliferation of many state Christian Right organizations (Reed 1994, 193). Moreover, the administration of Ronald Reagan may have also played a role in encouraging Christian Right activity. Not only was President Reagan openly sympathetic to the Christian Right (in word if not always in deed), but his policy of devolving power and responsibility to the states and localities may well have provided Christian Right organizations with the incentive necessary to organize effectively at the grassroots level.

A third reason for the success of the Christian Right in Michigan has been the growing political sophistication of at least some of its organizations. This is evident, for example, in the choice of issue agendas. Groups such as RTLM and ADA have found it very useful to focus their resources on a relatively narrow set of political issues, thereby maximizing their impact on those issues. Other Christian Right groups have used different tactics to allocate scarce resources, targeting a limited number of key electoral contests rather than spreading their resources more broadly. In addition, most of the successful Christian Right organizations have learned to coordinate their activities with those of other groups that share their objectives.

The political sophistication of the Christian Right manifests itself in a variety of other ways as well. For example, as we have seen, most of the groups have become adept at fund-raising and most have developed relatively complex organizational structures (sometimes in response to complex Internal Revenue Service rules). In addition, the past five years have seen a tremendous increase in the use of electronic technology by Michigan Christian Right groups. Almost all of them now maintain websites, fax networks, and e-mail lists. This technology has greatly reduced the cost of communication with both supporters and government officials while increasing the speed of such communication.

Finally, a fourth reason for the continuing success of at least some of Michigan's Christian Right organizations concerns changing political rhetoric. To a large extent, the Christian Right has replaced its earlier language of moralism with the language of liberalism (Moen 1997). Rather than framing public policy issues in moralistic, sectarian terms, they have moved to recast many of their arguments in terms of the language of rights, freedom, and equality that is associated with liberal democratic thought. This approach was evident in discussion of Proposal B (in the 1998 election), a measure dealing with assisted suicide. The Christian Right opponents of the proposal explicitly avoided "culture war" terminology in favor of secular language and argumentation through their advertising campaign of "B is bad legislation."

On the other hand, the Christian Right in Michigan is far from all-powerful, and certain organizations, including the Christian Coalition of Michigan, have been notably unsuccessful both in terms of organizational maintenance and in terms of pursuing their policy objectives. What accounts for the limited success of the Christian Right in Michigan? One explanation for its mixed success is that the movement has been hampered by internal conflict. It may not be particularly surprising that as the Christian Right has institutionalized, transforming itself from a social movement to a more formally organized set of interest groups, internal disputes have arisen, pitting purists against pragmatists. In the case of the more successful organizations, including RTLM and CTV, strong leadership and a sense of mission have helped resolve such conflicts or at least helped to minimize their deleterious impact. However, in the case of other organizations, most notably CCM, internal divisions (as well as conflict between state and national organizations) have seriously weakened the organization and limited its political impact.

A second explanation for the limited impact of the Christian Right in Michigan politics has to do with political immaturity, manifested particularly in the early years of the movement. Although, as we have seen, Christian Right organizations in the state have grown in political sophistication and have increasingly sought to work "within the system" to effect change, that has not always been the case. For example, the early stridency and outspokenness of some Christian Right organizations offended even some of the movement's potential supporters. Thus, as we have seen, the 1988 Robertson campaign deeply offended some party regulars in the GOP. More recently, the harshly antigay rhetoric of organizations such as AFA of Michigan has produced more friction than political success.

An early lack of political sophistication has also led some Christian Right organizations to make a number of crucial strategic errors. Perhaps most problematic has been the attempt of some groups to pursue an exceedingly broad policy agenda, thereby dissipating their resources and, perhaps, engendering more internal conflict than was necessary. Groups such as RTLM, which have maintained their focus, have tended to be more politically successful than other Christian Right organizations.

Finally, the Christian Right in Michigan has been limited by group countermobilization. Groups such as Planned Parenthood and the ACLU, for example, have sought to counter the activities of RTLM. And the antigay activities of AFA of Michigan have fostered a considerable amount of opposition from the state's gay community in places as diverse as Ann Arbor and Traverse City. And perhaps most interesting, the political activities of Christian Right clergy have prompted clergy on the left to countermobilize. For example, shortly before the November 2000 election, representatives of a (Washington-based) nonpartisan, clergy-led group, the Interfaith Alliance, met in Grand Rapids to publicly attack the Christian Coalition for placing voter guides in churches (Prichard 2000).

What can we expect from the Christian Right in Michigan as we enter a new millennium? Most likely the Christian Right will continue to have a significant, though limited, impact on politics and policy in Michigan. To be politically successful, the movement will have to balance tension between purists and pragmatists. It will have to continue to develop its political skills. And, as a distinct minority in state politics, it will have to work cooperatively with like-minded citizens and organizations to achieve its policy objectives.

NOTES

1. Christian Right voters are operationally defined here as those white voters who willingly classified themselves as "part of the conservative Christian political movement, also known as the religious right." Using the same operational definition with the 1996 exit poll data, 15 percent of Michigan voters in 1996 could be classified as part of the Christian Right—the same percentage as that found in 2000.

2. However, the 1996 Michigan exit poll data revealed that Christian Right voters were more likely to be found among older, rather than younger, voters as the percentage of Christian Right voters increased from 12 percent for those under age thirty to 21 percent for those aged sixty and older.

3. The 1996 Michigan exit poll data also revealed rather small differences between males and females in terms of percentage of Christian Right members, though in 1996 a somewhat higher percentage of Christian Right voters was evident among females (16 percent) than among males (13 percent).

REFERENCES

American Decency Association. 2001. "Who Is ADA?" www.americandecency. org/who.htm.

American Family Association. 2001. "About AFA." www.afa.net/about.asp.

American Family Association of Michigan. 2001. "AFA of Michigan." www.afamichigan.org.

Barone, Michael, Richard E. Cohen, and Grant Ujifusa. 2001. *The Almanac of American Politics 2002*. Washington, D.C.: National Journal.

Berkowitz, Laura, and John C. Green. 1997. "Charting the Coalition: The Local Chapters of the Ohio Christian Coalition." Pp. 57–72 in *Sojourners in the Wilderness: The Christian Right in Comparative Perspective*, ed. Corwin E. Smidt and James M. Penning. Lanham, Md.: Rowman & Littlefield.

Cain, Charlie. 1997. "Right to Life: In 25 Years, Michigan's Group Gains Enough Political Clout to Rival Unions." *Detroit News* (2 March).

Citizens for Traditional Values. 1997. "A Voice for Your Values." Brochure. Lansing, Mich.: CTV.

———. 2000. "A Voice for Your Values." Insert in summer/fall issue of CTV newsletter.

Conger, Kimberly H., and John C. Green. 2002. "Spreading Out and Digging In: Christian Conservatives and State Republican Parties." *Campaigns and Elections* 23 (February):58–60, 64–66.

Detroit News. 2000. "Dissecting the Vote" (22 February):1–3.

Dickerson, Brian. 2000. "Abortion Foes Scoring Quiet, Key Victories." *Detroit Free Press* (8 December).

Elazar, J. Daniel. 1972. *American Federalism: A View from the States*. 2d ed. New York: Thomas Y. Crowell.

Fenton, John. 1966. *Midwest Politics*. New York: Holt, Rinehart & Winston.

Hanley, James P., and Paul A. Rozycki. 2000. *Politics and Government in Michigan*. 3d ed. New York: McGraw-Hill.

Heinlein, Gary. 2000. "Abortion Limits a Signature Away from Law." *Detroit News* (20 December).

McDiarmid, Hugh. 1997. "Christian Coalition Pushes to Change Its Michigan Leadership." *Detroit Free Press* (13 May).

Michigan Family Forum. 2001. "About MFF." www.mfforum.com/index.htm.

Moen, Matthew. 1997. "The Changing Nature of Christian Right Activism: 1970s–1990s." Pp. 21–37 in *Sojourners in the Wilderness: The Christian Right in Comparative Perspective*, ed. Corwin Smidt and James Penning. Lanham, Md.: Rowman & Littlefield.

Penning, James. M. 1994. "Pat Robertson and the GOP: 1988 and Beyond." *Sociology of Religion* 55 (fall):327–44.

———. 2003. "Michigan: The End Is Near." Pp. 33–45 in *The Test of Time: Coping with Term Limits*, ed. Rick Farmer, David Rausch, and John C. Green. Lanham, Md.: Lexington Books.

Penning, James M., and Corwin E. Smidt. 2000. "Michigan: The 'Right Stuff.'" Chap. 9 in *Prayers in the Precincts: The Christian Right in the 1998 Elections*, ed. John C. Green, Mark J. Rozell, and Clyde Wilcox. Washington, D.C.: Georgetown University Press.

Potts, Laura. 2001. "Michigan Republicans Try to Woo Catholic Voters." *Detroit News* (7 July).

Prichard, James. 2000. "Interstate Alliance Vetoes Voter Guides." *Detroit News* (19 October).

Reed, Ralph. 1994. *Politically Incorrect: The Emerging Faith Factor in American Politics*. Dallas: Word Publishing.

Rozell, Mark J., and Clyde Wilcox. 1996. *Second Coming: The New Christian Right in Virginia Politics*. Baltimore: Johns Hopkins University Press.

Scott, Sara, and Barton Deiters. 2001. "Abortion Still Prime Legislative Target." *Grand Rapids Press* (16 July):A1, A4.

Smidt, Corwin, and James M. Penning. 1997. "Michigan: Veering to the Left?" Pp. 147–68 in *God at the Grassroots 1996: The Christian Right in the American Elections*, ed. Mark J. Rozell and Clyde Wilcox. Lanham, Md.: Rowman & Littlefield.

Squire, Peverill. 1992. "Legislative Professionalization and Membership Diversity in State Legislatures." *Legislative Studies Quarterly* 17 (February):69–79.

State of Michigan. 2000. State Budget Office, "Michigan Census 2000."

Zagaroli, Lisa. 1999. "Michigan Is a Priority, Christian Coalition Says." *Detroit News* (14 October).

SIX

Iowa: Crucible of the Christian Right

Donald P. Racheter, Lyman A. Kellstedt,
and John C. Green

THE COMMON IMAGE OF THE CHRISTIAN RIGHT AS AN IMPORTANT
grassroots movement was largely born in Iowa. It was there that Pat
Robertson's 1988 bid for the Republican presidential nomination had
an unexpected success, laying the groundwork for the Christian Coalition in the 1990s (Reed 1994, 1993). These dramatic events were part
of broader developments in the Hawkeye state: the growth of effective
Christian Right organizations, a strong presence within the Iowa GOP,
a small but significant voting bloc, and growing influence in the state
legislature. By 2002, the Christian Right had become a key Republican
constituency and an important player in state politics.

To many observers, Iowa is an unlikely place for the Christian Right
to take root. A midwestern state with a reputation for moderation and
competitive elections hardly seems fertile ground for a conservative
movement explicitly opposed to modernist trends in American culture.
Yet Iowa's reputation masks considerable political diversity, including
a vigorous conservatism. The ability of the Christian Right to successfully exploit elements of this conservatism in the crucible of Iowa politics reveals much about its strengths and limitations.

THE POLITICAL AND SOCIAL CHARACTERISTICS OF IOWA

Elazar characterized Iowa as having a mix of "moralistic" and "individualistic" cultures (1972, 117). The northern and western portions of the
state resemble the moralistic culture of Minnesota, which sees politics
as a search for the public interest. The eastern and southern reaches

reflect the individualistic culture common in Illinois. This perspective stresses politics as a means of advancing private interests. This mix of cultures encourages diverse constituencies to organize and compete to define the public interest.

Iowa's political culture operates in the context of decentralized state government, traditional political parties, and an open political process. As one observer put it, Iowa "is a two-party state whose politics are competitive, clean, and open" and "highly pragmatic, non-programmatic, cautious, and moderate" (Winebrenner 1998, 11). Party registration reflects this characterization. In 2002, Republicans and Democrats each accounted for 30 percent of registered voters, with the remaining 40 percent independents. A good illustration of Iowa's competitiveness is the 2000 presidential election, where Al Gore carried the state by about 4,000 votes out of 1.3 million ballots cast. In this context, diverse constituencies have strong incentives to organize aggressively, but also to temper their demands.

The epitome of Iowa politics is its party caucuses, which since 1972 have become the opening event in the major party presidential nomination contests (Cook 2000, 24). In an age of media-centered campaigns, the caucuses share with the New Hampshire primary the distinction of being "retail" politics, where presidential candidates seek support by extensive grassroots contact with individual citizens. However, the party caucuses are not principally presidential events, but are instead local party organizational meetings. The Republican and Democratic caucuses are actually held every two years to elect delegates to county conventions. These caucuses and conventions elect party leaders and write the party platforms—and in presidential years, select delegates to the national conventions, while state and local candidates are nominated by primary.

Demographically, Iowa is fairly homogeneous compared with the country as a whole but hardly monolithic. It is overwhelmingly white, older, and oriented toward agriculture. Iowa's population is well educated and participates in a wide range of occupations and industries, arrayed across several large cities, numerous small ones, and rural areas. Despite losing population for the last three decades, its per capita income is relatively high, and it lacks the extremes of poverty and wealth that characterize the nation as a whole. Iowa is also fairly diverse in terms of religion. Mainline Protestants, led by the United Methodist Church, account for 36 percent of the population, followed by Catholics at 23 percent. Evangelical Protestants are numerous, at about 14 percent, slightly less than the secular population at 18 percent. All other religious groups combine for a total of 9 percent.[1]

These demographic characteristics are the source of active constituencies in both the major parties, which help explain the conservative tilt of the GOP and the liberal tendency of the Democrats. The Republicans draw support from business groups, especially the National Federation of Independent Business and the Chamber of Commerce. Other important groups are Iowans for Tax Relief, Iowans for Right to Work, the National Rifle Association (NRA), and its affiliate, the Iowa Sportsmen's Federation. Farm groups are divided, reflecting the fact that Iowa farmers are a swing constituency.

The Democrats are strongly supported by labor unions, and first among equals is the Iowa State Education Association (ISEA), followed by the American Federation of State, County, and Municipal Employees (AFSCME) and the United Auto Workers (UAW). Feminists are important, including the National Abortion Rights Action League and Voters for Choice. Environmentalists are led by the Iowa Citizens' Action Network, but are less of a factor, as are peace, civil rights, and gay-rights groups. Democrats are well organized on the twenty-six college and university campuses around the state, and are supported by groups of young professionals, such as the 21st Century Forum. These differences manifest themselves in the political geography of the state. Democrats count on the urban areas, the small towns are strongly Republican, and it is the purely rural townships that usually decide elections.

CHRISTIAN RIGHT ORGANIZATIONS IN IOWA

Religious conservatives began organizing in Iowa in the mid-1970s. The right-to-life activists, many of whom were Roman Catholics, were the first to engage in grassroots mobilizing and by 1978 had achieved success in primary and general elections. Indeed, their tactics, including the leafleting of Catholic and Protestant churches the Sunday before the election, were dubbed the "Iowa model," and copied across the country in 1980 (Hershey 1984). Another active group was antifeminists, working against the Equal Rights Amendment (ERA).

By 1980, affiliates of the newly formed Christian Right groups were active in Iowa, particularly the Moral Majority and Christian Voice. And by the mid-1980s, these groups were joined by Concerned Women for America and the Freedom Council, a group headed by Pat Robertson.

As in the rest of the country, these original movement organizations drew on different religious constituencies, concentrated among evangelical Protestants. For example, the religious base of the Moral Majority was the fundamentalist Baptists and that of the Freedom Council was charismatics and Pentecostals. While these first-generation groups were quite effective in particular campaigns, most were unable to build and/or sustain grassroots organizations until the 1990s, when a second generation of Christian Right groups appeared.

The second generation of the Christian Right was headlined by the Christian Coalition of Iowa (CCI), which remains a potent organization at present despite the decline of the Christian Coalition at the national level. Because of the importance of the CCI, and a serendipitous opportunity to survey their membership in 2001, we will discuss it first and in some detail. Then we will turn to the other important organizations, which are at various stages of development.[2]

Christian Coalition of Iowa (CCI)

Ione Dilley and other veterans of Pat Robertson's 1988 presidential campaign organized the CCI in January 1991. It was active in the 1992 election, helping to defeat a proposed state Equal Rights Amendment. In this and subsequent elections, the CCI produced and disseminated voter guides, worked in campaigns, and became a player in Republican Party politics. For example, in 2000, the CCI mobilized over 1,000 volunteers to turn out the vote in selected precincts in cooperation with the Republican Party and other conservative groups.

The CCI has developed relationships with evangelical churches throughout the state and has been quite successful in the larger and midsized counties, but less so in smaller, rural counties, where there are few evangelical churches. It also has developed and trained a network of local activists, producing an "Iowa Political Handbook" for the biennial party caucuses, the conventions that follow, and the elections held that year.

The CCI also works hard to maintain contact with its activist corps. For example, an email dated January 28, 2002, asked members to attend a precinct caucus informational meeting to be held at a Pentecostal church in Des Moines. In the message, members were encouraged to stand for election to their county central committees, volunteer as delegates to their county conventions, and prepare issues for consideration for the state party platform. The message also encouraged attendance at one of ten "house parties" to be held throughout the state in 2002 to set the stage "for the largest turnout of pro-family voters in Iowa history." Attention was also directed to a special election for a state senate seat that resulted from a resignation. Finally, the message included an update on the pressing issues facing the Iowa legislature by a legislator who supports CCI causes. Such communication is common in an effort to keep members informed and alerted to upcoming events.

At its annual fund-raising dinner in 2001, CCI turned out 600 contributors and members only four days after the tragedy on September 11 and with no campaign under way. Approximately 200 of the assembled filled out a questionnaire distributed by the authors while mingling with friends, eating dinner, hearing patriotic songs, and listening to speakers (publisher Steve Forbes via satellite and Senator Charles Grassley in person). Close to one-quarter of the survey respondents were not formal members of the CCI but had contributed a substantial amount of money to attend the event. In the following analysis, we group these contributors with short-term CCI members (less than seven years) because the two groups had similar survey responses. These short-term activists comprised 71 percent of the respondents; the remaining 29 percent were longer term members (members for more than seven years).

As can be seen in table 6.1, the CCI activists are well educated and well heeled. Over three-fifths have college degrees, including one-quarter with postgraduate education. More than one-half have incomes of over $50,000 per year. They are also predominantly male, married, and middle-aged. Long-term members are somewhat less educated and affluent, and are somewhat older than their short-term counterparts, but the differences are not of great magnitude. CCI membership is overwhelmingly evangelical Protestant in religious makeup; it is also very active in church and holds orthodox religious beliefs (such as a literal view of the Bible).

In these regards, the 2001 CCI activists resemble the original Robertson activists. However, they differ in one important respect: they are somewhat more diverse in religious terms. About one-sixth of the CCI activists are mainline Protestants and about one-tenth Catholic. More diversity is also apparent among the evangelicals, with fewer respondents identifying as "charismatic" or "Pentecostal"—groups that were the backbone of the Robertson campaign (where fully 75 percent of donors to the 1988 Robertson campaign identified as either charismatic or Pentecostal, see Guth et al. 1995, 63). These differences are

Table 6.1   Christian Coalition: Social-Demographic and
Religious Variables

Social–Demographic Variables	All Members (%)	Contributor/ Short-Term Members (%)	Long-Term Members (%)
Education			
High school or less	9	10	6
Some college	28	26	33
College graduate	37	35	41
Postgraduate	26	28	20
Income			
Under $50K	45	39	61
Greater than $50K	55	62	39
Gender			
Male	57	57	58
Female	43	43	42
Marital status			
Married	88	87	90
Single	12	13	10
Mean age	49	47	55
Religious variables			
Evangelical	74	71	81
Mainline	15	16	14
Catholic	9	11	6
Other	1	2	0
Charismatic identification	20	17	28
Pentecostal identification	23	20	32
Born-again	61	53	79
Weekly or greater attendance at church	91	88	98
Belief in Bible as literal word of God	84	82	89

Source: Survey of contributors to and members of the Iowa Christian Coalition, September 2001.

also evident between the short-term activists and long-term CCI members. The former have more mainline Protestants and Catholics and fewer born-again Christians. These figures suggest that the CCI has broadened its religious base since the Robertson campaign and its beginnings in Iowa.

As one might expect, the CCI activists hold very conservative views on social issues. For example, nearly 100 percent are prolife (see table 6.2). They also feel close to other Christian conservative groups (from Focus on the Family to Concerned Women for America) and to Pat Robertson himself. They strongly oppose rival liberal groups: gay-rights advocates, feminists, the National Education Association, labor unions, and environmentalists. Not surprisingly, most strongly identify with the Republican Party,[3] and almost all voted for George W. Bush in the 2000 election. In these regards, they bear a close resemblance to the original Robertson activists. However, long-term CCI members were more conservative, stronger Republicans, and more favorable to Pat Robertson than the short-term activists. Almost one-half of the latter backed George W. Bush in the 2000 caucuses, while more than one-half of the long-term members supported publisher Steve Forbes. Neither of the movement candidates, Gary Bauer or Alan Keyes, received much support.

Table 6.2   Christian Coalition: Political Attitudes and Behaviors

Political Factors	All Members (%)	Contributors/Short-Term Members (%)	Long-Term Members (%)
Prolife	93	90	100
Support for conservative groups and individuals			
Focus on the Family	96	94	98
Right to Life Groups	93	91	98
Prison Fellowship	85	80	98
Concerned Women for America	69	60	91
Pat Robertson	75	68	93
Opposition to liberal groups and individuals			
Environmental groups	55	48	72
Unions	61	56	72
National Education Association	76	72	85
Feminist groups	82	77	94
Gay rights groups	90	89	93
Party identification: Strong Republican	57	54	65
Voting			
Bush—2000 general election	98	97	100
Bush—2000 caucus	43	48	32
Forbes—2000 caucus	35	27	53
Bauer and Keyes combined—2000 caucus	18	20	13

Source: Survey of contributors to and members of the Iowa Christian Coalition, September 2001.

In table 6.3, we see the intense levels of political participation engaged in by CCI activists. Even allowing for some exaggeration, the CCI is "hyperactive" compared with the mass public (see Rosenstone and Hansen 1993). However, there appears to have been some lessening of activity on the part of the short-term activists, with the exception of running for office.[4] Such intense activism, rooted in religious values and communities, helps explain the staying power of the CCI, which begins the twenty-first century with a strong base of support and with the potential for getting stronger.

Table 6.3   Political Participation of Christian Coalition Contributors and Members in 2000 or 2001

Activities	All Members (%)	Contributors/Short-Term Members (%)	Long-Term Members (%)
Campaign activity			
Attended a campaign rally	76	68	94
Made a campaign donation	74	68	91
Engaged in fund-raising	43	41	46
Campaigned door to door	32	29	39
Passed out voter guides	44	35	67
Involved in a phone bank	27	32	57
Registered new voters	17	23	35
Canvassed churches	17	11	32
Ran for public office	5	7	2
Other participation			
Signed a petition	79	74	93
Contacted a public official	60	54	74
Wrote letter to an editor	35	33	41
Participated in a boycott	23	18	35
Participated in a protest demonstration	11	8	19
Christian Coalition activities[a]			
Gave money beyond dues	78	68	87
Worked with allied groups	71	55	86
Attended local meetings	67	53	80
Helped to organize events	51	44	58
Served as a leader	44	33	55
Percent of sample	100	71	29

Source: Survey of contributors to and members of the Iowa Christian Coalition, September 2001.
[a]Responses exclude contributors and include only members.

Iowa Family Policy Center (IFPC)

While the CCI has an electoral orientation, IFPC is more policy oriented, but both work together to further the movement's goals. The IFPC is a nonprofit, research, and education organization associated with James Dobson's Focus on the Family and the Family Research Council, founded in January 1997. Its purpose is to strengthen Iowa's families, and it attempts to do so through a number of interrelated efforts. It has a small, full-time staff that lobbies the legislature on issues of marriage and the family, abortion and euthanasia, homosexuality, gambling, and education. Its current executive director, attorney Chuck Hurley, served three terms in the Iowa legislature and is a veteran of the 1988 Robertson campaign.

Apart from the lobbying effort, IFPC has established a legal arm to tackle religious liberty cases as they arise; this operation uses a team of over two dozen Christian lawyers throughout the state. IFPC publicizes its views through a regular newsletter (claiming a mailing list of 12,000) and sixty-second "legislative updates" aired over radio stations in the state. Following a pattern of other statewide arms of Focus on the Family, IFPC has just begun a program of working through churches, creating "SALT Committees" to educate members on issues and candidates.

Iowans for Life (IFL) and the Iowa Right to Life Committee (IRLC)

The IFL was organized in 1972 by Carolyn Thompson, R.N., to coordinate opponents of legalized abortion in Iowa, and the 1973 *Roe v. Wade* decision caused an explosion in its membership. IFL created a Political Action Committee (PAC), which supports prolife candidates in the state. Group leaders supported different presidential candidates in the run-up to the 1988 caucuses, and differences over an official endorsement resulted in the formation of a new Iowa Right to Life Committee (IRLC). The two groups are still separate organizations (although the issue that caused the split has long been moot), but work together on prolife issues, especially before the legislature.

Concerned Women for America (CWA)

Maxine Sieleman organized the Iowa CWA in 1986. Less visible in the state than CCI or IFPC, CWA nonetheless packs some punch. Organized in prayer-action chapters, the members respond to efforts by the national organization to contact members of Congress and executive branch officials.

CWA is also very active in lobbying and electoral campaigns in Iowa, cooperating with other Christian Right organizations. Its "legislative liaison" keeps the state membership informed about issues of interest in the Iowa legislature. In addition, CWA has a radio talk show that runs on many Iowa radio stations to share its policy concerns. One movement insider called CWA "an important part of what happens in Iowa," but then observed that it was no longer in the forefront of movement activity in the state.

Eagle Forum of Iowa

In the early 1970s, Donna LaPorte organized a group titled "Iowa Women Against the ERA," which eventually coalesced with similar local groups into a state affiliate of the Eagle Forum; LaPorte heads the state affiliate. When legislative leaders pushed ratification of the ERA through the Iowa legislature in 1972 with no debate, these antifeminist groups began to lobby for repeal. In response, the legislative leaders proposed state ERAs, which the Eagle Forum and allies (such as CCI) helped defeat in 1980 and in 1992. Phyllis Schlafly called the 1992 defeat of the state ERA a significant bright spot in an otherwise disappointing election year (Mayer and Nesmith 1995, 196). Observers suggest that the Eagle Forum is now a minor player in the politics of the Christian Right in Iowa.

Iowa Family Alliance

The manager of the Iowa Buchanan and Bauer presidential campaigns, Loras Schulte, organized a PAC in 2001 to raise funds for a limited number of electoral campaigns. Other Christian Right leaders were excited about the possibilities for this PAC in the near future because it gives activists a way to fund candidates who strongly support the Christian Right agenda.

Iowa Center-Right Information Exchange (ICRIE)

Technically, ICRIE is not a Christian Right organization, but it is a bridge between the Christian Right and other Republican groups. ICRIE was organized in February 2000 to heal rifts from Iowa caucuses and to foster cooperation among conservative activists.[5] ICRIE meets on the second Wednesday of each month to share information and discuss political problems. During the 2002 electoral cycle, ICRIE has been interviewing candidates for statewide and federal offices about their positions on issues of concern.

THE CHRISTIAN RIGHT AND THE IOWA
REPUBLICAN PARTY

From the earliest days of the movement, Christian conservatives have operated within the confines of the Iowa Republican Party. Overall, the Christian Right has reinforced other conservatives in a conservative/moderate struggle that has been a staple of Iowa GOP politics for twenty-five years. The role of the movement in the party can be shown in two ways: the growing presence of Christian Right activists in the party organizations and their influence on the party platform.

Organizational Influence

Christian Right activists first became a presence in local Republican organizations in the 1986 caucuses, when Moral Majority and Freedom Council members obtained nearly one-half of the convention delegates in Polk and Dallas Counties (the Des Moines metropolitan area). Indeed, moderate Mary Louise Smith, a former chair of the Republican National Committee was barely elected as a delegate (Schwartz 1986). One goal of this activism was to influence the 1988 presidential contest. After 1988, Christian conservatives steadily gained positions on local committees and the state central committee. By 1994, the Christian Right was judged to have a strong role in the state party organization (Persinos 1994), a situation that persisted in 2000 (Conger and Green 2002).

In 2002, the state GOP chair was Chuck Larson, a strong Christian conservative and state legislator. The executive director of the state central committee, Marlys Popma, and approximately three-fifths of the members also identify with the movement, with only two members considered "hostile" to a Christian Right agenda. Observers also estimate that the movement is a dominant force in two-thirds of the largest counties in the state and an important player in many others. As noted above, the Christian Right is less influential in many smaller counties because of a paucity of evangelical churches.

The Great Iowa Republican Party Platform Wars

During the 1960s and 1970s, the moderate faction of the Iowa Republican Party was able to dominate the creation and adoption of the every-other-year state party platform because of its numerical dominance. But as moderates began to decline by the mid-1970s, they supplemented their control by a clever use of rules. For example, only 60 percent of the delegates to the state party platform committee were elected by the rank and file in the districts, while those in power appointed the other 40 percent. Another was the use of appointed "temporary chairmen," who inevitably were elected permanent chairmen at the outset of the committee gathering. By these means, moderates were able to include liberal platform planks, provoking an increasingly bitter struggle between them and conservative activists.

The turning point in this conflict came in 1982 when a last-minute coalition of "traditional conservatives" (concerned about taxes, right-to-work laws, and guns), and Christian conservatives (concerned about abortion, prayer in the schools, and vouchers) were able to elect, by a single vote, a permanent chairman with a foot in both camps.[6] Subsequently, the rules were altered and the character of the state platform began to change. As shown in table 6.4, the number of liberal planks declined to zero, while Christian Right planks increased to roughly one-quarter of the total. Traditional conservative planks constituted the bulk of the platform over the entire period.

THE CHRISTIAN RIGHT AND IOWA ELECTIONS

In the 1970s, moderates exemplified by Governor Robert Ray dominated the Iowa Republican Party, and liberals, such as U.S. Senators Dick Clark and John Culver, were prominent among the Democrats. By

Table 6.4   Types of Planks in the Iowa Republican Party Platform, 1978–2002

Year	Liberal (%)	Conservative (%)	Christian Right (%)
1978	18	79	3
1980	15	80	5
1982	15	81	4
1984	11	83	6
1986	6	84	10
1988	1	84	15
1990	3	80	17
1992	0	80	20
1994	0	72	28
1996	0	80	20
1998	0	74	26
2000	0	72	28
2002	0	73	27

the mid-1970s, however, conservatives were on the march in both parties. More conservative Democrats allowed Jimmy Carter to do well in the 1976 caucuses (finishing second behind "uncommitted" with 29 percent of the caucus goers), and conservatives helped Ronald Reagan to nearly upset President Gerald Ford (42 percent to 45 percent of the straw vote). In 1978, prolife forces helped conservative Lieutenant Governor Roger Jepsen win the U.S. Senate nomination over a moderate Republican, and then defeat liberal incumbent Dick Clark (Hershey 1984).

At least some of the activists involved in the 1976 and 1978 campaigns supported the newly formed Moral Majority in 1980. Once again, Ronald Reagan finished second in the Iowa caucuses, this time to moderate George H. Bush, his eventual running mate (30 percent to 32 percent). Reagan and Bush then carried Iowa in the fall against President Carter and independent John Anderson (52 percent to 39 percent to 9 percent, respectively). Table 6.5 provides some sense of Christian Right impact using exit poll data; although these data must be viewed with some caution, they provide a minimum estimate of the Christian Right's electoral constituency.[7] In 1980, this constituency made up 8 percent of the electorate, and it voted about the same way as the other Republicans. Although only modestly more conservative, these voters put greater stress on moral issues.

The Christian Right also contributed to the defeat of a state Equal Rights Amendment on the ballot in 1980, and to the victory of conservative Charles Grassley over liberal incumbent John Culver in the U.S. Senate race. As with Senator Clark in 1978, many forces converged to defeat Culver (Hershey 1984). But Grassley represented what would become a winning formula for the Christian Right in future races across the country. A three-term congressman, Grassley had good conservative credentials (he was a protégé of the archconservative congressman H. R. Gross) as well as mainstream GOP connections (moderate Governor Ray campaigned for him in the primary). He was an evangelical Protestant and a lay preacher who campaigned effectively in churches by simply testifying about his faith. A speaker at the 1980 "Washington for Jesus" rally, Grassley was *for* the movement's agenda, but not *of* the movement itself (Herbers 1980). Grassley eventually became a conservative fixture in Iowa politics, reelected in 1986, 1992, and 1998. In 1982, movement activists helped then Lieutenant Governor Terry Branstad succeed retiring Governor Ray in a close race (he won with 53 percent). A conservative Roman Catholic, Branstad would be a movement ally on key issues for almost two decades, although, like Grassley, never a part of the movement itself.

Table 6.5 Iowa General Election Christian Right (CR) Supporters Compared with Other Voters, 1980, 1988, 1996, and 2000 (Whites Only) (%)

Political Factors	1980 CR GOP	1980 No CR GOP	1980 Ind./Dem.	1988 CR GOP	1988 No CR GOP	1988 Ind./Dem.	1996 CR GOP	1996 No CR GOP	1996 Ind./Dem.	2000 CR GOP	2000 No CR GOP	2000 Ind./Dem.
Ideology												
Liberal	0	0	23	0	7	35	0	15	29	2	6	26
Conservative	55	50	29	65	67	25	79	45	16	81	47	20
Importance of moral issue	36	0	11	32	10	12	68	0	14	75	50	30
GOP house vote	96	94	37	84	90	29	96	79	19	100	92	25
Prior presidential vote												
Democrat	27	23	66	0	3	53	4	13	71	7	16	64
Republican	64	68	22	89	92	36	85	70	14	75	59	12
Current presidential vote												
Democrat	5	5	47	15	15	76	7	30	77	5	8	69
Republican	91	90	42	85	85	23	86	62	15	92	92	27
% Sample of electorate	8.0	14.9	77.2	7.9	19.0	73.1	12.9	18.7	68.3	9.9	23.7	66.4

Source: These data were obtained from the Roper Center at the University of Connecticut.

The Iowa Christian Right once again supported Ronald Reagan in 1984. There was little controversy over this decision, although some Iowa national convention delegates talked about replacing Vice President Bush with a more conservative candidate. The Reagan-Bush ticket swept Iowa, but the Christian Right encountered mixed results in congressional and state races. Liberal congressman Tom Harkin defeated Senator Jepsen by a narrow margin, but conservative farm broadcaster Jim Lightfoot took Harkin's congressional seat. In 1986, Governor Branstad survived a close reelection bid, winning by 52 percent.

The 1988 Watershed

As the 1988 election approached, Iowa Christian conservatives began deploying their resources for the GOP nomination battle. Although the Moral Majority was by then in decline, CWA and IFL were quite active (Balmer 1989, chap. 6). Many of these activists backed Congressman Jack Kemp, an evangelical Protestant with conservative economic credentials, while others (following Jerry Falwell) endorsed Vice President Bush or Senate Majority Leader Bob Dole. Pat Robertson was also organizing in Iowa, with a cadre of politically savvy recruits like Ione Dilley and Steve Scheffler. Although Robertson scored an early victory in a party straw poll during the summer of 1987, observers consistently underestimated his strength, reinforced by the *Des Moines Register* polls that showed low levels of support for his candidacy (Winebrenner 1998, 160, 164).

On caucus night, Robertson's "invisible army" appeared in force, giving him 25 percent of the straw vote and a second place finish behind "Iowa's Third Senator," Bob Dole (37 percent). The real news, however, was that Robertson had bested Vice President Bush (19 percent), the winner of the 1980 Iowa caucuses, and fellow evangelical Jack Kemp (11 percent) (Cook 2000, 24–25). Robertson's success came from bringing a host of new people to the caucuses, and into the Republican Party (Hertzke 1993, 135–69). The 1988 GOP caucus exit polls show these differences (see table 6.6).[8] Religion aside, the Robertson supporters were much younger and less affluent, less likely to identify as Republican, much more conservative, and far more focused on moral issues than the Bush supporters. Overall, Christian Right activists made up 31 percent of the caucus attenders; a little more than one-half of them supported Robertson, followed by Jack Kemp (data not shown).

The prominence Robertson gained from his Iowa success was short-lived, and Vice President Bush eventually won the Republican

Table 6.6   Characteristics of Voters for GOP Caucus Candidates in 1988, 1996, and 2000 (%)

Voter Characteristics	Robertson 1988 $(24.6)^a$	Bush 1988 $(18.6)^a$	Buchanan 1996 $(23.4)^a$	Dole 1996 $(26.3)^a$	Bauer and Keyes 2000 $(24.1)^a$	Bush 2000 $(43.5)^a$	Forbes 2000 $(32.4)^a$
Social variables:							
Income							
Low	74	50	64	56	53	42	50
High	26	50	36	44	47	58	50
Age							
Under 45	57	32	43	29	46	31	34
Over 45	43	68	57	71	54	69	66
Political variables							
ID with CR	NA	NA	65	26	71	31	34
GOP	76	90	NA	NA	87	89	78
Dem. or Ind.	24	10	NA	NA	13	11	22
Ideology							
Conservative	80	49	92	73	89	70	71
Liberal/Moderate	20	51	8	27	11	30	29
Key issues							
Deficit/taxes	43	56	52	32	4	25	48
Moral values	68	16	84	38	92	40	34

Note: NA = no data available.
[a]Percent of caucus vote received by the candidates.

nomination. The Bush campaign's efforts to unite the party fell short in Iowa, contributing to a narrow Democratic general election victory (55 percent to 45 percent). The exit poll data in table 6.5 show that the size of the Christian Right voting bloc was about the same in 1988 as in 1980, despite a greater level of mobilization.

After 1988, the original Christian Right organizations quickly faded from the scene (the Moral Majority was disbanded in 1989), but the Iowa activists did not disappear. In 1990, they worked for Governor Branstad, who easily won reelection, and helped elect Congressman Jim Nussle, a prolife conservative, in a very close race. Such activists were soon represented by a new organization, the CCI. By the 1992 elections, it was quite active, although as in 1984, the 1992 caucuses were of little interest because of a sitting Republican president. Christian conservatives took advantage of this low-key event to gain experience, influence, and positions within the party. Elsewhere commentator Pat Buchanan rallied conservatives against President Bush, and Ross Perot's quixotic campaign drew away other supporters. In the fall election, Bill Clinton carried Iowa on his way to the White House (43 percent to 37 percent for Bush and 19 percent for Perot).

Christian conservatives, however, enjoyed a victory in 1992 when they helped defeat another Equal Rights Amendment to the state constitution. The anti-ERA campaign increased the membership in all the Christian Right organizations, but especially the CCI. In the words of Ione Dilley, the stop-ERA movement was "one of our most productive means of organizing" (Mayer and Nesmith 1995, 197).

The 1994 midterm election was a Republican sweep of historic proportions, giving the GOP control of both houses of Congress for the first time in forty years. The Christian Right played a small but significant role in this victory, and Iowa was no exception. Thanks to the defeat of a thirty-six-year Democratic incumbent, the GOP controlled all the Iowa U.S. House seats. Most telling was the CCI's involvement in Governor Branstad's renomination battle, where its voter guides were a key to Branstad's slim 52 percent win over moderate congressman Fred "Gopher" Grandy (Grandy's nickname from his role on the TV program *The Love Boat*). CCI's Ione Dilley remarked, "We've never gotten involved in primaries previous to that election . . . and it certainly influenced a lot of people" (Mayer and Nesmith 1995, 199). Christian conservatives also helped Governor Branstad win reelection in the fall.

Could the Christian Right successes of 1992 and 1994 be carried over to a presidential election? As the 1996 election approached, the Iowa Christian Right activists were divided among the GOP presidential hopefuls, diminishing the movement's impact. CCI's Ione Dilley backed Senate Majority Leader Bob Dole, the front-runner, but others supported commentator Pat Buchanan's second try for the GOP nomination, or a new Christian Right candidate, Ambassador Alan Keyes. Dole repeated his 1988 win, but with just 26 percent of the straw vote. Buchanan finished second with 23 percent, a bit less than Robertson's 1988 showing, in both relative and absolute numbers. (Tennessee Governor Lamar Alexander's 18 percent resembled Vice President Bush's 1988 percentage, and publisher Steve Forbes's 10 percent was much like Jack Kemp's 1988 showing; Keyes received 8 percent [Cook 2000, 24–25]).

Buchanan's 1996 success had much the same effect as Robertson's in 1988, propelling him to prominence, but front-runner Dole secured the nomination. Buchanan's support was different from Robertson's, as can be seen in table 6.6. Buchanan's supporters stand between Robertson's 1988 backers and Dole's 1996 supporters in terms of income and age, but the "Buchananeers" were the most conservative and focused on moral issues. In 1996, some 36 percent of the caucus attendees were Christian Right supporters; 42 percent of whom supported Buchanan, with Dole coming in second with 19 percent. Had the Christian Right been united behind Buchanan, he might well have finished first.

The 1996 campaign ended in disappointment for the Christian Right. First, Clinton again carried Iowa on his way to reelection (50 percent to Dole's 40 percent and Perot's 10 percent). As table 6.5 shows, the Christian Right voting bloc had grown to 13 percent of the total electorate, reflecting in part the movement's new organizational muscle. When compared with voters in 1980 and 1988, these voters were markedly more likely to identify as conservative and Republican, and more likely to vote for GOP candidates than other Republicans. Second, the movement backed conservative congressman Jim Lightfoot against liberal incumbent senator Tom Harkin, but he lost by a slim 48 percent to 52 percent margin. Lightfoot did not work especially well with the Christian Right, a problem that would haunt him two years later.

If the 1994 campaign was a triumph for the Republicans and the Christian Right, then 1998, like 1996, was a defeat for both. The battle was fought in the shadow of the Monica Lewinsky scandal, and movement activists were dismayed by the fact that voters did not punish the Democrats for Clinton's transgressions. In Iowa, the disappointment included the loss of the governorship for the first time in thirty years. Four-term Governor Branstad retired and the GOP nominee, Jim Lightfoot, lost to Democrat Tom Vilsack, in what many regarded as the upset of the year; the margin of Lightfoot's loss—48 percent to 52 percent—was the same as that for his 1996 loss to Senator Harkin.

The 2000 Campaign

The Iowa Christian Right was again divided over the Republican presidential candidates as the 2000 campaign approached. Several candidates made Christian conservatives and the Iowa caucuses central to their strategies. Publisher Steve Forbes had moved to the right on social issues since his 1996 campaign with the hope of building a broader coalition. He shrewdly hired Steve Scheffler, one of the most experienced movement operatives in the state (and eventually chair of the CCI), to work in his campaign. However, Forbes faced serious competition for the Christian conservative vote from Ambassador Alan Keyes and a new candidate, Gary Bauer. A former head of the Family Research Council and an associate of Focus on the Family's James Dobson, Bauer hoped to replicate the Robertson campaign by mobilizing a new constituency—the "Focus network" of nondenominational evangelicals—which was not especially well organized in Iowa.

Still other candidates staked a claim on the Christian Right vote: commentator Pat Buchanan (back for a third try), former vice president Dan Quayle, prolife New Hampshire Senator Robert Smith, Congressman John Kasich, Senator Orrin Hatch, and even more moderate candidates such as Elizabeth Dole and Texas Governor George W. Bush. With this crowded field, Iowa became immensely important, and most of the candidates attended the Republican Party summer straw poll in 1999. Front-runner George W. Bush prevailed in the poll with 31 percent. When added to Bush's prodigious fund-raising, this result drove numerous candidates from the race, including Elizabeth Dole, Dan Quayle, Robert Smith, and Pat Buchanan (who eventually obtained the 2000 Reform Party nomination). However, Forbes's 21 percent was solid, and when combined with Bauer (9 percent) and Keyes (5 percent) supporters, it led observers to regard the 2000 caucuses as up for grabs.

But on caucus night, Bush prevailed with 41 percent of the vote. Forbes was second with 30 percent, with Keyes at 14 percent and Bauer at 9 percent. Overall, Christian Rightists made up 40 percent of the voters in the GOP caucus, the highest percentage ever recorded. Bush received the largest share, about one-third. Steve Forbes came in a strong second, followed very closely by Keyes, with Bauer trailing behind (data not shown). Bush's success reflected three things: his front-runner status, his careful commitments to elements of the movement's agenda, and his public professions of faith.

Table 6.6 shows some familiar distinctions among the 2000 supporters of the various candidates. The Bauer/Keyes backers were younger and less affluent than the Bush supporters, and also more conservative, focused on moral values, and identified with the movement. The Forbes supporters were also less affluent than the Bush backers, and were less Republican, conservative, and close to the Christian Right than the Bauer/Keyes supporters. The signature characteristic of the Forbes backers was a focus on fiscal issues. Thus, Forbes's moral issues strategy was not a great success, despite his support among long-term CCI members (see table 6.2). Still, if the movement had united behind Forbes, he might have won.

In the 2000 general election the size of the Christian Right voting bloc was down a bit from 1996 but as supportive of Bush as other Republicans (see table 6.5). This united GOP produced a near tie at the ballot box: Gore received 49 percent, Bush 48 percent, Ralph Nader 2 percent, and Pat Buchanan less than 1 percent. In such a close election, all groups can claim to have made a difference—for good or ill. Even modestly higher turnout of Christian conservatives or the absence of Pat Buchanan could have given Bush the state. Of course, if Ralph Nader had not been on the ballot, Gore might have won an outright majority.

The vicissitudes of particular elections aside, evangelical Protestants had become a solid voting bloc for the Iowa Republicans. Table 6.7 examines the GOP presidential vote in all ninety-nine Iowa counties from 1980 to 2000, and a summary measure of Republican votes over all the elections for multiple offices. Using a simple regression model, we look at the impact of religious groups and other demographic factors.[9] The single best predictor of Republican voting 1980–2000 is the evangelical population in the county, and this holds for all presidential elections except 1980 (where it is second). In addition, the relationship between evangelicals and Republican presidential vote became stronger over time. The percentage of Pentecostals in a county begins the time period with a moderate association with Democrat voting, but ends the period with a small association with the GOP.

Other religious groups drifted Republican or remained Democratic. The percentage of mainline Protestants in a county is strongly associated with GOP voting in 1980 but steadily declines over the period. The percentage of Catholic and Jewish population is associated with a higher Democratic vote, despite the fact that Catholics nationwide have trended Republican. These findings for religious groups are especially impressive because they survive controls for sociodemographic factors, which show the expected relationships, such as the strong link between low-income and minority populations, and the Democratic vote.

THE CHRISTIAN RIGHT AND IOWA PUBLIC POLICY

The major motivation for Christian activism is to restore traditional values in social policy, from abortion to public schools. As in many other states, the Iowa Christian Right has not obtained a large number of changes in public policy, although it has prevented the enactment of liberal policies. But over the last twenty years, movement organizations have made significant headway in their dealings with the legislature and are now poised to have considerable impact.

Table 6.7   Characteristics of Iowa Counties and the GOP Presidential Vote[a]

County Characteristics	2000	1996	1992	1988	1984	1980	GOP Vote: 1980 to 2000[b]
Religious factors							
Catholic	−0.28	−0.21	−0.21	−0.22	−0.17	−0.14	−0.09
Evangelical	0.54	0.54	0.52	0.44	0.40	0.46	0.44
Mainline	0.05	−0.02	0.03	0.08	0.12	0.31	0.22
Pentecostal	0.03	0.03	0.04	0.00	−0.07	−0.12	−0.07
Jewish	−0.18	−0.07	−0.08	−0.14	−0.19	−0.32	−0.30
Social factors							
White	0.33	0.18	0.15	0.20	0.26	0.47	0.38
Black	−0.35	−0.20	−0.16	−0.18	−0.24	−0.39	−0.31
Hispanic	−0.26	−0.16	−0.12	−0.06	−0.07	−0.21	−0.04
Median age	0.15	−0.03	−0.04	0.01	−.05	0.38	0.16
No. of farms in county	−0.01	0.15	0.17	0.07	0.08	−0.07	0.03
No. of people below poverty level	−0.11	−0.26	−0.32	−0.19	−0.20	−0.08	−0.15
No. of unemployed	−0.34	−0.35	−0.33	−0.18	−0.16	−0.19	−0.16
Median income	−0.11	0.08	0.16	0.02	−0.002	−0.25	−0.11
No. registered voters in county	−0.26	−0.12	−0.08	−0.16	−0.22	−0.38	−0.32
R square for above variables	.475	.451	.443	.344	.323	.489	.449

Source: Data in this table come from three sources: The 1990 Census of Churches and Church Bodies produced by the Glenmary Research Center provides data for the denominational breakdowns by county throughout the United States; socioeconomic and political data come from Goudy et al. (1999); and the authors compiled 2000 election statistics from public sources.

[a]The coeffficients are standardized regression weights.

[b]The final column includes GOP voting for president, U.S. Senate, U.S. House, and Iowa governor from 1980 to 2000.

According to a questionnaire sent to all candidates in 2000, at least eleven of the fifty Iowa senators, all Republicans, support the agenda of the CCI. The CCI asked legislators for their views on tax issues (including one involving tax credits for parents sending their children to private or parochial schools), capital punishment, and abortion. In the house, 40 of the 100 members, all Republican, say they support at least eight of nine CCI issue positions. These numbers track with IFPC Director Hurley's assessment that about a dozen of the 150 current legislators are "fully committed Christians" and another thirty or more are what he would call "religious conservatives."[10] In sum, the potential impact of the Christian Right on the Iowa legislature is significant at present. The leaders of movement organizations feel that cooperation is very good among the groups—particularly CCI, IFPC, CWA, and the right-to-life groups. The intensely competitive political environment in Iowa may well require compromise to enact their agenda, however.

CONCLUSIONS

The Christian Right has found fertile ground in the crucible of Iowa politics. Since 1980, it has developed several effective organizations, a significant presence in the state Republican Party, a small but significant voting bloc, and growing influence in the state legislature. Thus, the movement has become a key Republican constituency. In addition to these strengths, the Christian Right faces a number of challenges in the Hawkeye State. Its activists are frequently divided, a tendency that has limited the impact of the Christian Right in presidential caucuses and sometimes hurt the GOP at the polls. It has yet to organize the rural, swing townships. The movement faces fierce opponents, which when combined with the competitiveness of Iowa politics, reduces its ability to nominate and elect favorable candidates and change policy in the legislature. Many of the Christian Right organizations are new and their potential is yet to be realized. Maintaining and expanding these and the other Christian Right opportunities will be a challenge in the near future. All and all, the Christian Right is likely to be a continuing player in Iowa politics in the foreseeable future.

ACKNOWLEDGMENT

The authors would like to acknowledge the assistance of Corwin Smidt, Robert Vickery, and Jason Haas.

NOTES

1. These data come from Kosmin (2001).
2. Interviews were conducted by the authors with leaders of the major Christian Right organizations discussed in the text, with leaders of some groups

opposed to the Christian Right, as well as with academics and other observers of Iowa politics.

3. All long-term members identify as Republicans, while only 3 percent of the remainder fail to do so.

4. Two things may account for the latter finding. Many old-time members feel comfortable simply working behind the scenes. Second, many candidates for office, or potential candidates, were at the fund-raiser as "contributors," hoping to curry support from CCI members.

5. One the authors, Don Racheter, was the organizer of ICRIE.

6. One of the authors, Don Racheter, was the committee chairman in question.

7. The general election network exit poll data in table 6.5 are far from ideal. Unfortunately, the operational definition of "Christian Right" varies from exit poll to exit poll because different questions were used in the surveys. In addition, the Ns are small for Iowa; the exit polls are national in scope. For 1980, the category "Christian Right GOP" includes Republicans who are Protestants (or "other Christians") who are born again *or* hold moral issue positions (N for 1980 is 273). For 1988, the same category includes Republicans who are evangelical Protestants, *or* born again, *or* prolife on abortion (N for 1988 is 327). In 1996, the category includes Republicans who identify themselves as "Christian Right," *or* are prolife on abortion, *or* take other moral issue positions (N for 1996 is 217). Finally, in 2000, the category includes Republicans who identify as "religious right" *or* regard "honesty" as the most important quality they are looking for in a candidate (N for 2000 is a substantially larger 1,007). For more details, contact Lyman Kellstedt at charandbudk@juno.com. These data were obtained from the Roper Center at the University of Connecticut.

8. The Iowa network exit polls are used in table 6.6, where we compare GOP caucus voters in 1988, 1996, and 2000. Comparisons are made between voters for identifiable Christian Right candidates—Robertson in 1988, Buchanan in 1996, and Bauer and Keyes in 2000—and voters for major party candidates—Vice President Bush in 1988, Dole in 1996, and George W. Bush in 2000, with Forbes voters included in 2000 because of the candidate's strong effort to connect with Christian Right voters. Exit poll surveys in Iowa select respondents in randomly selected precinct caucuses held throughout the state and tend to be sizable. In 1988 Ns were 1,652; in 1996 Ns were 2,074; and in 2000 the figure was 1,700. For more details, contact Lyman Kellstedt at charandbudk@juno.com.

9. Data in table 6.7 come from three sources. The 1990 Census of Churches and Church Bodies produced by the Glenmary Research Center provides data for the denominational breakdowns by county throughout the United States. Socioeconomic and political data came from Goudy et al. (1999). Finally, the authors compiled 2000 election statistics from public sources. For more details, contact Lyman Kellstedt at charandbudk@juno.com.

10. These data were made available to the authors by CCI.

REFERENCES

Balmer, Randall. 1989. *Mine Eyes Have Seen the Glory.* New York: Oxford University Press.

Conger, Kimberly H., and John C. Green. 2002. "Spreading Out and Digging In: Christian Conservatives and State Republican Parties." *Campaigns and Elections* (February):58–64.

Cook, Rhodes. 2000. *Race for the Presidency.* Washington, D.C.: Congressional Quarterly Press.

Elazar, Daniel J. 1972. *American Federalism: A View from the States.* 2d ed. New York: Thomas Y. Crowell.

Goudy, Willis, Sandra C. Burke, and Margaret Hanson. 1999. *Iowa Counties: Selected Population Trends, Vital Statistics, and Socioeconomic Data.* Ames, Iowa: Census Services, Department of Sociology.

Guth, James L., John C. Green, Lyman A. Kellstedt, and Corwin E. Smidt. 1995. "Onward Christian Soldiers: Religious Activist Groups in American Politics." Pp. 55–76 in *Interest Group Politics,* 4th ed., ed. Allan J. Cigler and Burdett A. Loomis. Washington, D.C.: Congressional Quarterly Press.

Herbers, John. 1980. "Ultraconservative Evangelicals a Surging Force in Politics." *New York Times* (August 17).

Hershey, Marjorie. 1984. *Running for Office.* Chatham, N.J.: Chatham House.

Hertzke, Allen D. 1993. *Echoes of Discontent.* Washington, D.C.: Congressional Quarterly Press.

Kosmin, Barry A. 2001. *American Religious Identification Survey.* New York: Graduate Center of the City University of New York.

Mayer, Jeremy D., and Bruce Nesmith. 1995. "Iowa: Everything Comes up Rosy." Pp. 191–210 in *God at the Grassroots,* ed. Mark J. Rozell and Clyde Wilcox. Lanham, Md.: Rowman & Littlefield.

Persinos, John F. 1994. "Has the Christian Right Taken over the Republican Party?" *Campaigns and Elections* (September):20–24.

Reed, Ralph. 1994. *Politically Incorrect: The Emerging Faith Factor in American Politics.* Dallas: Word Publishing.

Rosenstone, Steven J., and John Mark Hansen. 1993. *Mobilization, Participation, and Democracy in America.* New York: Macmillan.

Schwartz, Maralee. 1986. "Fundamentalists Elected." *New York Times* (April 9).

Winebrenner, Hugh. 1998. *The Iowa Precinct Caucuses: The Making of a Media Event.* 2d ed. Ames: Iowa State University Press.

SEVEN

The Kansas Christian Right and the Evolution of Republican Politics

Allan J. Cigler, Mark Joslyn, and Burdett A. Loomis

RELIGIOUS INVOLVEMENT IN KANSAS POLITICS HAS A HISTORY that stretches back to the state's founding. The Kansas-Nebraska Act of 1854 led to an influx of a large number of Republican abolitionists from New England as the territory became a central battleground for contending free- and slave-state forces. The victory of the former, linked to what political scientist Daniel Elazar (1972) has termed the "moralistic culture," proved to be the catalyst for the 1861 creation of a Republican-dominated state. From statehood to the New Deal, Kansans played prominent national leadership roles in various religious and moralist movements, including abolition, populism, progressivism, and prohibition, all directly linked to the Republican Party.

Kansas's partisan tendencies survived even the powerful national forces that brought about the critical realignments of the 1890s and 1930s. In recent decades, Democrats have been able to gain occasional short-run advantage, especially at the gubernatorial level, by exploiting regionally based splits within the Republican Party, but durable voter shifts characteristic of partisan realignment have never been evident (Cigler and Loomis 1992). As the nation enters the twenty-first century, Kansas remains one of the most Republican of all states and stands as the only state not to have elected at least one Democratic U.S. senator since the 1930s.

Still, the tenor of Kansas politics has changed markedly over the last quarter century, largely through the resurgence of religious forces within the Republican Party. From the New Deal until the late 1980s, Kansas Republicanism generally embodied fiscal, not social, conservatism.

Nationally prominent Kansas Republicans, such as Senate majority leader and ex-presidential candidate Robert Dole and Senators Nancy Landon Kassebaum, James Pearson, and Frank Carlsen developed reputations as deficit fighters, uneasy with the expansion of government and the accompanying increasing tax burden, but not anxious to elevate social issues on the political agenda, whatever their own beliefs.

The late 1980s and 1990s witnessed the rise of a new breed of party activist and politician within the Republican Party: connected to the Christian Right, fiscally conservative, and firmly convinced that government actions must reverse the moral decline of the nation. The result has been a continuing internecine conflict within the party that has altered the style and intensity of the state's electoral politics and, to a degree, the content of state public policy.

THE SEEDS OF THE CHRISTIAN RIGHT IN KANSAS

Kansas has long had its share of adherents to the Christian Right's social and economic agenda. These citizens hold conservative views on abortion, gay and lesbian rights, school prayer, sex education, school vouchers, and related issues (Cigler and Loomis 1997). As elsewhere, members of the Kansas Christian Right are alarmed by unwholesome societal trends caused by the secularization of American culture; these include purported increases in crime, violence, sexual promiscuity, and social diseases, as well as erosion of the work ethic and performance in the public schools. Kansas's populist tradition is compatible with the Christian Right perspective, given its distrust of government, big business, and political party and mainstream media elites on one hand, and, on the other, suspicion of the underclass, particularly racial minorities, ostensibly the major beneficiaries of most social programs. From the New Deal to the early 1970s, however, religious-based, political efforts were rare in Kansas and typically appeared at the fringes of mainstream politics. The John Birch Society had a presence in Kansas, as did other groups whose message merged Christianity and anticommunism, such as Defenders of the Christian Faith, the Christian Patriots, and the Mid-America League for Constitutional Government.

The 1973 Supreme Court decision in *Roe v. Wade* proved to be the trigger event that prompted an active Christian Right movement in the state. The immediate post-*Roe* period in Kansas witnessed the active opposition to the decision from several Protestant church congregations and Catholic parishes, as well as the creation of a few right-to-life groups, as the abortion issue gave Christian activists the sharp focus that they had previously lacked (Sigman 1996). By far the most prominent group was Kansans for Life, an affiliate of the National Right to Life Committee, which had been organized and funded by the Catholic Church to oppose the legalization of abortion.

In these early years, the antiabortion groups were bipartisan and limited in their electoral activities. Groups like Kansans for Life, for example, published voter guides that encouraged supporters to base their vote solely on a candidate's position on the abortion issue but avoided direct participation in campaigns. The one notable exception occurred in 1974, when for the first time antiabortion activists played a pivotal role in a major election contest. Senator Dole was strongly challenged by Democratic Representative William Roy, a physician who had performed a modest number of abortions while practicing in Topeka. Two days before the election, with Kansans for Life playing a major role, antiabortion activists, including both Catholics and Protestants, engineered an extensive literature "drop" of an anti-Roy pamphlet, which included a picture of an aborted fetus. Caught off guard, the Roy campaign failed to respond, and Dole's small margin of victory gave weight to the apparent potential political clout of the antiabortionists (Cigler and Loomis 1997, 208–9). The mid-1970s were crucial to the development of the eventual Kansas Christian Right, as conservative Catholics and Protestant fundamentalists showed they could cooperate when they shared political goals.

Cooperation increased slowly in the late 1970s and early 1980s as the social agenda expanded beyond abortion politics. Until that time Kansas had on the books some of the most restrictive morality laws in the nation, reflecting the religious, rural character of the state. But the declining rural influence in the legislature and the state's deteriorating economic condition combined to create a new context for morality issues, which were elevated to the policy forefront through the larger debate over economic development. Economic growth in Kansas depended on agriculture and the rural-based oil and gas industry, sectors that had difficulty rebounding from the recession of the late Carter and early Reagan presidencies. In order to remake Kansas's image in hopes of attracting business to diversify the economy, various state decisionmakers in both parties supported efforts to revise the state's morality laws. A Democratic governor and a Republican legislature enacted statutes that permitted sales of liquor by the drink, established a lottery, and allowed for parimutuel wagering on dog and horse racing. These measures were widely viewed as both helping fill state coffers and contributing to the image of a more modern, cosmopolitan Kansas. Not surprisingly, the consideration of such intensely charged morality issues led to group mobilization across the Kansas political spectrum, including the rise of a large number of single-issue groups concerned with social issues (Cigler and Kiel 1993). Typically, the battles were fought out in the Kansas legislative arena rather than during electoral campaigns.

By the mid-to-late 1980s Kansas had in place a diverse collection of politically active, culturally conservative, organized interests, most religiously based. But cooperation and coordination among the groups was sporadic at best. Some were go-it-alone individual congregations; the most extreme was the Topeka Westboro Baptist Church, headed by the Reverend Fred Phelps. A registered Democrat, Phelps later developed a national reputation for his crusade against homosexuality by demonstrating outside gay bars and picketing the state's higher-education institutions, which had funded gay and lesbian groups. Although the Christian Right loosely included any number of churches and groups, including those with national affiliations, such as the Christian Coalition and the Eagle Forum, the most influential organization remained Kansans for Life, which had grown far beyond its original Catholic base. The Moral Majority had no organizational presence in the state.

Perhaps the most daunting obstacle facing any attempt to mobilize cultural conservatives into a movement was and remains the state's basic religious diversity, coupled with its low population density. According to survey data, Roman Catholic identifiers make up 20 percent of the state's population, mainline Protestants comprise 24 percent (led by 13 percent Methodist), with 23 percent of the population affiliated with a wide range of evangelical denominations. Among churches with an evangelical bent, Baptists represent the leading denomination (13 percent of the Kansas population), with Pentecostal/Assembly of God adherents and various Church of Christ denominations among the leaders of the many smaller evangelical denominations.[1]

Although evangelicals are dispersed throughout rural Kansas, the main element of the emerging Christian Right movement in the state was surprisingly concentrated—in the suburbs, where evangelicals have become far more politicized than those found in more rural areas of the state (Beinart 1998). The "outer-ring suburbs—where the city meets the countryside"—in the metropolitan areas of Wichita and Kansas City, have proved to be the hotbeds of Kansas Christian Right political activism, noted the *New Republic*'s Peter Beinart (1998, 26). These suburbs represent the fastest-growing areas within a state where the rural population has experienced a substantial decline over the past century. Moreover, a large proportion of the new suburban residents have migrated from the state's rural areas. These outer-ring suburbs provided the key venues for the clash between the traditional/religious and modernizing/secular cultures. This is where the political mobilization of the cultural conservative Christian elements eventually took place.

THE CHRISTIAN RIGHT AND THE CAPTURE OF THE KANSAS REPUBLICAN PARTY ORGANIZATION

Various forces converged in the late 1980s and early 1990s to propel social conservatives toward more unity and cooperation. The eventual goal became to capture the Republican Party, which would serve as a base for remaking state policy and sending to Washington a Kansas delegation committed to the Christian Right agenda. The first major effort to directly influence Republican Party decision making came in early 1988, when Pat Robertson's Christian Coalition supporters, largely made up of members of individual congregations throughout the state, attempted to stack the Republican state and local caucuses entrusted with the selection of national convention delegates. Senator Dole, the acknowledged leader of the state party and a presidential nomination contender, expressed considerable irritation at the Christian Right's efforts to embarrass him on his home turf. It took a major mobilization effort by party regulars during the two weeks prior to the caucuses for Dole to prevail, but tension between regular Republicans and insurgent Christian Right activists rose markedly.

The wedge between the Republican moderates and social conservatives soon extended into party business both inside and outside state government. In 1990, after a stormy legislative session in which a group of social conservative legislators had made life difficult for moderate Republican governor Mike Hayden, the governor and the Republican legislative leadership decided to cut off Republican political action committee (PAC) money to a number of emerging Christian Right leaders (Loomis 1994). The so-called rebels, led by state representative David Miller, had aggressively criticized the governor and the moderate legislative leadership for not pursuing a socially conservative agenda. Miller and his followers had concluded that the mainstream Republican leadership would never be responsive to the social conservative agenda and that Christian conservatives had no choice but to remake the state's Republican Party in their own image. Miller convinced Nestor Weigand of Wichita to challenge incumbent governor Hayden in the 1990 Republican primary, in part by agreeing to be his running mate. Hayden won a close primary race but enraged the Christian Right by denying his primary opponent the state party's voter identification lists. In the general election, many social conservatives crossed party lines to support a prolife Democrat, Joan Finney, who won a close gubernatorial contest.

From his post-1990 position as political director for Kansans for Life and later as executive director of the Kansas Christian Coalition, Miller, a Methodist, turned his attention to capturing the Republican Party organization. Like many one-party–dominated states, Kansas had a weak and permeable party organization (Mayhew 1986; Cigler and Loomis 1992). With particular emphasis in the suburban areas of Wichita and Kansas City, Christian Right elements conducted a concerted precinct-level effort to win control of the party organization. Since precinct positions often went vacant and were filled by appointment, in many precincts simply finding a candidate was tantamount to winning the position.

Johnson County (Kansas City suburbs) presents a vivid example of how the party was quickly altered at the local level (Sullinger 1996). In 1990 there were 330 candidates and 10 contested races for precinct committeeman/woman in Johnson County. These figures rose, respectively, to 487 candidates and 94 contested races in 1992, 759 and 221 in 1994, and 935 and 343 in 1996. Both Kansans for Life and various individual evangelical churches played major roles in developing slates of candidates and working to turn out conservative Republicans at precinct caucuses. Early on, the opposition moderates were largely unorganized, and by 1994 virtually all Republican county political organizations were controlled by the Christian conservatives.

In the Wichita area, Christian Right political mobilization to take over the party was aided by a catalyst event. In the late summer of 1991 the leadership of the national antiabortion group Operation Rescue targeted a number of abortion clinics in the city, focusing especially on the clinic run by Dr. George Tiller, nationally known for his willingness to conduct late-term abortions (Risen and Thomas 1998, 317–38; Johnson 1999). Early success in shutting down the clinics inspired evangelicals from throughout the country as well as Kansas, many of whom came to Wichita to join in the picketing and rallies in what has come to be known as the "Summer of Mercy." Crucial to the organizing efforts in Wichita besides groups like Kansans for Life were a number of local fundamentalist churches, especially Wichita's Central Christian Church, which acted as the banker and bookkeeper for Operation Rescue's efforts. Clinic picketing soon turned violent, with confrontations between police and demonstrators resulting in a large number of arrests, and eventually was ended only when judicial intervention and accompanying fines and imprisonment for protest leaders became prohibitive (Risen and Thomas 1998).

The "energy channeled into Wichita during the protests spilled over into the political arena," and by 1992 Christian Right adherents had captured the Sedgewick County Republican Party organization (Risen and Thomas 1998, 333). During the Operation Rescue rallies Mark Gietzen, head of a splinter party group called the Kansas Republican Coalition for Life, had used the rallies to recruit candidates to run for precinct committee positions. In the August 1992 Republican primary, fully 83 percent of elected committee members held antiabortion views. A few weeks after the election the new county committee elected Gietzen to become the new party chair (Risen and Thomas 1998).

With party delegations from the state's two largest metropolitan areas well in hand, it was only a matter of time before Christian Right supporters would be able to control the state Republican Party organization. After the 1994 election, Bob Dole's candidate for Republican State Chair (the incumbent) stepped down rather than face certain defeat. Now in control of the party, Christian Right adherents elected Miller as the new state chair—despite the opposition of long-time incumbent senators Dole and Nancy Kassebaum, as well as the newly elected governor, Bill Graves. The moderates, who had controlled the state party for decades, were now on the outside looking in.

1994–1998: "Every Family Has Its Ups and Downs"

The battle for the soul of the Republican Party continued unabated between 1994 and 1998 (a detailed description is found in Cigler and Loomis 2000). David Miller reigned as the party organization's chairman and continually opposed the agenda put forth by moderate Bill Graves, the highly popular GOP governor who had been elected in 1994. The social conservatives experienced real electoral success yet could not impose their agenda on the state legislature.

The Kansas delegation to Congress changed dramatically in this period (Cigler and Loomis 1997). As of October 1994, Kansas voters were represented by two traditional Republican senators to Washington (Dole and Kassebaum), along with two traditional Republican House members (Jan Meyers and Pat Roberts) and two moderate Democrats (Dan Glickman and Jim Slattery). But in 1994, in the context of a strong Republican year nationally, the Kansas electorate moved sharply to the economic and social right. Most surprising was the defeat absorbed by Glickman, an eighteen-year House Democratic veteran, who lost to first-term State Senator Todd Tiahrt, "who relied heavily on volunteer workers recruited during the Operation Rescue rallies" (Risen and Thomas 1998, 334). Tiahrt also benefited from redistricting that had increased the district's competitiveness and from the Christian Right-National Rifle Association electioneering cooperation that characterized the last weeks of the general election campaign. Sam Brownback, a former state agriculture secretary with a moderate background (and a conservative, prolife challenge in the primary) won Slattery's House seat convincingly over former governor John Carlin. Much to the discomfort of many moderate Republicans, Brownback embraced a thoroughly conservative agenda on both fiscal and social issues, a tack that he has followed throughout his legislative career in Washington.

The 1996 elections represented the apex of Christian Right electoral strength in the state, as two new social conservatives from the Christian Right movement, Jim Ryun and Vince Snowbarger, won congressional seats, emphasizing their strong antiabortion views during the campaign. Brownback, who had become a key spokesman for Christian Right views throughout the state and was now enthusiastically embraced by the movement, defeated U.S. senator Sheila Frahm in the GOP Senate primary. This election was especially significant in that Frahm, a moderate and former lieutenant governor, had been appointed by Governor Graves to the seat vacated by Senator Dole, who had resigned during his run for the presidency.

In two short years the ideological complexion of the Kansas congressional delegation had been drastically altered. The all-GOP Kansas delegation now consisted of four social conservatives (Senator Sam Brownback, Representatives Todd Tiahrt, Jim Ryun, and Vince Snowbarger) and two traditional Republicans (Roberts, now a senator, and Representative Jerry Moran). All the social conservatives benefited from the expanding organization power of the Christian Right, anchored by both the prolife movement and the newly captured Republican Party. At the same time, Roberts and Moran, while not tied to the movement, were conservative enough on social issues to retain the overall support of Christian Right adherents.[2]

Still, social conservatives did not dominate Kansas politics; their electoral successes in the 1996 encouraged David Miller to challenge Governor Bill Graves in the 1998 Republican gubernatorial primary. The extremely popular Graves, riding the mid-1990s economic surge, had cut taxes substantially while allowing government to grow at a modest rate. And he had proved a constant thorn in the conservatives' side, as he negotiated with Democrats in the state legislature and generally ignored the Christian Right agenda. In 1998 he did sign a bill that appeared to curtail third-trimester abortions (but in fact did nothing). Republican social conservatives were scarcely mollified and Miller declared his candidacy. Raising only $400,000 compared with Graves's $1.7 million, Miller never had a chance. He lost the August 1998 primary by an embarrassing 73 percent to 27 percent margin.

In addition, the Miller wing lost control of the party organization, largely because his candidacy had produced a strong countermobilization among moderate Republicans, led by the Mainstream Coalition, a group formed and led by a number of Johnson County (suburban Kansas City) ministers affiliated with mainstream Protestant denominations. After his defeat, Miller and other Christian Right activists did create a conservative party organization—the Kansas Republican Assembly—but this group did not succeed in attracting the membership of any significant GOP elected officials, regardless of their conservatism. To add insult to injury, Democrat Dennis Moore, buoyed by moderate Republicans in Johnson County, upset one-term Representative Snowbarger, who proved too conservative for his affluent suburban district (Cigler 1999; Loomis 2001).

Yet the Christian Right did register one set of election victories in 1998. Social conservatives elected a controlling faction of an obscure, yet symbolically important body: the Kansas Board of Education (KBOE).[3] The battle for control of this board would dominate Kansas's electoral politics in 2000, as the state once again had to answer the question, "What's the matter with Kansas?"

DÉJÀ VU ALL OVER AGAIN: EVOLUTION AS A (REPUBLICAN) POLITICAL ISSUE

The core of the Kansas Christian Right's education agenda focused on remaking the public schools to make them more compatible with Christian values. Across the state Christian Right advocates were encouraged to run for local school boards and given help in their efforts. By the mid-1990s attention turned to the state level, as Christian Right advocates created the Kansas Education Watch Network (KEW-NET), a group dedicated to electing Christian Right candidates to the KBOE. The aims of the organization included the elimination of sex education, advocacy of abstinence as the only proper approach to sex education before marriage, encouragement of Christian messages in public schools to give students a sense of right and wrong, and consideration of "intelligent design" as an alternative to the theory of evolution to explain the origin of mankind (Beem 1996).

In a manner similar to the so-called stealth campaigns that served the Christian Right so well in their early 1990s capture of the Republican Party organization, KEW-NET actively recruited and trained candidates for the low-profile, largely noncompetitive KBOE seats. The 1998 elections produced a slim board majority that was sympathetic to the Christian Right and KEW-NET's perspectives on a variety of key issues, most notably the question of evolution.

The 1999 KBOE Decision

The election results produced policy implications almost immediately. An August 1999 decision of the KBOE focused attention specifically on the moderate/Christian Right split in the state Republican Party and generally on the state of Kansas as it reopened controversies that drew comparisons to the Scopes trial of 1925. By a six-to-four majority the board adopted a set of science standards that were widely, if inaccurately, interpreted as prohibiting the teaching of evolution in the state's public schools. If newspaper headlines can frame public discussion and create powerful impressions, the image of Kansas could do nothing but suffer. A front-page *New York Times* story proclaimed, "Board from Kansas Deletes Evolution from Curriculum," while the *Cleveland Plain Dealer* flatly stated, "Kansas Schools Delete Darwin." Editorials over the next few weeks took their toll on Kansas's image, steadily reinforcing a negative impression of the state. For example, the *Atlanta Constitution* discussed "Ooze and Oz," the *Washington Post* weighed in with "Kansas Slides Down Evolutionary Chain," while the *Omaha World Herald* saw "The Scopes Trial Replayed in Kansas."

The reaction to the decision and its news coverage by most Kansas public officials and the state's business community was predictably defensive, reflecting a fear that the hard work of the past two decades to overcome the state's stereotypical "Oz" image had been for naught. Within a week of the board's decision, an Oregon firm announced that the KBOE action had caused it to rethink locating a new plant in Kansas. State educators took to wondering if Kansas high school students would be disadvantaged in their efforts to attend out-of-state colleges and universities, given the perception of Kansas education as unprogressive. Representative Jim Ryun and Senator Sam Brownback, attuned to their social-conservative constituencies, quickly endorsed the board's action, but most prominent Kansans condemned the decision, agreeing with Governor Graves, who called it "terrible, tragic, embarrassing" (Milburn 2001).

If perception becomes reality, the media's interpretations of the board's decision posed a problem. Although the majority's reasoning was clearly rooted in the creationist thinking of the Christian Right, the KBOE decision did not require the teaching of the faith-based notion of intelligent design, with its assertion that a higher power created the universe. The decision did not eliminate the teaching of evolution or the mention of Darwin from the public schools, but it did deemphasize the importance of the Darwinian theory of evolution. Well-informed by social conservative groups, the board understood that previous court decisions barred states from requiring the teaching of creationism. At the same time, questions dealing with the Darwinian theory of evolution would no longer be part of the state's science assessment tests, thus discouraging teachers from addressing the subject. The decision could be defended from a local-autonomy perspective, since it allowed local school districts to decide for themselves whether or not, and to what degree, the theory of "macro" evolution—based on the premise that all life descended from a common ancestor—would be part of the curriculum.

Despite the new guidelines, virtually all school districts in the state indicated that the decision would not alter their science curriculum. In practice, nothing had changed for most Kansas teachers and students, but the KBOE decision left the widespread impression that the Christian Right could dictate specific educational practices through its board majority.

The Christian Right's success on the evolution issue was scarcely an accident. In addition to its well-publicized attempts to affect the state's abortion policies, Christian Right elements had been paying close attention to state public education policy for over a decade. Although not given much press coverage, home schooling, for example, has been a major issue in Kansas. The Christian Coalition in the early 1990s was instrumental in creating the Christian Home Educators Confederation of Kansas (CHECK), a statewide organization that provides resources, including legal assistance, to help families begin their home schooling efforts (Christian Home Educators Confederation of Kansas 2002). CHECK also succeeded in the legislative arena, where it has largely prevented state government from imposing administrative regulations and state standards on the content of home schooling education.

In the end, however, the Christian Right reached its high-water mark in affecting Kansas public policy with its capture of a KBOE majority. In the wake of the fight over science curriculum standards, moderates within the Republican Party vowed to reverse the decision. To most observers, the decision was not really about science but about religion and politics. Creationists argued that the decision represented the will of Kansas, democracy at work. Opponents argued church/state boundaries had been breached, and that an unrepresentative minority, using stealth tactics, had usurped the power of the people. These low-profile contests became the fodder of national news, as Kansans fought an electoral battle at the cusp of the twenty-first century over an issue connected to a much earlier political era.

The 2000 Kansas Elections

The initial reaction of many state politicians and business leaders angered by the evolution decision was that its reversal should come about through constitutional/legal means rather than through the electoral process. "The question is whether [the board] is constituted in such a way to match the needs of the 21st century, or is it constituted in such a way to match the needs of the 19th century," noted Kansas House Majority Leader Kent Glasscock, a moderate Republican who expected that the appropriateness of an elected KBOE would dominate the 2000 legislative session (Hancock 1999, A-1). Republican moderates immediately opined that either members of the KBOE should be appointed by the governor in consultation with the state legislature or the board should be eliminated entirely or, at the very least, that the KBOE should be stripped of its power to act on educational matters without legislative direction (Hancock 1999).

Kansas continued to draw the attention of outside observers and groups. For example, a number of Washington advocacy organizations focused on the decision, and Americans United for Separation of Church and State promised legal intervention if it could be conclusively demonstrated that a religious motive fueled the board's actions. The American Civil Liberties Union was especially concerned with the potential censorship of teachers. An ACLU spokesman noted, "What can be dangerous is the silent chilling effect [of the decision]. We may never know that a biology teacher drops evolution for a year or teaches it for only one or a few days" (Carpenter 2000, A-1).

Governor Graves viewed the decision as "one further step toward some serious legislative consideration about whether or not Kansas should be asked to reconsider the value of an elected State Board of Education" (Petterson and Dvorak 1999, B-1). He appeared ready to lend his prestige to an effort to change the Kansas Constitution to create a board appointed by the governor.

But political reality soon set in. In 1990 Kansas voters had overwhelmingly rejected a constitutional proposal designed to allow the state legislature to decide how the board would be elected. Even before an amendment could be placed on the ballot, two-thirds of both state houses would have to approve it, a daunting task in light of the size of the conservative contingent in the Kansas House. Upon reflection, opponents of the KBOE decision, including the governor, were uneasy with attempting to take direct voting power out of the hands of the people. Even the Democratic House Minority Leader, Jim Garner, appalled by the decision, reluctantly concluded, "I think the solution is in electing better people to the state Board of Education. Maybe this incident will heighten interest and increase the awareness of the importance of this office" (Petterson and Dvorak 1999, B-1). Moderates were encouraged by a *Kansas City Star* statewide poll indicating that 52 percent of those surveyed disagreed with the board's decision to adopt science standards that downplayed evolution (Beem 1999). Slightly less than a third supported the change. Within weeks after the KBOE decision it became clear that the battle over the teaching of evolution in the state's public schools would be fought out in the arena of public opinion and, ultimately, at the ballot box.

Much of the fall of 1999 and early winter of 2000 witnessed an extensive public dialogue over the KBOE decision and its implications. Amid much media coverage, a number of debates between scientists and creationists took place. It became clear that the board had relied heavily on material from the Creation Science Association of Mid-America in constructing its new science standards. Sixteen passages in the new state science education document were "borrowed" nearly word for word from that organization's publications. The creationist organization's president observed, "[W]hat difference does it make? So they borrowed a few phrases from people who don't build their religion around evolution" (Beem 2000b, 1). In reaching its decision the board had paid little, if any, attention to the guidelines on the teaching of evolution developed by its own advisory committee, consisting of twenty-seven science teachers and professors, who had relied upon documents from the National Academy of Sciences, the American Association for the Advancement of Science, and the National Science Teachers Association.

The August 2000 Republican primary soon became a focal point of both those in favor of the decision and those who wished it overturned. Four of the five seats to be contested, on the ten-member board, were currently held by Christian conservatives who had voted for the controversial new science standards. The other was held by a Democrat who had opposed these standards. By mid-March three of the four Christian conservative board members, including its chair, had decided to seek reelection, and Republican moderates had lined up candidates to contest all four seats.

The primary campaign was reminiscent of the 1990s battles between Christian Right activists and moderates over control of the Republican Party, a contest that many thought had ended with David Miller's crushing defeat in his challenge to Governor Graves in the 1998 gubernatorial primary. In the 2000 reprise, the Graves-led Republican moderates confronted the Christian conservatives led by the Kansas Republican Assembly, whose members took great pleasure in referring to themselves as "the Republican wing of the Republican Party."

One major difference this time, however, was the large number of grassroots, organized interests that had been activated by the KBOE's evolution decision, including nonprofit groups that were prevented by law from direct political action (Beem 2000a). But such groups were not forbidden from issue advocacy in an attempt to influence the climate of opinion. For example, as early as January, drivers along a suburban Kansas City interstate were greeted by a billboard that depicted a Bible in the background and the words, "Science textbook in Kansas public schools. NO!!! Vote Aug. 1, 2000." The billboard was paid for by an ad hoc group organized in the fall called Save Our Schools. Later in the spring commuters heading home from Missouri into the bordering Kansas suburbs were greeted by another billboard on the interstate proclaiming, "If you don't want evolution to stop at the Kansas border join us." The organization responsible for the sign was Kansas Citizens for

Science, another ad hoc group that claimed 120 members and was anxious to recruit more in anticipation of the August primary.

In the past, KBOE candidates (in both the primary and general elections) had campaigned with budgets of less than $1,000, which came from their personal funds and from their friends' pockets. PAC contributions by organized interests were very unusual. Endorsements by prominent politicians, especially in the primary, played no role. The 2000 Republican primary, however, encouraged both extensive press coverage and substantial involvement by forces never previously active in the board elections.

The most high-profile race occurred in the affluent Kansas City suburbs of Johnson County, where KBOE chair Linda Holloway, the most outspoken member of the board's majority, faced reelection. Her primary challenger, Sue Gamble, was a past president of the Kansas Association of School Boards, a current member of a district school board and a vehement opponent of the evolution decision. Gamble had been approached to run for the office by the Mainstream Coalition, a group dominated by moderate Republicans who originally came together in the early 1990s to oppose the Christian Right takeover of the party organization.

Holloway raised and spent over $90,000 on her reelection effort, while Gamble spent nearly $40,000 in her challenge (Beem 2000c). Holloway's major financial support came from individual social conservatives connected to the Kansas Republican Assembly, which earlier in the year had sponsored a "Back the Board" fund-raising dinner for those members who had voted for the new science standards. The Free Academic Inquiry and Research Committee (FAIR), a PAC affiliated with the group, contributed the maximum allowed ($500) to Holloway's campaign, as well as to the other social conservatives running for reelection. Gamble's support, in contrast, came largely from small contributions; educators throughout the state were particularly important. The Kansas National Education Association (KNEA) took a special interest in communicating with its members about the race, and its affiliated PAC made a $500 contribution to the Gamble campaign as well as to the candidates it supported in the other KBOE races.

Holloway took the unusual step of spending $20,000 on cable television ads. She hoped such ads would overcome what she called the press's "liberal bias," which had led Kansans to think that the teaching of evolution had been banned and the teaching of creationism mandated (Carpenter 2000; Beem 2000d). The ads showed the incumbent explaining her views, as she attempted to make clear that the KBOE decision did not prevent the teaching of evolution but simply let parents and school board members decide what their children should learn.

Senator Brownback, a longtime friend, endorsed Holloway, indicating that he supported the KBOE's decision on the evolution issue. "I agree with Governor George W. Bush of Texas," he said, siding with the then Republican presidential candidate. "Decision-making is best done at the local level. The decision of whether to teach creation, evolution, or both, should be made between local school boards, and parents" (Ranney 2000, A-1). Governor Graves, who formally endorsed three of the other challengers to KBOE incumbents and clearly preferred Gamble, stayed out of the race because Gamble did not ask for his endorsement, largely as a tactic to keep attention focused on Holloway.

By early summer it was apparent that, despite the extensive campaigning in all four of the contested districts, opinion divisions among the Kansas electorate on the evolution issue had changed little since soon after the decision was first announced. In our statewide survey, among those who were aware of the KBOE decision, 21 percent agreed with the decision and 11 percent strongly agreed.[4] However, intensity of opinion was stronger among those who felt the board majority was wrong. More than half the sample said they disagreed with the decision, and fully 34 percent indicated strong disagreement.

In the same poll, using the same language employed by national Gallup surveys, respondents were asked a question addressing the beliefs of Kansans about evolution. Thus, comparisons could be made between the beliefs of Kansans and those of the nation as a whole. The question read: "Which of the following statements comes closest to describing your views about the origin and development of human beings? God created man pretty much in our present form at one time within the last 10,000 years. Human beings developed over millions of years from less advanced forms of life. God had no part in the process. Or, human beings developed over millions of years from less advanced forms of life, but God guided this process, including man's creation?" The first statement identifies what is generally considered a creationist perspective, while the second represents the naturalistic, Darwinian account. Finally, the third statement has come to be known as the theistic evolutionist position. Figures 7.1A and 7.1B display a comparison of the distribution of responses on the question from the June 2000 survey of Kansans and the results of an August 1999 (the closest date to our survey) Gallup Poll on the evolution issue. The most obvious, and perhaps most remarkable, finding is the striking correspondence between Kansans and the rest of the country. Fully 49 percent of Kansans believe in the creationist view, while 42 percent ascribe to the theistic evolutionary perspective. Only 5 percent of Kansans have beliefs corresponding to the pure Darwinian position. The survey results indicate that Kansans, like most Americans, separate their personal beliefs about the origin of life from their thoughts concerning what is appropriately taught in public school science classes.

Figure 7.1A   U.S. Citizens' Beliefs about the Origin and Development of Human Beings

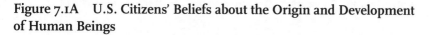
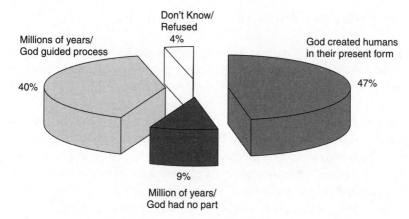

Source: Survey by the Gallup Organization, August 1999.

Figure 7.1B   Kansas Citizens' Beliefs about the Origin and Development of Human Beings

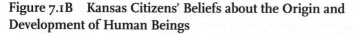
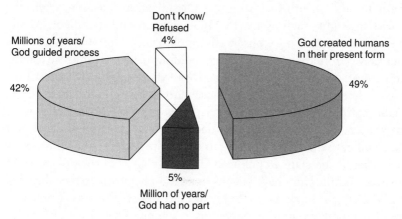

Source: Survey by the Survey Research Center, University of Kansas, June 2000.

The poll results were confirmed in the August 1 primary. Voters rejected Holloway and two other conservatives by comfortable margins, and the moderate Republican winners would go on to post easy victories in the November general elections. Within a month of being sworn in, the new board voted seven to three to approve revised science standards that emphasized evolution. Unfortunately for the image of the state, the national media barely noted this reversal in fortune, and Kansas would have its rural, out-of-step reputation reinforced.

THE CHRISTIAN RIGHT AND KANSAS POLITICS

Building on a long populist tradition, even in the face of a declining rural population, social conservatives in Kansas have proven resilient since the mid-1980s. The state's Christian Right remains a reliable, core element of Republican support for the party's national presidential ticket.[5] It has won and lost control of the state's Republican Party.[6] It has won and lost control of the Kansas Board of Education. Three of the state's current six-person congressional delegation are strong Christian Right loyalists. The Christian Right has consistently elected about a third of the state legislature. Prior to the 2002 elections, the movement coalesced around one major GOP candidate for both governor and attorney general.

From an organizational perspective, especially in its capacity for consistent mobilization of conservative voters, the Christian Right movement in Kansas is currently a far cry from its halcyon days of the early to mid-1990s. The movement now faces a fully mobilized and better-funded group of moderates in the party, unlikely to be caught off guard again by any stealth-like strategy. Organizational leaders from the Christian Right, such as David Miller, have found it difficult to ally themselves with many conservative politicians, who have distanced themselves from the purist perspectives of those who created the Kansas Republican Assembly as an alternative to the Republican State Committee. Even dedicated social conservatives like congressmen Todd Tiahrt and Jim Ryun and Senator Sam Brownback, whose careers were spawned by the movement, have deemphasized abortion as a political issue and have made extra efforts to cooperate with the moderates now in charge of the state Republican Party. Finally, the state's press and business communities have become increasingly hostile to the Christian Right, seeing it as a threat to the economic future of the state. For many, the effort to eliminate the mandatory teaching of the theory of evolution in the state's public school was the last straw, as it signaled a conscious turning away from accepted educational standards within the scientific community. Given the growth of information-based businesses in Johnson County and a major push to make the Kansas City metro area a center for medical and biological research, bowing to creationist forces was seen as the worst kind of publicity.

In the end, despite some organized efforts from the Mainstream Coalition and a variety of smaller, ad hoc groups such as science teachers, the core opposition to the Christian Right came from moderates within the Republican Party. These individuals had more to lose than anyone else from a strong social conservative movement.

Ironically, the Christian Right has fared better in economic policy-making than on social issues. Abortion policy remains moderate in Kansas, and school vouchers have never gained much support in a state with a strong public education tradition. But when socially conservative Republicans have cooperated with the more moderate wing of the party, especially on taxation issues, they have had a major impact on state policies. Thus, they supported Governor Graves's tax reduction plans, and pushed him to make deeper cuts, thus reducing the growth of government, especially as revenues declined in the post-2000 period of recession. Strangely enough, such a "victory" may lead Kansas to legalize casino gambling and slot machines in order to obtain more revenue. In the end, although the Christian Right remains a major force in Kansas political and social life, its triumphs have been limited.

NOTES

1. The data on denominational identification come from two sources: Kosmin 1990, 2000 and the 1990 Glenmary Census of Churches. Results from the surveys were provided to us by John Green. He notes that some of the self-identified evangelicals were really black Protestants.

According to a statewide random digit dialing survey we conducted for this project, our results generally mirror the findings from the above surveys: 18.49 percent of our respondents identified themselves as Catholics, 10.74 percent as Methodists, and 8.15 percent as Baptists. Roughly a quarter of our respondents identified with evangelical churches. Interviewing for the survey took place during early June 2000. The poll was conducted by the Survey Research Center at the University of Kansas and had 330 respondents.

2. All of the four social conservatives have voted 100 percent of the time for the Christian Coalition position during their years in Congress (Snowbarger

served only one term). Senator Roberts and Congressman Moran tend to vote along the lines supported by the Christian Coalition in most instances. For example, in 2000, Roberts scored 92 percent on the CHC support index, while Moran scored 93 percent (National Journal 2002).

3. The statewide board is made up of ten members, five selected every two years to serve four-year terms. The state is divided into ten regions for election purposes and candidates run under party labels.

4. For a full discussion of our survey results see Cigler and Joslyn (2001).

5. According to the 2000 election exit polls conducted in Kansas, those identified as "white religious right" supported Republican George W. Bush with 71 percent of their votes, compared with Democrat Al Gore's 25 percent (CNN 2000).

6. Two previous studies of the relative influence of Christian conservatives in state Republican parties, one conducted prior to the 1994 elections and one just after the 2000 elections, have classified the Christian Right's influence in the Kansas Republican Party as "moderate" (Persinos 1994; Conger and Green 2002). Both assessments were probably accurate when the researchers' data were gathered. However, for the period between the 1994 elections and the 1998 elections we would classify the Christian Right's influence in the Kansas Republican Party as "strong," since Christian Right elements dominated party decision making.

REFERENCES

Beem, Kate. 1996. "Kansas Lobbying Group Triumphant in Elections." *Kansas City Star* (7 November).

———. 1999. "Poll: A Belief in God and Evolution." *Kansas City Star* (7 November).

———. 2000a. "Ballot in Spotlight for Kansas." *Kansas City Star* (9 January).

———. 2000b. "Evolution: New Standards May Not Pass the Lemon Test." *Kansas City Star* (12 January).

———. 2000c. "Holloway Outspending Gamble in Race for Campaign Money." *Kansas City Star* (27 July).

———. 2000d. "State Board of Education Incumbent Buys TV Ads." *Kansas City Star* (18 July).

Beinart, Peter. 1998. "Battle for the 'Burbs.'" *New Republic* (18 October).

Carpenter, Tim. 2000. "Board Official Bashes Media." *Lawrence Journal World* (10 February).

Christian Home Educators Confederation of Kansas. 2002. www. kansashomeschool.org/getstart.htm.

Cigler, Allan J. 1999. "The 1998 Kansas Third Congressional District Race." Pp. 77–92 in *Outside Money: Soft Money and Issue Advocacy in the 1998 Congressional Elections*, ed. David B. Magleby. Lanham, Md.: Rowman and Littlefield.

Cigler, Allan J., and Mark Joslyn. 2001. "What Do Kansans Think about Evolution? An Analysis of the Beliefs and Perceptions of Kansas Citizens." Paper presented at the meeting of the Western Political Science Association, Las Vegas, 5–17 March.

Cigler, Allan J., and Dwight Kiel. 1993. "Kansas: Representation in Transition." Pp. 94–116 in *Interest Groups in the Midwestern States*, ed. Clive Thomas and Ronald Hrebener. Ames: Iowa State University Press.

Cigler, Allan J., and Burdett A. Loomis. 1992. "Political Realignment in Kansas: Two-Party Competition in a One-Party State." Pp. 163–78 in *Party Realignment in the American States*, ed. Maureen Moakley. Columbus: Ohio State University Press.

———. 1997. "Kansas: The Christian Right and the New Mainstream of Republican Politics." Pp. 207–22 in *God at the Grass Roots, 1996: The Christian Right in American Elections*, ed. Mark J. Rozell and Clyde Wilcox. Lanham, Md.: Rowman and Littlefield.

———. 2000. "After the Flood: The Kansas Christian Right in Retreat." Pp. 227–42 in *Prayers in the Precincts: The Christian Right in the 1998 Elections*, ed. John C. Green, Mark Rozell, and Clyde Wilcox. Washington, D.C.: Georgetown University Press.

CNN. 2000. "Exit Polls for Kansas." www.cnn.com/ELECTION/2000/epolls/.

Conger, Kimberly H., and Green, John C. 2002. "Spreading Out and Digging In: Christian Conservatives and State Republican Parties." *Campaigns and Elections* (February):58–64.

Elazar, Daniel J. 1972. *American Federalism: A View From the States*. 2d ed. New York: Thomas Y. Crowell.

Hancock, Peter. 1999. "Legislators Take Aim at BOE." *Lawrence Journal World* (17 October).

Johnson, Victoria. 1999. "The Strategic Determinants of a Countermovement: The Emergence and Impact of Operation Rescue Blockades." Pp. 221–40 in *Waves of Protest: Social Movements Since the Sixties*, ed. Jo Freeman and Victoria Johnson. Lanham, Md.: Rowman and Littlefield.

Kosmin, Barry. 1990. *American Religious Identification Survey*. New York: Graduate Center of the City University of New York.

———. 2000. *American Religious Identification Survey*. New York: Graduate Center of the City University of New York.

Loomis, Burdett A. 1994. *Time, Politics and Policy: A Legislative Year*. Lawrence University Press of Kansas.

———. 2001. "Kansas's Third District: The 'Pros from Dover' Set Up Shop." Pp. 123–59 in *In the Battle for Congress: Consultants, Candidates and Voters*, ed. James A. Thurber. Washington, D.C.: Brookings Institution.

Mayhew, David R. 1986. *Placing Parties in American Politics*. Princeton, N.J.: Princeton University Press.

Milburn, John. 2001. "Evolution Debate Continues." *Lawrence Journal World* (17 February).

National Journal. 2002. www.nationaljournal.com/members/almanac.

Persinos, John. 1994. "Has the Christian Right Taken Over the Republican Party?" *Campaigns and Elections* (September):20–24.

Petterson, John L., and John Dvorak. 1999. "Elected Board Again a Target." *Kansas City Star* (18 August).

Ranney, David. 2000. "Senator Endorses Holloway." *Lawrence Journal World* (14 April).

Risen, James, and Judy L. Thomas. 1998. *Wrath of Angels: The American Abortion War.* New York: Basic Books.

Sigman, Robert P. 1996. "The Religious Right Is More Than Just an Army of Zealots." *Kansas City Star* (23 August).

Sullinger, Jim. 1996. "Precinct Divisions Seen as Important amid Party Divisions." *Kansas City Star* (14 June).

EIGHT

Strong Bark, Weak Bite:
The Strengths and Liabilities of the
Christian Right in Minnesota Politics

Christopher P. Gilbert and David A. M. Peterson

THE POST–WORLD WAR II POLITICAL IMAGE OF MINNESOTA HAS a decidedly liberal bent. Home to Democratic Party and liberal icons Hubert Humphrey, Eugene McCarthy, Walter Mondale, and Paul Wellstone, Minnesota appears to be one of the last bulwarks of the national Democratic Party's shrinking liberal wing. The existence of a strong Christian conservative movement in such a liberal Democratic state might seem anomalous. But for nearly three decades Christian Right groups and activists have worked assiduously, progressing from political outsider status to insider roles, to seize control of the state Republican Party and to guide its policy stances.

The rise of Minnesota's Christian Right coincides with a general decline in support for the Democratic-Farmer-Labor (DFL) Party. The most dramatic evidence of this decline came in the 1998 and 2000 election cycles—a humbling third-place finish for DFL gubernatorial candidate Hubert Humphrey III in 1998 behind surprise winner Jesse Ventura, and a closer-than-expected win for Al Gore in the 2000 presidential election. Match these results with the state Republican Party's takeover of the Minnesota house of representatives in the 1998 legislative elections, and two key questions arise. First, in what ways are the overall decline of the Minnesota DFL and the rise of the Minnesota Republican Party linked? Second, how much of the state GOP's success is attributable to the efforts of the Christian Right?

In many respects the Minnesota GOP is indebted to the state's Christian Right movement. More significantly, these same connections that have worked in electoral politics have drastic limitations when it comes to changing policy. The Christian Right has become a minor player in Minnesota state politics today, doing more harm than good to the state GOP when its actions are publicly visible, and doing less well than it should in electoral politics. The limitations of Christian Right influence, and the backlash against visible Christian Right activism, help to explain the remarkably divided nature of Minnesota politics today.

THE POLITICAL AND RELIGIOUS CULTURE OF MINNESOTA

Few states have ever been able to claim as much diversity in electoral representation as Minnesota. The parameters of this diversity are not altogether coherent—a third-party governor; a state house controlled narrowly by the Republicans, and a state senate with a clear Democratic majority;[1] two of the nation's most distinctively liberal U.S. senators; and a U.S. House delegation of five Democrats and three Republicans that votes four to four on most legislation. Toss in the considerable support for third parties since 1992,[2] and clearly Minnesota has become a more volatile electoral battleground than it was twenty years ago. What accounts for these outcomes, and how does the Christian Right figure into the picture?

Political Culture and Structural Factors

Elazar classified Minnesota as having a moralist political subculture, with "a commitment to using community power to intervene in private activities for the good or well-being of the polity" (Elazar, Gray, and Spano 1999, 206). Debates in Minnesota tend to be issue-oriented; hence party labels are less cohesive, and for years Minnesota voters were more likely than U.S. citizens generally to label themselves as independents (Elazar, Gray, and Spano 1999, 207). High voter turnout is another feature of state politics, driven in part by registration at the polls, but more so by a strong tradition of civic engagement; Minnesota deserves its high rank on Putnam's social capital index (Putnam 2000, 292–93).

Within such a political culture—focusing on issues, citizen participation, and crossover voting—it is not surprising that Minnesota ranked eighth in the nation in the number of organized interest groups (Elazar, Gray, and Spano 1999, 54). The influence of interest groups on public policy formation is considered weak by interest group scholars, however, because of citizen distrust of organized interests in the policy-making process (Elazar, Gray, and Spano 1999, 57).

Interest group activity instead can be focused on electoral politics because of the structure of Minnesota's candidate selection process. In early March of an election year, major political parties hold local precinct caucuses, which adopt policy proposals and choose delegates to county and congressional district conventions. These conventions endorse candidates for legislative and congressional races, and select delegates to each party's state convention. Later in the spring, the state conventions endorse candidates for the major statewide offices.

Minnesota's accessible caucus system is ideal for committed, focused activists such as Christian conservatives. Fewer than 1 percent of the state's citizens attend any party caucus; those who show up are thus in control, and in the last two decades Christian Right activists have shown up in force to dominate the process in Republican caucuses.

The primary election is not held until September. Candidates losing the endorsement fight historically drop out of the primary, but in recent years more primary elections have been contested. Indeed, the mobilization of conservative Christians on precinct caucus night in late February or early March virtually forces more moderate Republicans to contest the primary, since it has become far more difficult to gain endorsement. The rules of the primary election encourage challenges as well—voters may take either party's ballot in the primary, and crossover voters are often crucial to the outcome.

The party endorsement carries obvious advantages. Endorsees have a built-in organization. Lists of campaign contributors and poll data are readily available. Sample ballots assist with name recognition. Even the state fair in late summer serves to enhance the stature of the party's endorsed slate; nonendorsed candidates cannot distribute literature or have their photos displayed at their party's booth.

Religious Composition

Minnesota has always been a strongly religious state; 65 percent of state residents belong to a church, one of the highest percentages in the nation (Bradley et al. 1992). The strong outcry from across the theological spectrum to Governor Ventura's disparaging comments about organized religion in September 1999 (Sherer 1999) points to the fact that attending church and drawing connections between faith and public life are typical activities of Minnesotans. The prevailing religious traditions are Lutheran and Catholic. The 1990 Census of Churches found roughly equal numbers of each—about 1.2 million people. Together Lutherans and Catholics comprise 80 percent of all Minnesota church members (Bradley et al. 1992).

Since 1980, as in most states, evangelical Protestant denominations have grown significantly, although they still comprise a small portion of Minnesota's population. Assemblies of God membership nearly doubled from 1980 to 1990, although this group is still only 1 percent of the state's population (Quinn et al. 1982; Bradley et al. 1992). Several evangelical-oriented megachurches have formed in the Twin Cities area, and observers generally agree that Minnesota's evangelical churches are making inroads, especially among younger churchgoers (Allen 2002).

The strong social conservatism of the Lutheran Church-Missouri Synod and other smaller Lutheran bodies, added to the growth of evangelical churches, creates a base of about 10 percent to 15 percent of the state's adult population attending churches that are usually associated with Christian Right political activism. This segment is enhanced by a strong Catholic presence but also overshadowed by the prevailing social liberalism embodied by the Evangelical Lutheran Church in America (ELCA), other mainline Protestants, and sizable numbers of Catholics. This constellation of factors helps explain why the most visible Minnesota Christian Right organizations are centered on opposition to legal abortion—the issue where the interests of evangelicals and conservative Catholics coincide. However, this same set of factors also explains the limits of Christian Right political influence, for Minnesota also possesses organized interests that bring a very different set of religious tenets to policy debates. In other words, in Minnesota's moralistic political culture, the Christian Right does not have the only "moral" voice.

RELIGIOUS AND LIBERAL VOICES IN OPPOSITION
TO THE CHRISTIAN RIGHT

Founded in 1971 as the first interfaith public interest lobby group in the United States., the Joint Religious Legislative Coalition (JRLC) advocates for social justice issues at the state and local levels. Sponsors of the JRLC include eleven Protestant denominations through the Minnesota Council of Churches,[3] the Minnesota Catholic Conference, and the Jewish Community Relations Council of Minnesota and the Dakotas.

Affiliated and observer groups include the African Methodist Episcopal Church, the Reformed Church in America, the Minneapolis Friends (Quakers) Meeting, the American Muslim Council (Minnesota chapter), and the Minnesota Eastern Orthodox Clergy Association. The JRLC website outlines the group's mission:

> Guided by basic Jewish and Christian moral vision, JRLC strives to further the cause of social justice in Minnesota by proposing and promoting responsible legislation; assisting congregations in the task of discerning and teaching God's vision of justice; and calling communities of faith to prophetic, unified action (Joint Religious Legislative Coalition 2002).

Activities include a network of 7,000 citizens to contact state lawmakers; a well-publicized conference each February to highlight issues of concern; and reports and position papers on a wide range of social justice issues—a partial list includes Native American issues, corporate responsibility, capital punishment, disability issues, gun control, human rights and sexual orientation, minimum wage laws, rural life, term limits, and tobacco (www.jrlc.org).

With such a visible, religiously based liberal group, it is difficult for Minnesota Christian Right groups to claim the sole moral voice in political debate. The JRLC also represents a much broader cross-section of the state's population in terms of religious affiliation, ethnicity, and race. Individual denominations such as the ELCA also have access to lawmakers as a result of their size and distribution throughout the state. In contrast to other states, where evangelical denominations have gained numerical superiority over fading mainline churches, mainline Protestantism is alive and well in Minnesota, and its religiously based social activism creates a sharp contrast with evangelical-inspired political messages.

The JRLC, Jewish groups, and mainline Protestant churches are the primary religiously affiliated actors who can be said to oppose the Christian Right in Minnesota, but other players contribute perspectives that generally run counter to Christian Right interests. Environmental groups such as the League of Conservation Voters (LCV) and the Sierra Club are well represented, while other liberal advocacy groups such as the Children's Defense Fund and the Minnesota Alliance for Progressive Action stand opposed to Christian Right initiatives on school vouchers and gay rights, among other issues (Elazar, Gray, and Spano

1999, 59). Minnesota companies and the state government have been national leaders in extending job-related benefits to employees' same-sex domestic partners (Associated Press 2002). Minnesota's congressional delegation is far more likely to receive high scores from liberal groups than from Christian Right organizations—for example, Democratic members typically score zero on the Christian Coalition's ratings and close to 100 from the LCV; Republicans receive the opposite ratings (Barone, Cohen, and Ujifusa 2001, 820–52).

Religious Voices in GOP Party Politics

Division in the Party

Minnesota's Republican Party is best understood as two distinct entities, whose differences were for many years captured in the party's name. The old label Independent Republican, or IR (adopted during the Watergate years and dropped in 1995), stood for two competing political ideologies—a primarily secular constituency advocating moderate to progressive social policies combined with fiscal restraint (the "I" side), and the increasingly Christian Right-dominated "R" wing that stressed a social agenda centered on opposition to abortion and the restoration of traditional values and family structures.

The 1980s were marked by a successful marriage of convenience between the party's two wings. This alliance worked most effectively to support former GOP Representative Vin Weber. Articulate and politically savvy (and notably not a Christian conservative), Weber understood the importance of combining the party's two wings in order to advance any agenda:

> In Minnesota, we have had this phenomenon for over 10 years. . . . By and large I have found that the vast majority of those folks become good, solid, responsible Republican activists and they don't give up their beliefs but they learn in the course of one election cycle the role of compromise, a proper understanding of the separation of church and state and they become very responsible activists in the process. (Haas 1992)

Weber's Christian Right support during the 1980s was centered in right-to-life groups, who won adoption of a strong prolife statement in the IR party platform but made little headway in the state legislature

(Elazar, Gray, and Spano 1999, 75). The Moral Majority and other national groups were never major players in Minnesota Republican circles. Despite little policy impact at the state or national level in the 1980s, the alliances forged by Weber laid the foundation for the public emergence of the Christian Right in the 1990s (Schmickle 1996).

Weber showed that Christian conservatives can work effectively within the state GOP. But the eight-year governorship of Republican Arne Carlson (1991–99)—who stood with the "I" wing of the state GOP—demonstrates that Christian conservatives can also be left behind if they are unwilling to compromise. Carlson won the 1990 gubernatorial election after a peculiar series of events brought down the original Republican nominee, who was a Christian conservative (Barone and Ujifusa 1993, 681; Hoium and Oistad 1991). Carlson overcame a contentious first two years on the job and easily won reelection in 1994 despite losing his own party's endorsement to another Christian Right leader.

Carlson embodies the problem that the Christian Right faces within the GOP and in the state as a whole. Carlson's Republican ties are based on fiscal conservatism; on social issues his stances fit quite well with the JRLC—he has been consistently prochoice and has advocated ending discrimination based on sexual orientation. In the 1990s, this combination of positions made Carlson a crossover voter's dream—he had something to offer Republicans, Democrats, and independents. Finally, Carlson's faith (Lutheran) was always presented in subtle terms to voters.

Christian Right Groups and State Politics

The dominant issue for Minnesota's Christian Right is abortion. The centrality of opposition to abortion helps explain why the Christian Coalition has never developed a strong presence in Minnesota (in fact no state chapter was even constituted until 1994). When one of the authors visited the state headquarters of the Christian Coalition in 1995, he found it staffed by one person with an active membership of perhaps twenty citizens. Christian Coalition activity in Minnesota amounted to faxes to news organizations and holding occasional candidate training seminars run by the national office. The Minnesota Christian Coalition tried distributing voter guides for school board races in 1995, but this had little impact (Gilbert et al. 1996).

The Christian Coalition barely functions in Minnesota because the main political interests of Christian conservatives are already well represented by the state Republican party and two other interest groups:

Minnesota Citizens Concerned for Life (MCCL) and the Minnesota Family Council (MFC).

MCCL was founded in 1968, when Minnesota was one of several states considering more lenient abortion laws. After the 1973 *Roe v. Wade* decision permitting legal abortion in the United States, MCCL became the state affiliate of the National Right to Life Committee. It has since developed into a grassroots organization with 225 local chapters and a claimed membership of 67,000 (Minnesota Citizens Concerned for Life 2002). Besides abortion, MCCL is engaged in the debate on euthanasia and supports free speech actions to protect the rights of prolife demonstrators.

For most of the 1980s and 1990s, MCCL Executive Director Jackie Schwietz has been considered the state's single most influential lobbyist (Elazar, Gray, and Spano 1999, 59). Under her leadership and the mobilization of local chapters, MCCL has put some aspect of legal abortion on the legislative agenda (and beyond) nearly every year for almost thirty years. Just about every facet of abortion politics has been covered—parental notification laws, waiting periods, public funding, partial-birth abortions, access to clinics, birth control and sex education in schools, and legal rights of prolife protestors. In 1996 MCCL urged defeat of two state supreme court justices who were prochoice, and election of three lower court judges who were prolife; while only one of MCCL's candidates won election, the groups action's demonstrate its willingness to politicize all aspects of Minnesota politics (Elazar, Gray, and Spano 1999, 143).

The MCCL's most recent initiative, in 2002, centers on a proposed amendment to the state constitution. In anticipation of a shift in the U.S. Supreme Court due to eventual Bush appointees, the amendment in question would require that the Supreme Court's interpretation of abortion law be applied to state abortion cases (Whereatt 2002). The Minnesota Supreme Court has ruled that abortion is permitted under the state constitution; the ruling is based on privacy rights language and thus is similar to the reasoning of *Roe v. Wade*. This amendment failed in the legislature but its consideration opens yet another avenue MCCL will pursue.

While Minnesota Democrats are strongly prochoice,[4] for the last ten years the state legislature (including the senate with a current DFL majority of forty-one) has become almost exactly divided over abortion. MCCL proposals thus stand a chance of passing both houses, although the slim majorities that occasionally pass restrictive abortion measures cannot override gubernatorial vetoes (Governor Ventura is staunchly prochoice, as was Carlson).

The MCCL's ally in abortion disputes is the Minnesota Family Council, which bills itself as "the largest nonprofit, nonpartisan, profamily organization in the state" (Minnesota Family Council and Minnesota Family Institute 2002). Like its national parent group, the Family Research Council, MFC works principally in five areas: combating the secular and liberal media; presenting profamily news and information; lobbying the legislature on public policy issues; building grassroots support for profamily legislation; and supporting lawsuits on profamily causes through the Northstar Legal Center (Minnesota Family Council and Minnesota Family Institute 2002). Led by director Tom Prichard, a frequent commentator in the Twin Cities media, the MFC in recent years has focused on opposing gay marriage and the extension of benefits to same-sex partners of state employees. To the extent possible it supports Republican candidates and officeholders, and lobbies at the state capitol through grassroots efforts.

WIN SOME, LOSE MOST: CHRISTIAN RIGHT ELECTORAL ACTIVISM

Most Christian Right activism in Minnesota has centered on electoral politics, both within the Republican Party and in statewide general elections. In the 1980s, the first wave of Christian Right activists moderated their positions in order to work more effectively with specific officeholders and to seek incremental change in policies. Since 1990, however, Christian Right activists have chosen to push their own candidates for office, often creating conflict within the state GOP. Several recent case studies serve to illustrate how the Christian Right has fared in Minnesota electoral politics: the 1994 Republican gubernatorial primary, the 1994 U.S. Senate race, the 1996 Republican National Convention; and the 1998 state legislative elections.

The Race for Governor, 1994

Arne Carlson won the 1990 gubernatorial election following the late withdrawal of the GOP primary winner, who was backed by Christian Right party activists (Hoium and Oistad 1991). Carlson's solid fiscal record led to a 60 percent approval rating by late 1993 (Smith 1993). In just about any other party in any other state, this track record would have assured Carlson the party endorsement and made him a strong bet for reelection.

But on precinct caucus night in March 1994, supporters of former state legislator Allen Quist turned out in large numbers and thus controlled the selection of delegates to county conventions and the state convention. A member of a small Norwegian Lutheran synod and noted for his fervent faith and conservative social agenda, Quist had declared his candidacy against Carlson in July 1993, declaring his fellow party member to be "left of center" on social issues (Whereatt 1993). Once Quist declared his candidacy, nine months of mobilizing efforts among Christian Right allies leading to precinct caucus night were deemed so successful that Carlson made no full attempt to counter, preferring to conserve his resources for the state convention and September primary election (Gilbert and Peterson 1995, 173–74). At the state convention in June delegates gave Quist the party endorsement for governor, generating national attention as a result of the party's rejection of Carlson (Whereatt 1994; Berke 1994).

The insular caucus system was exploited successfully by Quist and his Christian Right allies, but Quist's June endorsement was his campaign's last success. The exclusion of moderate Republicans from party endorsements alienated many Republicans. A Quist remark about men's being "genetically predisposed" to head families proved hard to play down, especially among women voters. The resulting flap made it difficult for Quist to convince non–Christian Right supporters that he was more than a fringe candidate (Smith 1994a, 1994b).

On primary election day in September 1994, substantial numbers of Republicans and crossover voters gave Governor Carlson an easy victory over Quist, with 64 percent of the vote. Quist received over 160,000 votes, normally a winning total in a Minnesota primary. But Carlson trounced Quist in the Twin Cities suburbs, generally considered a swing region in state elections, and Carlson managed to hold his own in counties where Quist was thought to have an edge. Quist generated substantial support from self-described born-again Christians, according to exit polls, but moderates and independents overwhelmingly supported Carlson (Smith 1994a; von Sternberg 1994b). An estimated 100,000 voters may have crossed over to vote in the Republican primary; most did so exclusively to oppose Quist (von Sternberg 1994b).

Carlson went on to victory by a record two-to-one margin in the general election—Quist earned 24,000 write-in votes (von Sternberg

1994a). Quist briefly attempted another bid for governor in 1998, but the negative reactions left over from 1994 sank his chances well before precinct caucus night. The open primary system clearly harmed Quist's chances of winning in 1994, and Quist's own statements also dragged his campaign down. An analysis of media coverage from the 1994 campaign also shows that the framing of Quist in religious terms contributed to his marginalization among voters who were not associated with the Christian Right movement (Gilbert and Peterson 1995, 176–80). Ironically, just as the Christian Right had become a strong influence within the state Republican Party (Persinos 1994), Quist and four other Christian Right-backed, endorsed party candidates failed to win the primary or general election.

The 1994 U.S. Senate Race

The media-driven connection of Quist with the Christian Right, which created a negative association among Minnesota voters, stands in sharp contrast to media portrayals of another Republican candidate that same election year. United States Representative Rod Grams, a former Twin Cities television news anchor serving his first term in Washington, earned the Republican U.S. Senate endorsement in June 1994 with strong backing from the "Quistian" wing of the party. Grams had received a 100 percent rating from the national Christian Coalition based on his congressional voting record (Schmickle and McGrath 1994). Grams's impeccable Christian Right credentials created a sharp contrast to his principal opponent, Lieutenant Governor Joanell Dyrstad. Like her 1990 running mate Arne Carlson, Dyrstad drew support from the "I" wing of the Republican Party, favoring abortion rights and prudent fiscal policies. Also like Carlson, Dyrstad recognized that Christian conservative dominance in the convention meant that she would have to focus resources on the September primary, effectively conceding the endorsement to Grams (Baden 1994b). Receiving a larger share of the vote from born-again primary voters than Quist did (von Sternberg 1994b), Grams handily defeated Dyrstad by a two-to-one margin. Grams went on to win the general election narrowly and served one term in the U.S. Senate.

Why did Grams attract moderate and crossover voters while Quist failed to do so? Once again, media coverage helps to explain the outcome. No other candidate was as open or aggressive as Quist in stressing social issues in religious terms (Smith 1994b). Media coverage thus rarely applied religious terminology to Grams, whereas the religious (Christian Right) framing was always present in stories about Quist. In effect, Minnesota voters received few cues that would have led them to reject Grams in the way that they rejected Quist: Grams took care not to highlight his Christian Right support; press coverage rarely focused on Christian Right support for Grams; and Grams's opponents consistently failed to press this point (Gilbert and Peterson 1995, 176–81; McGrath and Baden 1994).

We conclude from this evidence that *support* for the agenda of Christian conservatives works to a candidate's advantage in Minnesota, whereas *identification* of a candidate with the Christian Right is a clear disadvantage. The 1994 general election exit poll data show that Grams won substantial majorities among voters opposing abortion (77 percent support among those opposed to all abortions), gun owners (59 percent), and voters who wanted new people in government (58 percent) (von Sternberg 1994a). An election eve poll also showed that voters who considered family values and morals the most important issue would favor Grams over his Democratic opponent by 59 percent to 23 percent (McGrath 1994). This category represented 27 percent of the total electorate, further evidence of the strength of the Christian Right in Minnesota elections.

A Right Turn to San Diego: 1996 GOP Convention Delegates

The composition of the Minnesota delegation to the 1996 Republican National Convention in San Diego reveals that despite notable 1994 electoral setbacks, the Minnesota Christian Right understood how to use its influence inside the party for other purposes. Minnesota delegates to the GOP national convention are selected in the same state convention that endorses statewide candidates. Thus the composition of this delegation indicates exactly where the power in the party rested in 1996. It turns out that Christian conservatives dominated the Minnesota Republican convention delegation like few others in the country.

Based on surveys of convention delegates, table 8.1 shows the thirty-three–member Minnesota delegation sitting further to the right than national convention delegates. Abortion views were the key indicator for delegate selection. Minnesota sent no prochoice delegates to San Diego, and its delegates were quite active in prolife organizations. The Minnesota delegates were also more likely to emphasize social issues over fiscal ones and more likely to support an increased role for the Christian Right in the GOP. Minnesota delegates were also less

Table 8.1   Opinions of Minnesota versus National Republican Convention Delegates on Social Issues

Issue Positions	Minnesota Delegates (%)	National Delegates (%)
Abortion		
Should be up to a woman and her doctor	0	24
Should be legal only in cases of rape, incest, or when mother's life is at risk	64	47
Should be illegal in all circumstances	27	12
Support antiabortion group	64	47
Issue importance		
Social issues more important	39	21
Fiscal issues more important	21	56

Source: Smith 1996b.

wealthy than GOP convention delegates generally (Smith 1996b), and far less likely to hold elective office (just 6 percent did so, versus 38 percent of all delegates). The Minnesota delegation in San Diego reflected Christian Right control of the caucus-convention delegate selection process. This control extended to presidential politics, as Minnesota's delegation was lukewarm toward Bob Dole, actively supporting first Phil Gramm and then Pat Buchanan (Smith 1996a, 1996b).

Overall, the San Diego delegation may be the best indicator of the dominance of Christian conservatives in Minnesota. National convention delegate positions are chosen from within the ranks of party activists and elected officials. Leaders of the three key state Christian Right groups—MCCL, MFC, and the Minnesota Christian Coalition—were all members of the Minnesota delegation (Smith 1996b). Several other delegates represented conservative groups or were often spokespersons in the Twin Cities and statewide media. The strong social conservative slant of this delegation indicates that Christian conservatives remain well positioned in the state GOP, regardless of the outcome of endorsement, election, or legislative battles.

Retaking the State House, 1998

In 1998 the Minnesota Republican Party reclaimed majority status in the Minnesota House of Representatives for the first time since 1987.

The Democrats held a seventy-to-sixty-four advantage heading into November 1998, and seemed to have a superior campaign organization to contest close races (Spano, Leary, and Janecek 1998). But in the general election, the Republicans won seventy-one seats, taking firm control of the House.

Shortly after this victory, the Minnesota Family Council led several Christian Right organizations in claiming responsibility for the Republican takeover of the state house. Although the party lost the governor's race to Ventura and made no inroads in the state's congressional delegation (all eight incumbents won reelection), MFC head Tom Prichard argued that the state GOP was indebted to Christian conservatives; party executive director Tony Sutton credited the mobilization efforts of conservative groups as essential to the party's triumph (Hallonquist 1998).

What empirical evidence supports these claims? In a close election, clearly any single group's support can affect the outcome, and we have seen that Christian conservatives are an important part of the state GOP voting bloc. But other factors also played a significant role in explaining the 1998 results. First, Minnesota has been moving from a Democratic-majority state to rough parity between the major parties since the early 1990s. Minnesota Republicans began winning a majority of the state house *vote* in 1994, but only in 1998 did these votes translate into enough districts to swing the state house majority to the GOP. The Christian Right definitely deserves credit for much of this swing.

A second explanation for the 1998 Republican state house takeover is that it was a byproduct of the huge turnout boost caused by the Ventura candidacy. Minnesota's 1998 voter turnout was the highest in the nation, and 12 percent of these voters registered on election day to support Jesse Ventura (Voter News Service 1998). While the Voter News Service (VNS) exit polls did not ask gubernatorial voters how they voted in state house races, our ecological inference analysis concluded that 72 percent of Ventura voters chose Republicans for the state house—enough to make the difference in eight districts and thus to give the state house to the GOP (Gilbert and Peterson 2000, 218–21; Gilbert and Peterson 2001, 177–78).

Ventura's issue stances clearly do not agree with the Christian Right. And the public backlash against obvious Christian Right electoral influence—so critical to Allen Quist's 1994 primary defeat—was if anything even stronger by 1998. On the basis of the empirical evidence, we conclude that support from Christian Right organizations and voters was critical to bringing the Minnesota Republican Party up to close parity with the Democrats by the middle of the 1990s, but the Ventura voters' support was required to push the Republicans over the top in 1998.

LESSONS FROM 2000

In the 2000 general elections the state GOP maintained its control of the state house, losing two seats but keeping an edge of sixty-nine to sixty-five (boosted by longtime incumbent officeholders, Democrats maintain clear control of the state senate). The most watched races in 2000, however, revealed again the somewhat tenuous position of the Christian Right in Minnesota politics. The worst outcome occurred when the main standard bearer of the Christian Right in the state, Senator Rod Grams, was defeated for reelection by Democrat Mark Dayton. More promisingly, the state GOP nearly pulled off a major upset in the presidential race, as Al Gore (47.9 percent) squeaked past George Bush (45.5 percent) (Minnesota Secretary of State Office 2000).

The 2000 election results demonstrate the reach and the limitations of state Republicans generally, and the Christian Right specifically. A reanalysis of state Republican parties again classified Minnesota in 2000 as having strong Christian Right influence (Conger and Green 2000). Rod Grams had maintained his high Christian Coalition ratings throughout his U.S. Senate term, but in 2000 his opponent was able to portray Grams as too conservative for Minnesota voters. Coupled with a lengthy media blitz for Democrat Mark Dayton, Grams could not keep up even with solid Christian Right support, and his attempts to sound more moderate in debates and advertising failed.

George W. Bush was not the first choice of Minnesota Republicans in early 2000; reflecting the Christian Right's control of the party, Alan Keyes was the preferred option. In a nutshell this fact is telling: Keyes never had a chance of winning, while Bush almost did win the state in November 2000, despite minimal campaigning. The general election results were close primarily because Vice President Gore lost substantial ground to Ralph Nader in traditionally strong Democratic regions (Barone, Cohen, and Ujifusa 2001, 829–30). Still, as evidenced by 2000 and other recent elections, Republicans and Democrats in Minnesota are now roughly even, with a relatively strong third-party presence. Christian Right supporters comprise a key portion of the Republican electoral coalition, which needs all its components to maintain parity with the Democrats statewide.

ASSESSING THE CHRISTIAN RIGHT IN MINNESOTA POLITICS, TODAY AND TOMORROW

It seems ironic that while the Christian Right was a key player in elevating the GOP's electoral fortunes through the 1980s, leading to the characterization of Christian Right influence in the state party as strong in 1994 and 2000, the present state GOP electorate is probably less Christian Right-influenced today than ten years ago. The 1994 Quist candidacy has had a lasting, negative impact on the ability of Christian Right activists to run for office statewide, and with the open primary system and weakening of the endorsement process it is likely that Christian Right candidates will remain hampered in seeking statewide office for years to come. The one consolation— and it is a major one—is that Christian Right electoral support is now given to a Republican Party that stands equal to the Democrats, rather than running second.

In state government the Christian Right's influence also remains limited. The state legislature is closely divided on abortion restrictions; this is the one area where any Christian conservative group stands a chance to enact favorable public policy. But the state's electorate overall is more prochoice than prolife, and the enactment of any significant restrictions on abortion would most likely benefit Democrats in ensuing elections. On other issue fronts the prevailing state sentiment continues to run against Christian Right positions—for example, a recently concluded contract with the largest state employees union included benefits for same-sex partners (Associated Press 2002). Sexual orientation issues in Minnesota are invariably framed by media discourse as human rights issues, and Christian Right groups have been unable to introduce terms of debate more favorable to their views.

Party politics remains the area where Christian Right activists wield significant power. The Republican state house delegation is more conservative than ten years ago, because Christian Right activists have controlled the local endorsement process (which is much more likely to lead to primary election victory) and the allocation of state party funds to close general election races, tipping the balance in districts where prolife Republicans run against prochoice Democrats (Baden 1994a). As long as Christian Right supporters are more apt to attend precinct caucuses and resulting conventions, the state Republican Party apparatus will remain in Christian Right hands and can be used to further this group's policy and electoral goals.

The Christian Right in Minnesota does not offer the sole Christian point of view on political and social issues, and it must operate in a religious environment that is more hostile to its religious as well as its political viewpoints. In addition, the tendency of groups like MCCL to work alone rather than in concert with obvious allies has prevented a true Christian Right movement from emerging. It seems more appropriate to say that Minnesota has several Christian Rights, rather than one movement, and this conception also makes more clear the idiosyncratic nature of Christian Right strengths and weaknesses in state politics. As long as the Minnesota Republican electorate remains divided on social issues, the ability of the Christian Right forces in Minnesota to achieve long-standing goals will remain circumscribed. Nonetheless, no Minnesota Republican statewide office seeker can afford not to have Christian Right votes on his or her side in an election year, and this fact ensures the importance of the Christian Right well into the twenty-first century.

NOTES

1. "Democrat" will be used in this chapter to denote the DFL Party.

2. Besides the 1998 election of Jesse Ventura, third parties and candidates have had several impressive outings. In 1992 Ross Perot won 24 percent of the Minnesota vote; Ralph Nader received 5 percent of the statewide vote for president in 2000 (and over 10 percent in some regions); and two Green Party candidates were elected to the Minneapolis City Council in November 2001. The Independence and Green parties are classified as "major" under Minnesota law on the basis of these results. For decades Minnesota voters have been more willing than most to consider alternatives to the major parties (Gilbert et al. 1999, 46, 103–6, 113–16).

3. These include the regional organizations of the following denominations: American Baptist Churches USA, Disciples of Christ, Church of the Brethren, Episcopal Church, ELCA, National Association of Congregational Christian Churches, Moravian Church, National Baptist Convention, Presbyterian Church (U.S.A.), United Church of Christ, and the United Methodist Church (www.jrlc.org).

4. For example, at the 1996 state DFL convention, only 8 percent of delegates were prolife (Elazar, Gray, and Spano 1999, 76). The most visible prolife Democrats in the last two decades have been former U.S. Representative Tim Penny (whose prolife stance helped greatly in his conservative district), former St. Paul Mayor Norm Coleman (who left the party in 1997), and current St. Paul Mayor Randy Kelly (a former state senator whose replacement in that body is prochoice).

184 THE CHRISTIAN RIGHT IN AMERICAN POLITICS

REFERENCES

Allen, Martha Sawyer. 2002. "Yes, You Can Be Questioning and Faithful in College." *Minneapolis Star Tribune* (26 January).
Associated Press. 2002. "State, Unions Act to Preserve Same-Sex Benefits." *Minneapolis Star Tribune* (21 May).
Baden, Patricia Lopez. 1994a. "Religious Right Sees Its Influence in IR House Wins." *Minneapolis Star Tribune* (23 November).
———. 1994b. "U.S. Senate Candidates Solid But Not Charismatic." *Minneapolis Star Tribune* (4 September).
Barone, Michael, Richard E. Cohen, and Grant Ujifusa. 2001. *The Almanac of American Politics 2002*. Washington, D.C.: National Journal.
Barone, Michael, and Grant Ujifusa. 1993. *The Almanac of American Politics 1994*. Washington, D.C.: National Journal.
Berke, Richard. 1994. "Advances Posted by Religious Right in Several States." *New York Times* (3 June).
Bradley, Martin, Norman M. Green, Jr., Dale E. Jones, Mac Lynn, and Lou McNeil, eds. 1992. *Churches and Church Membership in the United States*. Atlanta: Glenmary Research Center.
Conger, Kimberly H., and John C. Green. 2000. "Spreading Out and Digging In: Christian Conservatives and State Republican Parties." *Campaigns & Elections* (February):58ff.
Elazar, Daniel J., Virginia Gray, and Wyman Spano. 1999. *Minnesota Politics and Government*. Lincoln: University of Nebraska Press.
Gilbert, Christopher P., Jeffrey Gustafson, Joel A. Johnson, and Paul Mueller. 1996. "Strategy, Issues, and Voter Impact: Christian Right School Board Candidacies in Urban and Suburban Contexts." Paper presented at Midwest Political Science Association Annual Meeting, Chicago, 18 April.
Gilbert, Christopher P., and David A. M. Peterson. 1995. "Minnesota: Christians and Quistians in the GOP." Pp. 169–89 in *God at the Grassroots: The Christian Right in the 1994 Elections*, ed. Mark J. Rozell and Clyde Wilcox. Lanham, Md.: Rowman & Littlefield.
———. 2000. "Minnesota 1998: Christian Conservatives and the Body Politic." Pp. 207–25 in *Prayers in the Precincts: The Christian Right in the 1998 Elections*, ed. John C. Green, Mark J. Rozell, and Clyde Wilcox. Washington, D.C.: Georgetown University Press.
———. 2001. "From Ross the Boss to Jesse the Body: Did the Perot Phenomenon Spawn the Ventura Victory?" Pp. 163–82 in *Ross for Boss: The Perot Phenomenon and Beyond*, ed. Ted Jelen. Albany: State University of New York Press.
Gilbert, Christopher P., David A. M. Peterson, Timothy R. Johnson, and Paul A. Djupe. 1999. *Religious Institutions and Minor Parties in the United States*. Westport, Conn.: Praeger.
Haas, Cliff. 1992. "Life of the Party: Issues and Ideas Man Vin Weber Sets His Sights on Reviving GOP." *Minneapolis Star Tribune* (22 November).

Hallonquist, Sarah. 1998. "In Year of Mavericks, DFLer Mike Hatch Finally Wins." *Minneapolis Star Tribune* (5 November).

Hoium, David, and Oistad, Leo. 1991. *There Is No November.* Inver Grove Heights, Minn.: Jeric Publications.

Joint Religious Legislative Coalition. 2002. www.jrlc.org.

McGrath, Dennis. 1994. "Senate Race Tight; Carlson Keeps Big Lead." *Minneapolis Star Tribune* (6 November).

McGrath, Dennis, and Patricia Lopez Baden. 1994. "Wynia Made Missteps and Missed Opportunities." *Minneapolis Star Tribune* (10 November).

Minnesota Citizens Concerned for Life. 2002. www.mccl.org.

Minnesota Family Council and Minnesota Family Institute. 2002. www.mfc.org.

Minnesota Secretary of State Office. 2000. General Election Returns—President, State Representatives. www.elections.sos.state.mn.us/ENR2000_General/elecmenu.htm.

Persinos, John. 1994. "Has the Christian Right Taken Over the Republican Party?" *Campaigns & Elections* (September):20–24.

Putnam, Robert. 2000. *Bowling Alone: The Collapse and Revival of American Community.* New York: Simon & Schuster.

Quinn, Bernard, Herman Anderson, Martin Bradley, Paul Goetting, and Peggy Shriver, eds. 1982. *Churches and Church Membership in the United States, 1980.* Washington, D.C.: Glenmary Research Center.

Schmickle, Sharon. 1996. "It's a Different GOP for McKasy and Boschwitz." *Minneapolis Star Tribune* (3 June).

Schmickle, Sharon, and Dennis McGrath. 1994. "Rod Grams [candidate profile]." *Minneapolis Star Tribune* (25 August).

Sherer, Michael. 1999. "Church Leaders, Members Rankled by Ventura's Remarks." *Metro Lutheran* (November).

Smith, Dane. 1993. "Carlson Must Speak Softly and Carry the IR Right." *Minneapolis Star Tribune* (13 September).

———. 1994a. "Carlson Victorious; Marty Is Surprise Winner: IR—Win Quells Revolt of Party's Right Wing." *Minneapolis Star Tribune* (14 September).

———. 1994b. "Primary Lessons: Caucuses Will Stay and the Right Is Healthy." *Minneapolis Star Tribune* (18 September).

———. 1996a. "Buchanan Wins Support from Quist and Others Who Had Backed Gramm." *Minneapolis Star Tribune* (17 February).

———. 1996b. "State Delegates Will Be on the Right at GOP Convention." *Minneapolis Star Tribune* (4 August).

Spano, Wyman, D. J. Leary, and Sarah Janecek. 1998. "The Battle for Control of the Legislature." *Politics in Minnesota* 17(6):3–6.

von Sternberg, Bob. 1994a. "Different Election, Same Outlook: Exit Polls Show Minnesota Voters Haven't Changed Much." *Minneapolis Star Tribune* (9 November).

———. 1994b. "Undecided Voters Held Sway in Three-Way DFL Battle." *Minneapolis Star Tribune* (14 September).

Voter News Service. 1998. *1998 Exit Poll Dataset*. Storrs, Conn.: Roper Center for Public Opinion Research, University of Connecticut.

Whereatt, Robert. 1993. "Ex-legislator Takes Aim at Governor's Job." *Minneapolis Star Tribune* (29 July).

———. 1994. "IR Delegates Give Quist a Historic Win." *Minneapolis Star Tribune* (18 June).

———. 2002. "Two Abortion Amendments to Be Considered." *Minneapolis Star Tribune* (27 January).

NINE

The Christian Right and the Cultural Divide in Colorado

Robert Zwier

IN FRONT OF CITY HALL IN THE WESTERN COLORADO TOWN OF Grand Junction stands a small monument containing the Ten Commandments. The display has been on this property for more than four decades, but a recent renovation of the municipal building provoked a controversy. Under the threat of a lawsuit from the ACLU and seeking a middle ground, the City Council voted early in 2001 to retain the monument on municipal property but to include a disclaimer that the display did not constitute the establishment of a religion and to include other historical documents—such as the Magna Carta and the Declaration of Independence—in the display. The mayor, who opposed the compromise plan and favored removing the display, was running for reelection in April. The Christian Coalition of Colorado (CCCO) mobilized through its local county chapter and through a letter-writing campaign that generated 7,000 letters from its Denver headquarters. The mayor lost his reelection bid and the CCCO claimed victory. Ironically, the lawsuit was dropped because the complainants feared that an adverse judicial ruling would be an incentive for even more communities to allow similar displays.

Nearly a decade earlier, the Christian Right brought Colorado to national attention by promoting a ballot initiative called Amendment 2—a state constitutional amendment that would prohibit gay rights laws, including those already approved in the liberal enclaves of Aspen, Boulder, and Denver. The center of the Amendment 2 movement was in Colorado Springs (El Paso County), which is home to several evangelical Christian organizations, most notably Focus on the Family, led by Dr. James Dobson. The amendment was approved by 53.4 percent of the voters—ironically, the same year in which the state cast its presidential votes in favor of Bill Clinton. Although eventually ruled unconstitutional by the U.S. Supreme Court, Amendment 2 cast an image of Colorado, and particularly Colorado Springs, that lives on to this day. This battle activated cultural conservatives, gave them a taste of victory, and suggested the viability of citizen initiatives as a political strategy.

Thus, the "culture war" is alive and well in Colorado. Like the more than fifty snow-capped "fourteeners" (mountain peaks above 14,000 feet) rising to dominate the arid eastern plains, the Christian Right has risen in an effort to dominate the diverse social and political landscape of the Centennial State. The vast inmigration of the last twenty years has brought not only a stream of nonreligious, social liberals to mix with the strong antigovernment individualism that is part of the political heritage of Colorado but also a host of evangelical Christians and their organizations, including Focus on the Family. From the so-called granola belt of the mountain ski resorts to Colorado's version of the "Bible belt" centered in Colorado Springs, the battle over moral values has been engaged. Despite a mixed record of successes and disappointments, the Christian Right has become influential in Colorado politics.[1]

THE SOCIAL LANDSCAPE OF COLORADO

The political sociology of Colorado is marked by significant population growth. The 2000 census shows a population of more than 4.3 million, up more than 30.6 percent in ten years. About 60 percent of the growth is due to inmigration, including both West Coast social liberals and evangelical Christians. Of particular note has been the influx of organizations such as Focus on the Family, the International Bible Society, the Association of Christian Schools International, and the Navigators, all headquartered in Colorado Springs. Indeed, some have labeled the city "the Vatican of the Religious Right," much to the dismay of city officials responsible for promoting business development and tourism.

Nearly 80 percent of Colorado's population lives along the Front Range, a line of rapidly growing urban areas from Fort Collins and Greeley in the north, through Denver, and south to Colorado Springs. The Denver metropolitan area itself includes about one-half of all Colorado residents. The Front Range is home to a high-tech boom, with several large telecommunications companies leading the way. Business development and entrepreneurship are critical ingredients in Colorado growth.

Predominantly white (83 percent of Colorado residents, compared with a national average of 75 percent), Colorado has relatively small African American and Asian American populations. However, it has a large number of Hispanics (17 percent of the state's population), with many of these people living in southern Colorado and in Denver. The Hispanic population grew 73 percent in the 1990s. Catholic Hispanics, while not identifying themselves with the Christian Right, have been key allies in political contests on prolife and profamily issues.

In terms of religion, Colorado mirrors other states in its blending of traditional Protestant and Catholic churches, including several rapidly growing megachurches within the conservative, evangelical subculture. By far, the denomination with the largest number of adherents is the Roman Catholic Church, including 23 percent of the population in 2000. White evangelical Protestants were a little less numerous at about 20 percent, followed closely by mainline Protestants at 19 percent. In addition to these traditional loyalties, however, newcomers have brought both New Age philosophies and a solid core of those for whom religion is not particularly important. In fact, this diverse secular population is the largest "religious preference" at 27 percent.

Elazar has described Colorado's political culture as "moralist" with a secondary strain of "individualism" (1994, 242). The recent increase in the number of evangelical organizations making their home in Colorado enhances even more the emphasis on traditional morality fostered through public policies on abortion, gay rights, and educational choice. This mixed political culture provides fertile ground for the Christian Right. The movement has also taken advantage of the openness of the Colorado political system, including the ease with which initiatives can be placed on the ballot (Cronin and Loevy 1993).

A multitude of groups opposed to the Christian Right have also taken advantage of these political opportunities. The environmental movement is especially strong for several reasons: the huge coverage of federal lands and the resulting battles over land use, the fascination with the "outdoors," and the visible brown cloud of air pollution over Front Range cities. Rapid population growth has aggravated the battles over land use, propelling this problem to a top-tier political issue in recent years. In addition, feminists and gay rights advocates have a presence in the state's liberal enclaves.

Religious counterparts to the Christian Right include the Colorado Council of Churches, an ecumenical group of moderate and liberal Protestant denominations. This group has done some lobbying in the state legislature on justice issues, such as housing, environmentalism, and racism. With a very small staff and with the struggles inherent in being a coalition of denominations, the Council of Churches appears to have minimal effect on Colorado politics. Colorado also has a chapter of the Interfaith Alliance, a coalition of mainstream Protestant, Catholic, and Jewish groups that have reacted to the Christian Right by calling for more civility in political campaigns. These groups are often allied with the Colorado chapters of the Anti-Defamation League, the Freedom from Religion Foundation, and the American Civil Liberties Union (ACLU). After the Amendment 2 campaign, People for the American Way set up an office in Boulder, but it is no longer visible in Colorado politics.

THE POLITICAL LANDSCAPE

Colorado increasingly leans Republican but has offered significant opportunities for Democrats. Statewide voter registration data suggest a Democrat plurality for much of the last forty years, but a significant Republican growth spurt in the past decade. The percentage of registered Republicans has increased from 30 percent in 1970 to 35 percent in 1998, producing a Republican plurality of more than 170,000 voters at the time of the 2002 elections. This compares with a small Democratic margin of 12,000 voters in 1992. Among those moving into Colorado in the last decade, Republicans have a 44 percent to 28 percent edge over Democrats. With a large number of independent voters, however, nearly every statewide election is up for grabs, and Colorado has witnessed extensive ticket splitting.

Table 9.1 shows the voting patterns for national and gubernatorial elections in Colorado over the last fifty years. In presidential elections since 1952, Colorado has overwhelmingly favored Republican candidates, with only two exceptions: the 1964 LBJ landslide, and the 1992 Clinton election, where Ross Perot captured 23 percent of the popular vote. In contrast, gubernatorial elections since 1958 have resulted in seven Democratic governors and only four Republicans. Current Republican Governor Bill Owens is the first Republican to occupy that office since the 1970s. United States Senate elections since the mid-1950s have resulted in victories for both parties, but more so for Republicans. In the U.S. House of Representatives, the Republicans have enjoyed a slight edge in recent years (four to two), following a more even split throughout most of the 1980s. In the state legislature, the Republicans have dominated, controlling both houses for the last thirty years, until the 2000 elections, where the Democrats eked out a one-seat majority, to the great dismay of the Christian Right. Consequently, divided government has been the norm for most of the last three decades.

Table 9.1   Colorado Voting History

Office	Time Period	Democratic Victories	Republican Victories
President	1952–2000	2	11
Governor	1958–1998	7	4
U.S. Senate	1954–1998	6	10[a]
U.S. House	1968–2000	43	50

[a]Senator Campbell switched from the Democratic to the Republican Party in 1995.

One illustration of the competitive nature of Colorado politics is its U.S. senators in the 1980s: conservative William Armstrong (a favorite among Christian Right supporters) and liberal Gary Hart (a source of Christian Right embarrassment). On the same day in 1978 that Coloradans voted to send Armstrong to the Senate, they also voted to return liberal Richard Lamm to the governor's mansion—and both candidates received 59 percent of the statewide vote.

Areas of Democratic strength within Colorado include Denver (with blue-collar industries and higher concentrations of minorities), Boulder (home of the University of Colorado), Pueblo (dominated by the steel industry), largely Hispanic and Catholic southern Colorado, and the wealthy, culturally liberal ski resorts. In contrast, the areas of Republican strength include the declining eastern plains, the western slope, and the rapidly growing region from the southern suburbs of Denver through Colorado Springs (Douglas and El Paso Counties).

Indeed, the most distinct partisan and ideological difference within Colorado is between Boulder and El Paso Counties. Boulder is a university town, replete with liberal interest groups, from feminists to environmentalists, and the home of the Naropa Institute, a center for Buddhist studies. It lies in the Second Congressional District, which has been held by the Democrats since 1974. El Paso County includes Colorado Springs, home of dozens of evangelical organizations and churches, and the U.S. Air Force Academy. It is in the Fifth Congressional District, which has been in safe Republican hands since 1972. The 1992 Amendment 2 election shows the contrasting voting patterns between the two counties: while the statewide margin was 53.4 percent in favor, El Paso County voted for it by 65.9 percent, and Boulder County rejected it by 60 percent.

Each party, however, is a broad coalition, with important elements that are not active participants in the "culture wars." For example, not all Colorado Democrats are culturally liberal like those in university towns and ski resorts. Blue-collar residents of Pueblo, ethnic minorities in Denver, and Catholic Hispanics in southern Colorado are traditionally religious and support portions of the Christian Right's profamily agenda, but not the Republican Party.

So, too, within the GOP there are at least two other groups that see things differently from the Christian Right. As a western frontier state, Colorado is home to a rugged individualism and an antigovernment ethos not particularly rooted in religious perspectives. Often decidedly libertarian on the social issues, these "frontier individualists" have been a thorn in the flesh of the Christian Right. In addition, there are fiscal conservatives whose priorities are economic growth and limited government, not abortion, homosexuality, or education vouchers. Within this cacophony of voices, the Christian Right has a seat at the Republican table but has not been able to set the table's agenda. Indeed, the movement's issues have rarely attracted the attention of the governor or the state legislature. However, the Christian Right's profamily agenda has been a persistent undercurrent in state politics for the last twenty years, and nearly every election has brought forth ballot initiatives reflecting this agenda, occasionally provoking a tidal wave of national visibility, such as with Amendment 2 in 1992.

THE COLORADO CHRISTIAN RIGHT

The Colorado Christian Right began when the Moral Majority set up a state chapter in the early 1980s. However, its focus was largely on national elections and issues, with very little attention to state or local matters, and it quickly faded from view. Most of the current Christian Right organizations arose in the early 1990s, with a greater focus on state and local issues. As in other states, the movement consists of a number of groups, each with its own constituency and leadership. Alliances have formed for the purpose of influencing elections and legislation, but differences in personality, style, and, on occasion, issue positions have prevented the formation of a monolithic force in Colorado politics.

The Christian Coalition of Colorado (CCCO)

The CCCO was formed in 1990 as a 501C(4) organization; contributors cannot claim a tax deduction for their gifts, but the group enjoys a wider scope of political activity than other groups that are 501C(3) nonprofit organizations. Its Denver headquarters has two full-time staff persons, and its current director suggests that there are about 5,000–6,000 financial contributors and 200,000 supporters throughout the state. The organization has county chapters in sixteen counties, although their activity varies widely. In the early days, the organization followed the model of the national Christian Coalition by focusing on general elections for president and Congress, but in the last few years the focus has clearly shifted to state and local elections, with particular emphasis on primary elections, school board contests, and party caucuses. These are venues where the impact of a small group of citizens can be maximized. The group's resources are devoted to voter education activities (1.2 million publications distributed in the last three years) and to recruiting and training candidates for future elections. Perceptions of the CCCO's impact vary widely. One respondent called it a "sleeping tiger," and another said it is "a force to be reckoned with" in Colorado politics. In contrast, two other conservative evangelicals said that its impact has been inconsistent in the last decade. Not all Christian Right allies appreciate what they perceive to be the aggressive, confrontational, and sometimes deceptive tactics of the CCCO.

Focus on the Family

The most visible evangelical organization is Focus on the Family, an evangelical ministry that was born in California in the 1970s and moved to Colorado Springs in 1991. Founded and led by Dr. James Dobson, Focus has emerged as a leading profamily advocate. Dr. Dobson's radio program reaches millions of listeners nationwide and regularly discusses current political issues. The organization assists Christian radio stations throughout the country through its news service, called Family News in Focus. Focus also distributes a monthly print magazine, *Citizen*, which emphasizes public policy issues at the national level and includes features and news reports about activities at the state level; there is also an electronic report called Citizen-link. One respondent estimated that Focus has a Colorado mailing list of nearly 60,000.

Focus employs about 1,300 people in Colorado Springs, working on a wide variety of projects, most of which are not directly related to public policy. In fact, less than 5 percent of the Focus budget is allocated to public policy projects. The organization has employed a lobbyist at the state level and hosted an annual legislative breakfast at the state capitol. One of the biggest impacts that Focus has on Colorado politics comes through its employees who participate in local and state politics; for example, a Focus vice president is also vice chair of the El Paso County Republican Party (see Minnery 2002, 120–21). Another significant impact of Focus is its culture-defining activities with conservative Christians throughout the state.

An offspring of Focus on the Family is the Rocky Mountain Family Council (RMFC), which began in 1991. The RMFC concentrates on the Colorado legislature, with weekly legislative updates on its website when the legislature is in session. It has a staff of three people in its Denver headquarters, with about 10,000 people on its mailing list and about 1,000 active supporters, mostly along the Front Range. The organization has, in recent years, put more emphasis on research and education through its Colorado Marriage Project, which is geared less toward political impact and more toward social transformation. It has also produced and distributed voter guides.

Prolife Groups

Abortion is a key issue for many Christian Right groups, including Colorado Right to Life, which started in 1971. It is a small organization, with about 2,500 members in the state and with one full-time staff person at the headquarters in Denver. There are county chapters throughout the state, but their activity and impact vary considerably. Their political activity focuses on the state legislature and on state elections, often working hand in hand with another group, Citizens for Responsible Government (CRG). Recently a rift developed among prolife groups in Colorado, particularly between Colorado Right to Life and a new group, the Colorado Pro-Life Alliance, which is fighting to become the official state chapter of the national Right to Life Committee. The two groups were on opposite sides of a 2000 prolife ballot initiative.

Citizens for Responsible Government (CRG)

CRG was formed in the early 1990s by a housewife-turned-politico, Pat Miller. She ran unsuccessful races for the school board, was elected to the state legislature, but then lost two subsequent elections for the U.S. House. As a lobbying organization and a political action committee, CRG produces voter guides and assists in recruiting and training candidates for office. It has a mailing list of 15,000 people centered along the Front Range. Several respondents pointed to CRG as an important part of the Christian Right effort largely because of the proactive personality of its leader and her network in the Colorado legislature, although the group's activities and influence vary with its financial condition.

Other Groups

Will Perkins, a Colorado Springs car dealer and a leader in the Amendment 2 battle, founded Colorado for Family Values (CFV) in 1992. Based largely in El Paso County, this group has tried to bring together evangelicals and others who support traditional families. Although CVF mobilized numerous activists and extensive finances during the Amendment 2 campaign, it became less of a factor in subsequent years.

The home-school movement is also active in Colorado, with data suggesting a tripling of home-schooled children in the decade of the 1990s. While not consistently or pervasively involved in state politics, the Christian Home Educators of Colorado (CHEC) has lobbied the legislature and proposed ballot initiatives to support alternatives to public education. CHEC hosts an annual "Home School Day" at the state capitol and sends out a quarterly magazine to 12,000 Colorado residents.

Another organization that has not been directly involved in Colorado politics but has affected its cultural environment is Promise Keepers, a Christian men's ministry. Founded in 1990 by popular former University of Colorado football coach Bill McCartney, the organization expanded rapidly and is most notable for its large stadium rallies throughout the county. Like Focus on the Family, Promise Keepers has an impact on Colorado through its employee base and through its efforts to develop a conservative profamily culture.

THE CHRISTIAN RIGHT AND COLORADO ELECTIONS

Following the example of national Christian Right groups, the Colorado organizations have consistently been involved in candidate elections. The most visible manifestation of their activity has been the cycle of candidate voter guides, in which several different groups (Christian Coalition, Citizens for Responsible Government, and the Rocky Mountain Family Council) have sought to compare the stands of candidates on issues dear to the movement—abortion, homosexual rights, same-sex marriages, support for private schools and home schooling, taxation on churches and other nonprofit organizations, and the like. Depending on the tax status of the particular group, there may or may not be an explicit or implied endorsement of particular candidates, but careful readers can easily discern who deserves their vote. These voter guides are distributed not only to members, but also in church bulletins and through the leafleting of church parking lots on the Sunday before election day. In the 2000 election, for example, the CCCO claims to have distributed between 250,000 and 300,000 voter guides. Movement opponents and even some supporters have suggested that the CCCO has occasionally misrepresented candidates' positions on issues.

The Colorado movement groups have also assisted congenial candidates in both primary and general elections. At the presidential level, the Colorado primary is scheduled too late in the sequence to have much impact. Exit poll data from the 2000 general election indicate that the white religious right made up 16 percent of the electorate and voted 79 percent for Bush. This voting bloc is not critical in a state that has typically gone Republican at the presidential level, but it has the potential to influence close state and local contests.

A key political ally of the Christian Right is former U.S. Senator William Armstrong, who served two terms in the Senate (1978–90), following service in the House (1972–78) representing the Fifth District (El Paso County), and a leadership role in the Colorado state senate (1969–72). An owner of a Christian radio station, he is unafraid to articulate the connection between his religious faith and his political conservatism (see Thomas and Dobson 2000, 195–203). Staunchly prolife, Armstrong provided support and visibility for the initial efforts of the Colorado Christian Right in the late 1970s and 1980s. Following his retirement from the Senate, he offered critical support to the Amendment 2 battle in 1992. No other elected official since Armstrong has taken up the mantel of the movement in Colorado.

Among Armstrong's GOP successors, Wayne Allard is a far more significant supporter of Christian Right issues than is maverick Ben Nighthorse Campbell (who switched to the GOP after Republicans took control of the Congress in 1994). Allard needed the electoral support of Christian Right voters in his competitive 2002 reelection campaign. Abortion has been a key issue in all of Allard races, including 1996, when Allard defeated Gail Norton (Secretary of the Interior in the Bush administration) in the Republican primary with the support of prolife voters.

Within the U.S. House delegation, Joel Hefley represents the Colorado Springs region and moves comfortably within Christian Right circles; the lack of Democratic competition in the district allows him to engage with conservative Christians without being co-opted. Congressman Tom Tancredo, representing suburban Denver, won a narrow victory in 1998 with the help of conservative Christians and agrees with much of their agenda. His background, however, with the libertarian-minded Independence Institute, suggests a different shading of priorities involving antitax, antigovernment, anti-immigration, and anti–gun-control efforts.

Despite the increased activity and occasional victories, however, the Christian Right does not always prevail in elections, even in areas with organizational strength. For example, Will Perkins, the leader of the Amendment 2 battle, was not successful in becoming mayor of Colorado Springs because of competition from other Republicans in the primary. CRG leader Pat Miller was unsuccessful in races for the school board and the U.S. House of Representatives (see Hertzke 1994). Abortion has been a key issue in several races, but the prolife candidates have a mixed record of success. In 1992, despite the success of Amendment 2, only one prolife candidate won among the eleven state legislative races targeted by the prochoice group the National Abortion Rights Action League (NARAL).

Governor Bill Owens received the crucial support of Christian Right voters in his narrow victory in 1998, but he has not made their agenda his own. For example, during the campaign, he commented about the abortion issue that 80 percent of Coloradans were going to cast their gubernatorial votes on issues that "were more appropriate" at the state level. Owens is a Bush-like Republican, who understands the political importance of social conservatives but gives greater emphasis to economic issues. The movement has had some success in state legislative elections; there are a small and growing number of Christian Right allies in the legislature, including Marilyn Musgrave, Doug Lamborn, and Mark Paschall.

THE CHRISTIAN RIGHT AND PARTY POLITICS

Although there are mixed views about the influence of the Christian Right in the Colorado Republican Party, there is no doubt that the movement has become significantly stronger and more visible in the 1990s. Comparative studies of Christian Right influence in 1994 and again in 2002 clearly demonstrate the growing power of the movement in the party apparatus (Persinos 1994; Conger and Green 2002). El Paso County (Colorado Springs) has a Republican Party organization dominated by Christian Right supporters and they have influenced both nomination and general election contests in that region. Among the state's delegation to the 2000 Republican Party convention, for example, approximately one-fourth of the delegates were reported to be financial contributors to the CCCO and about three-fourths were supporters of a prolife, pro-family agenda. A previous chairman of the Colorado Republican Party, Steve Curtis, made no secret of his Christian faith, although his authoritarian management style led to a short tenure and may have diminished the reputation of the Christian Right for a time. There were allegations that Curtis used party funds to support social conservative Republican candidates in primary fights against fiscal conservatives, who were social moderates, and frontier individualists, who were social liberals.

In fact, the Christian Right has also become deeply involved in what some observers describe as a "war for the soul" of the Colorado GOP. Several fiscal conservative Republicans in the state legislature have been surprised, and occasionally defeated, by fiscally *and socially* conservative candidates who took exception to legislative votes, particularly on abortion. The reverse is also true: moderate Republicans, sometimes including the local party leadership, have targeted conservative Christian incumbents. The Christian Right runs a clear risk in challenging other Republicans, because the bitter primary campaigns have resulted in Democratic victories in the general election. In 1992, for example, the Democrats picked up four seats in the House and four in the Senate, in part because of the squabbling among Republican factions. This intra-party warfare may also have been a factor in the 2000 elections, with the Democrats regaining control of the Colorado Senate for the first time in forty years. Several respondents noted that socially moderate Republicans crossed party lines to vote for Democratic candidates rather than vote for candidates supported by the Christian Right.

As noted above, the Colorado Republican Party is an uneasy alliance of different kinds of conservatives. The business interests are mostly concerned with economic growth, transportation, and low taxes, showing little interest in issues like abortion and homosexuality. The frontier individualists are strongly antigovernment and antitax, but their libertarian tendencies lead them to oppose government efforts to restrict abortions and gay rights. Likewise, the military has a strong presence in Colorado and vocal advocates among elected officials, particularly along the Front Range and in Colorado Springs, but their agenda does not always include social issues. The complex alliances between the Christian Right and other kinds of conservatives can be seen most clearly in ballot initiatives.

THE CHRISTIAN RIGHT AND BALLOT INITIATIVES

As in other western states, it is relatively easy to place initiatives on the ballot in Colorado, and every election brings forth a host of measures. The Christian Right has joined with the other conservatives to impose term limits and to support tax initiatives, such as the 1992 Tax-Payer Bill of Rights (TABOR), which limited the rate of growth in government spending and required popular approval of tax increases. There is a strong Second Amendment movement in the state, which has occasionally allied with Christian Right supporters, although these efforts have become more cautious in the wake of the shootings at Columbine High School. The Christian Right has developed its own measures, which are supported by other conservatives when they have an antigovernment character. Table 9.2 lists the most important of the initiatives backed by the Christian Right.

Table 9.2   Voting on Ballot Initiatives

Year Issue	Topic	Statewide Vote (%)	El Paso County Vote (%)	Boulder County Vote (%)
1988 Amend. 7	Repeal ban on state funding of abortions	Defeated 41–59	Defeated 31–69	Passed 50.1–49.9
1992 Amend. 2	Ban gay rights laws	Passed 53–47	Passed 66–34	Defeated 39–61
1996 Amend. 17	Recognize parental rights	Defeated 43–57	Passed 50.1–49.9	Defeated 30–70
1998 Amend. 11	Ban on partial-birth abortions	Defeated 49–51	Passed 59–41	Defeated 35–65
1998 Amend. 12	Parental notification for teen abortions	Passed 55–45	Passed 66–34	Defeated 38–62
2000 Amend. 25	Informed consent for abortions	Defeated 40–60	Defeated 48–52	Defeated 31–69

Note: See text and notes for more details on amendments.

Colorado was one of the first states to ban state funding of abortions, and this occurred via a ballot initiative in 1984, winning approval by a very narrow 50.4 percent margin. Christian conservatives supported this effort, but it also received support from fiscal conservatives. In 1988, liberal groups proposed Amendment 7, an attempt to repeal the state-funding ban. It was rejected by a strong statewide margin of 60 percent to 40 percent. As table 9.2 shows, this measure actually passed in the liberal bastion of Boulder.

The most visible triumph for the Christian Right in Colorado was the passage of Amendment 2 in 1992 (see Bransford 1994). The amendment was a reaction to city ordinances in Aspen, Boulder, and Denver that provided civil rights to homosexuals, and it called for outlawing any such effort within Colorado, dubbed as "special rights" for gays and lesbians. Led by Will Perkins and CVF, the initiative generated interest and financial support from across the nation. Supporters of Amendment 2 saw it as a way to stop or at least slow the gay-rights movement; opponents saw it as another example of discrimination by self-righteous Christian zealots.

Polls taken just a few days before the election predicted a defeat for the amendment, but on election day, 53.4 percent of the voters approved it. Voting returns showed that only fifteen of the sixty-three counties voted against the proposal, and in El Paso County the amendment was approved by nearly two to one. In contrast, Boulder County rejected it by about the same margin. Getting the amendment on the ballot and winning approval from the voters was an uphill struggle, and thus a significant accomplishment for the Christian Right. This effort brought together movement groups that had not cooperated actively before 1992 and led Christian activists to see ballot initiatives as a prime strategy for social change.

The battle did not stop on election night, however. There were immediate calls for national organizations to boycott Colorado as a site for conventions, and Colorado Springs officials were clearly worried about a significant decline in tourism dollars. Legal challenges shortly brought the issue to the Colorado courts and ultimately to the U.S. Supreme Court, which ruled the proposal unconstitutional in *Romer v. Evans.* The Christian Right had triumphed at the ballot box but not before the bar. This incident, and similar ones throughout the country, have led the Christian Right on the one hand to decry the ability of judges to overturn popular decisions and, on the other hand, to emphasize the importance of judicial appointments in legislative and executive elections.

Overall, the record on Christian Right initiatives is decidedly mixed. For instance, the 1998 Amendment 11 banning late-term abortions lost 51 percent to 49 percent. Christian conservatives took some solace in the fact that another measure also on the ballot, Amendment 12 requiring parental notification of possible teen abortions, passed with 55 percent of the vote. However, a federal appeals court also eventually overturned this amendment. El Paso and Boulder counties took almost opposite stands on both these initiatives.

The Christian Right suffered serious defeats in two other ballot contests, partly because the movement itself was divided. One was the 1996 Amendment 17 concerning parental rights over children.[2] The movement was divided on this poorly drafted measure, with former senator William Armstrong refusing to support it. The initiative was defeated 57 percent to 43 percent statewide and passed only by a slim majority in El Paso County. A similar fate awaited the 2000 Amendment 25 requiring informed consent for an abortion,[3] which was opposed by Colorado Right to Life. It was defeated by 60 percent statewide and lost even in El Paso County.

Table 9.3 offers a deeper look at voter support for these initiatives. Using county-level data and a simple regression model, this analysis considers the impact of eight variables on the percentage of support for the Christian Right position on these initiatives.[4] There are four religion variables: the percentage of white evangelical and mainline Protestants, black Protestants, and Catholics within each county. The movement could reasonably have expected some support from these religious traditions.

The other four variables are demographic: the percentage of Hispanic and college-educated, population density (a proxy for urbanization), and the rate of population growth over the preceding decade. Culturally conservative Hispanics are an important voting bloc in Colorado. The remaining three measures have traditionally been seen as proxies for the culturally liberal and secular population, and certainly high levels of education and urbanization characterize the liberal bastions in the state. Population growth, however, may have a mixed impact. In the 1970s and 1980s, migration to the state tended to be liberal and cosmopolitan, but in the 1990s, it turned more conservative, including the arrival of Focus on the Family.

The results of this analysis are revealing. First, note the percentage of variance explained by these simple models (the adjusted R^2): it tracks well with the degree of the ballot box success for the movement. For example, this handful of variables explains one-half of the variance when

Table 9.3 Support for Christian Right Ballot Initiatives in Colorado, 1988–2000 (%)

Voter Characteristics	1988 Amend. 7 (Abortion)	1992 Amend. 2 (Gay Rights)	1996 Amend. 17 (Parental Rights)	1998 Amend. 11 (Abortion)	1998 Amend. 12 (Abortion)	2000 Amend. 25 (Abortion)
Protestant						
Evangelical	0.28[a]	0.38[a]	0.33[a]	0.34[a]	0.38[a]	0.25[c]
Mainline	0.34[a]	0.23[b]	-0.20[c]	0.33[a]	0.31[a]	-0.18[c]
Catholic	-0.44[a]	-0.37[a]	-0.18[c]	-0.33[a]	-0.35[a]	-0.26[c]
Black	0.19	0.09	0.27	0.31[b]	0.29[b]	0.26
Hispanic	0.20[b]	0.53[a]	0.22[a]	0.40[a]	0.42[a]	0.20[c]
College-educated	-0.25[b]	-0.14[c]	-0.04	-0.32[a]	-0.30[a]	-0.33[a]
Population density	-0.40[a]	-0.32[b]	-0.47[a]	-0.40[a]	-0.40[a]	-0.35[a]
Population growth	-0.15[c]	-0.15[c]	0.20[b]	0.09[c]	0.05	0.13[c]
Adjusted R^2	0.44	0.54	0.30	0.44	0.50	0.23

Notes: See text and notes for variable coding; N = 63. The coefficients are standardized regression weights.
[a]Significant at .05 level or better
[b]Significant at .10 level or better
[c]Significant at .15 level or better

the Christian Right did best (1988 and 1998), a little less than one-half for close elections (1992 and 1998), and less than one-third for the big losses (1996 and 2000). This finding suggests that the success of these ballot initiatives required a broad alliance of conservatives, extending beyond the movement's core constituency of evangelical Protestants.

However, the evangelical population was certainly associated with support for all these initiatives, as demonstrated by the positive coefficients in all the columns in table 9.3. Interestingly, mainline Protestants were often positively associated with these positions—except for the 1996 and 2000 issues that lost badly at the polls. A similar but weaker pattern held for the black Protestant population, which is quite small in Colorado. The Hispanic population (much of which is Catholic) also strongly supported the Christian Right's positions on all the ballot initiatives.

In contrast to Protestants and Hispanics, the Catholic population was always negatively associated with the Christian Right's position on the ballot issues. The patterns for mainliners and Catholics are a bit surprising in light of the conventional wisdom that the former are moderate to liberal on cultural questions and the latter moderate to conservative. Of course, these are aggregate data, and may reflect the differences between conservative and liberal counties. High levels of education and urbanization are also negatively associated with support for all the ballot measures (although the level of statistical significance varies). The most varied pattern occurs for population increase: in 1988 and 1992, growth was negatively associated with Christian Right positions on the ballot initiatives, but beginning in 1996, the relationship becomes positive. This may well reflect the changing nature of migration to Colorado.

Taken together, these data starkly reveal the dimensions of the culture war in the Centennial State, and the difficulties in assembling a broad conservative coalition. Two further findings reinforce these conclusions (data not shown). Including the county Republican presidential vote in the analysis substantially eliminates the influence of white Protestants, who, as in other states, tend to vote Republican. A similar result is obtained if mean household income is included: the impact of Hispanic and black Protestants vanishes because these groups are located in low-income areas. Put another way, low-income Hispanics and black Protestants may vote with the Christian Right on such ballot initiatives but are unlikely to vote for Republican candidates; likewise, wealthy and well-educated libertarians support GOP candidates but only reluctantly back ballot measures that strongly implement traditional values.

Reflecting on this mixed record on ballot initiatives, several Christian Right groups have recently chosen to redirect their efforts away from ballot initiatives, citing the high costs of such campaigns, the despair created when courts overturn election results, and the difficulty of mobilizing and maintaining citizen enthusiasm year after year. With a Republican governor now in place for the first time in twenty years, and with more prolife and profamily state legislators, the groups are more hopeful that they can secure governmental support for their agenda.

THE CHRISTIAN RIGHT AND THE STATE LEGISLATURE

In the legislative arena, the Christian Right has developed a presence through lobbying efforts and also through the increasing numbers of profamily legislators. For the most part, the Christian Right's agenda has not been prominent in recent legislative sessions, so movement groups put few resources into lobbying in the 1990s. Still, there was a persistent trickle of legislative proposals on topics such as abortion, parental notification and consent, same-sex marriages, and, to a lesser extent, tax credits for private schools. These legislative initiatives have come from newly elected social conservatives who challenged moderate or socially libertarian incumbent Republicans, or who have taken advantage of opportunities created by the eight-year term limits approved in 1990. Clearly, one of the strategies of Christian Right supporters in the legislature is to force roll-call votes on specific issues, so that the recorded votes can become campaign fodder in the next primary or general election. Some state legislators who have received electoral support from the movement have walked a tightrope between gratitude for electoral support and the stigma of being too visibly aligned with the movement.

Despite the paucity of big victories in the state legislature, there is growing support among legislators for the profamily agenda of the Christian Right. Several respondents estimated that nearly one-third of current state legislators are supportive of this agenda, a dramatic change from a decade ago when only about 10 percent were supportive. One respondent was so bold as to suggest that there will be a prolife, profamily majority in the legislature within four years. Indeed, several group leaders suggested that this gradual accumulation of electoral successes is the most significant result of Christian Right activities in the last decade.

Perhaps the biggest victory for the Christian Right agenda in the Colorado legislature took place in the mid-1980s when the legislature passed a law prohibiting state funding of abortion. Despite several attempts to overturn the legislation, the prohibition remains on the books and has recently led to a controversial reduction in state funding for Planned Parenthood. Given current trends toward more prolife legislators, it seems unlikely that this will change in the near future.

Despite this new potential, the overall policy impact of the Christian Right in Colorado has been minimal. From the 1970s to the late 1990s, liberal Democratic governors were largely able to ward off efforts by a Republican legislature to enact the Christian Right agenda. In fact, the influence within the Republican Party and within the legislature of fiscally conservative but socially moderate or libertarian Republicans has also worked against the Christian Right's influence on state policy. In recent years, the policy emphasis on growth, education reform, and budget constraints, coupled with a Republican governor who has not pushed a social issues agenda, has not provided a fruitful environment for the Christian Right.

Summary and Conclusions

Just as the continental divide runs through Colorado's geography, so, too, a cultural divide runs through Colorado politics, resulting from demographic and political changes in the Centennial State. Each battle in this war is fought in a competitive political environment, and no outcome is preordained.

The Christian Right has made a difference in Colorado: winning such legislative battles as the ban on state funding of abortion and increasing the number of legislators who support a profamily agenda; winning ballot box initiatives on gay rights and parental notification of teen abortions; and keeping the social agenda of the movement visible in the legislature and at nearly every election cycle. These gains are the result of a significant migration of fiscal and especially religious conservatives during the last decade, the persistent dominance of Republicans in the state legislature, and the existence of several viable movement organizations.

The overall impact of the Christian Right, however, has been diminished by several factors. The migration that brought Focus on the Family and other evangelicals to Colorado also brought high-tech business people, wealthy retirees, ski buffs, and cultural liberals to reinforce the opponents of the movement's agenda. Indeed, the presence of fiscally conservative but socially moderate or libertarian Republicans has prevented the Christian Right from controlling the Republican Party, nominating congenial candidates, and passing ballot issues. Finally, the fact that the movement is split among several groups and organizations that often compete for money and support from the same constituents has diminished its effectiveness.

NOTES

1. Interviews were conducted in 2001 with the executive directors or political directors of movement groups in Colorado and with two state legislators noted for their support of the Christian Right agenda.
2. To recognize that parents have "the inalienable right to direct and control the upbringing, education, values, and discipline of children."
3. To require that women seeking an abortion be given detailed information about the procedure and about alternatives to abortion, and to require a twenty-four-hour waiting period between being informed and undergoing the procedure.
4. The dependent variable in each of these analyses is the percentage of the vote for the Christian Right position by county. These data came from the Colorado Secretary of State. The religion data came from the 1990 Census of Churches and Church Bodies produced by the Glenmary Research Center for Georgia. All the other data came from the U.S. Census. To make the analyses more comparable, 1990 census data were used in all the analyses, except for population growth. For the 1988, 1992, and 1996 analyses, the 1980–90 census was employed, and for the 1998 and 2000 analyses, the 1990–2000 growth rate was used. The use of 2000 census data produced very similar results.

REFERENCES

Bransford, Stephen. 1994. *Gay Politics vs. Colorado and America: The Inside Story of Amendment 2.* Cascade, Calif.: Sardis Press.

Conger, Kimberly H., and John C. Green. 2002. "Spreading Out and Digging In: Christian Conservatives and State Republican Parties." *Campaigns and Elections* (February):58–64.

Cronin, Thomas R., and Robert D. Loevy. 1993. *Colorado Politics and Government: Governing the Centennial State.* Lincoln: University of Nebraska Press.

Elazar, Daniel J. 1994. *The American Mosaic: The Impact of Space, Time, and Culture on American Politics.* Boulder, Colo.: Westview Press.

Herztke, Allen. 1994. "Vanishing Candidates in the 2nd District of Colorado." Pp. 82–100 in *Who Runs for Congress?* ed. Thomas Kazee. Washington, D.C.: Congressional Quarterly Press.

Minnery, Tom. 2002. *Why You Can't Stay Silent.* Wheaton, Ill.: Tyndale House.

Persinos, John F. 1994. "Has the Christian Right Taken over the Republican Party?" *Campaigns and Elections* (September):20–24.

Thomas, Cal, and Ed Dobson. 2000. *Blinded by Might.* Grand Rapids, Mich.: Zondervan.

TEN

The Christian Right in California: Dimming Fortunes in the Golden State

J. Christopher Soper and Joel S. Fetzer

> Californians are a race of people; they are not
> merely inhabitants of a state.
>
> —*O. Henry*

The history of the Christian Right in California is a study in contrasts (Soper 1995; Fetzer and Soper 1997). On the one hand, it is difficult to imagine a state that is less hospitable to the social, policy, and party goals of the Christian Right. California is among the least churched and most secular states in the union. On the issues most salient to Christian conservatives, particularly abortion and gay rights, public policy is liberal in California and has become more so over the past twenty years. Finally, to the extent that the political fortunes of the Christian Right are inextricably bound to those of the Republican Party, conservative Christian groups and causes have suffered in recent years as the state GOP has atrophied, perhaps because of the party's too-close identification with the Christian Right. The failures of the Christian Right are a reminder that California's political culture places strong limits on a movement whose religious, political, and policy views are not shared by a majority of the state's electorate.

On the other hand, Christian conservatives have had a significant political impact in California. In the past twenty years, the Christian

Right has become the dominant wing of the state Republican Party, it has helped to both nominate and elect candidates to public office, and persons closely identified with the movement have poured millions of dollars into the political process. Through the legislative initiative process, the Christian Right has also helped to bring a number of issues to public attention. The success of the Christian Right in California tells us much about the vitality of movement participants, their willingness and ability to engage the political process, and the permeability of the state's political structures to the activism of a well-organized movement. The story of the Christian Right in California, in short, is one of relative success within a political culture that limits the capacity of a conservative religious movement to have much of an impact at all.

OBSTACLES TO AND OPPORTUNITIES FOR
CHRISTIAN RIGHT MOBILIZATION

The primary obstacle to Christian Right political mobilization in California is that the state's religious environment is not conducive to conservative Christian activism. The Christian Right derives its principal strength from evangelical Protestants (Green 2000). In California, however, the denominations most closely associated with the Christian Right are not particularly strong, and the size of the evangelical constituency is fairly limited. The two largest "religious" categories in the state are Roman Catholics (28 percent) and nonreligious persons (13 percent), two groups that are not natural or easy allies of the Christian Right (Kosmin and Lachman 1993, 88–93). By contrast, the Southern Baptist Convention, the nation's largest Protestant denomination and the one most closely affiliated with conservative Christian politics, is not at all strong (1.7 percent).

This religious landscape does not mean that there is no market for the Christian Right in the state. According to a 1993 poll, 21 percent of Californians could be categorized as part of the Christian Right—people who are both religiously and politically conservative. Respondents whom the poll identified as belonging to the religious right had consistently conservative attitudes on a wide range of social issues, such as abortion, gay rights, and prayer in public schools, and nearly two-thirds (64 percent) are Republican. The poll also revealed, however, even larger populations of religious moderates (25 percent) and "secularists" (54 percent)—people who were not religious or were not religiously active (California Opinion Index 1993). Not surprisingly, the social and political views of religious moderates and secularists were far more liberal than the attitudes of their conservative counterparts.[1]

The political ideology of the state's population also acts as an impediment to Christian Right groups. Political conservatives are a minority of the state's active electorate. In the 1994 midterm elections, 29 percent of voters described themselves as conservative or very conservative, 17 percent as liberal or very liberal, and 46 percent as moderate. The percentage of self-described conservatives and liberals increased in the 2000 elections to 34 and 37, respectively, while moderates fell to 39 percent (*Los Angeles Times* Poll 2000). The state may not be as liberal as the media often assume, but neither is it as conservative as it would need to be for the Christian Right to be a dominant electoral force. The winning formula for elections in California was and still is to be found in the ideological center or slightly left of center, which is not where the Christian Right and the Republican Party have positioned themselves for much of the past two decades.

The state is also liberal or moderate on the social issues that matter most to the Christian Right. According to a 1997 poll, 62 percent of Californians supported first-trimester abortions, a majority favored publicly funded abortions for indigent women, and two-thirds (66 percent) preferred either the status quo or even less restrictive abortion laws (Field Poll 1997). Californians are more evenly divided on the rights of gays and lesbians, but here again the state is moderate to liberal. A 1997 poll indicated that 45 percent of the state's population believe homosexual relations to be always or almost always wrong, while a nearly identical percentage (47 percent) feel that homosexual relations are not at all wrong or only sometimes wrong (California Opinion Index 1997). A majority (56 percent) disapprove of allowing two people of the same sex to marry and benefit from regular marriage laws, but most Californians (67 percent) do approve of granting legal recognition of family rights to domestic partners, allowing child custody rights for homosexuals (69 percent), and permitting gays and lesbians to serve in the military (58 percent).

A final political obstacle to Christian Right mobilization in California is the electoral decline of the Republican Party in the state over the past two decades. After the 2000 election, the state's governor, Gray Davis, and California's two senators were Democrats. In addition, the Democrats comfortably controlled both houses of the state legislature, and the party held an advantage in its congressional delegation of thirty-two to twenty. Finally, the Democrats enjoyed an eleven-point advantage in party registration over the GOP. Whatever the cause of the electoral decline of the state GOP, it did not bode well for a politically conservative movement like the Christian Right, which is so closely identified with the Republican Party.

While California's political culture acts as a barrier to Christian Right activism, the state's political institutions provide an ideal context for social movement mobilization. Few states have been as affected by Progressive political reforms as has California. California was one of the first states to adopt the political primary election, the initiative, referendum, and recall votes, nonpartisan city elections, and the outlawing of preprimary endorsements by the political parties (Mayhew 1986; Gerston and Christenson 1995; Hyink and Provost 1998). What these Progressive innovations have made possible is for a well-organized social movement to have a dramatic political impact. Because they are structurally weak, political parties are open to takeover by groups willing and able to commit time and resources to party activism. Candidates for elective office need the support of active groups in the electorate that can mobilize voters for political primary elections. Finally, interest groups and their supporters dominate referendum and initiative campaigns. What the Christian Right discovered as it began to mobilize in the state in the late 1980s, in short, was that California's political system provided the movement with multiple points of access and potential influence.

CHRISTIAN RIGHT ORGANIZATION
AND ACTIVISM IN THE STATE

As in other states, the impetus for Christian Right activism in California was a growing dissatisfaction among conservative Christians with the state's liberal social policies on abortion, gay rights, and religion in public schools. From a resource perspective, conservative Christians proved to be ideal for political activism as group leaders recruited members through sympathetic evangelical and fundamentalist churches (Gilbert 1993). A number of groups emerged to challenge the state's liberal social policy, including the California Republican Assembly, the California Pro Life Council, the Traditional Values Coalition, and the Christian Coalition. Notably absent in California were the Moral Majority and Concerned Women for America, groups that have been politically significant in other states but have had little or no presence in California.

The California Republican Assembly (CRA) is a conservative, grassroots wing of the state GOP. Founded in 1934, the CRA endorses candidates for public office, contributes money to elections, and presses the party on social and economic issues. In the elections of 2000, for example, the group endorsed Gary Bauer's presidential bid and contributed $60,000 to various socially conservative Republican candidates. The 3,500-member group is very effective at the grassroots level and has a considerable presence within the state GOP.

The Traditional Values Coalition (TVC) was founded in 1981 and is the brainchild of the Reverend Lou Sheldon. The TVC claims a nationwide membership of 1,000,000, which is probably inflated. The group's national headquarters are in California, where Sheldon has had a high profile on gay-rights issues for the past twenty years. He led two efforts to restrict gay and lesbian rights, a 1979 initiative that would have prevented gay and lesbian people from teaching in public schools and a 1981 bill to retain the state's antisodomy law (Dunlap 1994). His failure at both of these convinced him of the need to organize a more lasting political movement.

The Christian Coalition has been active in California since shortly after Pat Robertson founded the group in 1989. Robertson had abandoned his presidential bid prior to the state's primary election in June of 1988, but he made a significant impact on Republican Party politics nonetheless. Most notably, Robertson encouraged persons active in his campaign to run for positions within the state Republican Party Committee. What had been a largely ineffective conservative Christian movement during the early 1980s became a significant force in state party politics by the early 1990s. Christian conservatives committed time and resources to party activism, turning out for party leadership elections to county and state committees to which few party members pay attention. It is instructive to note, for example, that John Fugatt, executive director of the Christian Coalition of California, is also a frequent delegate to the state's Republican Party convention (Fugatt 2001).

The Coalition remains the most significant grassroots Christian Right organization within the state. While its active membership is not particularly large, an estimated 5,000 between elections (Fugatt 2001), the group has proved adept at establishing a network of support through its sixty local chapters. Through these local chapters the Coalition mobilizes members for political activism and preelection voter guide distribution. In 2000, for example, the Coalition claimed to have distributed 2,500,000 guides for the primary election and an additional 4,000,000 for the general election. Each of the sixty chapters has a list of churches through which it distributes its voter guides (Fugatt 2001).

Once organized, conservative Christians turned to the political process with hopes of stemming the tide of liberal social policy coming out of the state. The movement's impact has been felt most dramatically in two areas: state Republican Party politics and initiative campaigns.

THE CHRISTIAN RIGHT AND STATE
REPUBLICAN PARTY POLITICS

One area where the Christian Right has had a significant political impact has been in the state Republican Party. Control of the California Republican Party has vacillated between moderates and conservatives in the past fifty years. In the 1950s, moderates controlled the party, but the migration of large numbers of midwesterners and southerners into the state in the 1940s and 1950s changed the state's political culture and fueled a conservative backlash in the state GOP (Elazar 1972). The party became far more conservative on law and order, taxation, labor, and racial issues. The transformation of the Republican Party eventually led to Ronald Reagan's two terms as California's Republican governor. At the time, no region in the country could match the fervor and organizational strength of the right wing in California, particularly in Orange County (Schupparra 1998; McGirr 2001).

As governor, however, Reagan was more a libertarian than a social conservative. In 1967, for example, he signed the Beilenson bill, which enacted the nation's most liberal abortion law (Cannon 1998). The same was largely true for Republican governors George Deukmejian (1982–90) and Pete Wilson (1990–98), for whom crime was the cornerstone social issue. The election of the prochoice Pete Wilson in 1990 solidified the movement of the state GOP in a socially moderate direction. As the Christian Right began to gain a foothold in the party in the early 1990s, however, antagonism grew between moderates and conservatives in the party. The annual party conventions in the 1990s became a public feud between Christian Right activists and the prochoice Republican governor, Pete Wilson. During his eight-year tenure as governor, Wilson urged the party to adopt a modified prochoice position, distanced himself from the state party leadership, and had an increasingly antagonistic relationship with Christian conservatives in the party. In response, some delegates to the party's 1991 convention tarred and feathered the governor in effigy (Peterson 1991).

According to evaluations of the state party, by 1993 conservative Christians controlled thirty-eight of the fifty-eight county GOP central committees and were a significant influence in the state Republican Party (Nollinger 1993; Persinos 1994). A more recent study of conservative Christian influence in state Republican parties (Conger and Green 2002) concluded that Christian conservatives had lost some ground in California but were still a moderate influence in the state GOP. One place where the Christian Right's impact has been felt is in the platform of the California Republican Party. Since conservative Christians became the dominant force within the party, the GOP platform has represented Christian Right views on abortion, school vouchers, and gay rights. The party platform adopted for 2000–03, for example, affirms the party's support "for the protection of innocent human life at every stage, from the pre-born to the elderly" and opposes "granting to homosexuals special privileges, including marriage, domestic partnership benefits, and child custody or adoption" (California Republican Party 2001).

The very forces that made the party susceptible to a takeover by the Christian Right have, however, limited what the movement has been able to accomplish within the state GOP. Because it is weak, the state party had few of the resources that candidates need and none of the sanctions that they fear. California's parties do not, for example, control the nomination process, and they have not historically contributed a very large percentage of the money needed for political campaigns. Nor has control of the party meant that the Christian Right has enjoyed the power to shape the issues debated within a given election. There is no state in the union where elections are more candidate-centered than in California; more often than not the Christian Right found itself responding to a set of issues defined for it by candidates or the media. Pete Wilson, for example, consistently used divisive wedge issues for his political purposes. The most notorious examples came in 1994, when he linked his reelection bid to support for Proposition 187, a referendum that called for cutting off undocumented immigrants' access to most public services, and in 1996, when he and the GOP supported an anti-affirmative-action measure, Proposition 209. Wilson easily won reelection in 1994, and Christian Right organizations endorsed both propositions, but immigration and affirmative action were not issues that were central to the movement's political self-understanding (Fetzer and Soper 1997).

Deep fissures remain within the party on abortion and gay rights, and they play themselves out in contests for state party leadership positions and in the party's primary elections. The most recent examples include the 2001 party convention, where conservatives retained control of the state party chair position despite a well-financed challenge from the party's moderate wing and support from the Bush White House (Barabak 2001; Wildermuth 2001), and the 2002 GOP gubernatorial primary election, which witnessed the surprising victory of social conservative Bill Simon over social moderate Richard Riordan (Cannon 2002).

The severe electoral decline of the state GOP in the past decade has further intensified the battles between social moderates and conservatives within the party. In the past three elections (1996, 1998, and 2000) the number of Republicans representing California's 52 congressional districts fell from 25 to 20. The Republican caucus in the 80-member state assembly declined from 41 to 30, and Republicans lost two seats in the 40-member state senate, dropping from 17 to 15. The GOP has also lost the last three presidential races in the state, the last gubernatorial campaign, and the last three contests for the U.S. Senate.

The demise of the Republican Party is, however, a relatively recent phenomenon in California. From 1952 to 1992, the Democrats won only one presidential contest in the state. Until Gray Davis won the race for governor in 1998, Republicans held that office for four consecutive terms, and six of the past eight. The state elected Republican senators in 1976, 1982, and 1988. After the 1994 elections, the GOP had a majority in the state assembly, and in 1993 the party narrowed its registration gap with the Democrats to a historic low of 7 percent. It is only recently that California has been transformed from a moderate, at times even conservative, state to one of the most Democratic states in the nation (Decker 2000; Cannon and Block 2001).

There are myriad reasons for the party's recent failures. First, Republican Party support for Proposition 187 mobilized the growing Latino population into the Democratic Party. This classic wedge issue proved effective for Governor Wilson and the GOP in the short run as it mobilized his base and divided Democrats, but the longer-term impact has been to reinforce an anti-immigrant, racist image of the GOP among Latinos. In the past Latinos had not been very politically active or predictably Democratic in party affiliation or voting. In the 1988 presidential election, for example, the Democratic plurality among Latino voters in the state was a mere 6 percent. Proposition 187 changed all that. By the 2000 presidential election, the Democratic margin among Latino voters had ballooned to a substantial 52 percent (Field Poll 2000). In addition, Latinos, who represent 30 percent of California's population and are the fastest-growing ethnic group in the state, began to register in large numbers after the 1994 elections. Nearly half of all Latinos currently on the voter rolls registered to vote since 1994; between 1994 and 1998, the Latino percentage of the electorate increased from 8 percent to 13 percent (Block 1998).

In some respects, Latinos are natural allies of the Christian Right. They are more religious than non-Latinos and less liberal ideologically, and they have more conservative views on social issues such as homosexuality and abortion (Field Poll 2000). When California voters approved Proposition 22, which banned the recognition of same-sex marriages, Latino voters gave the measure stronger support than non-Latinos (Meyerson 2001). But though they are to the right on social issues, Latinos are to the left of the electorate on economics and the rights of ethnic minorities. In order to be most effective the Christian Right must expand its base outside the white evangelical community, but Christian Right support for Proposition 187 limited the movement's capacity to do so in the growing Latino community.

Just as troubling for the Christian Right and the GOP is that the party's conservative positions on abortion, gay rights, school vouchers, gun control, and the environment have alienated California's moderate voters, many of whom are not registered with either of the two major parties. The fastest-growing part of California's electorate is those who "decline to state" their party affiliation when they register to vote; such voters increased from 9 percent to 14 percent of the electorate in the past ten years. These nonpartisan voters tend to be more moderate on social issues than the GOP (Lucas 2001). In the 2000 presidential election, Gore defeated Bush among self-described moderates by a healthy 58 percent to 39 percent margin. It is difficult to imagine that a candidate who opposes abortion rights and gun control, or favors school vouchers or very conservative restrictions on the rights of gays and lesbians could win a top-of-the-ticket race in California (Skelton 2000). Nonetheless, these views prevail within the state GOP, in large part because of the role that conservative Christians have assumed in the party.

THE CHRISTIAN RIGHT AND ELECTORAL POLITICS

The Christian Right has been able to take control of the state GOP, but the movement's electoral impact has been far less significant. As table 10.1 demonstrates, white evangelical Christians, the core of the Christian Right movement, are at best an important, but not controlling, faction among Republican voters. Evangelicals reached their high-water mark in the 1994 midterm election. In that contest evangelicals comprised 17 percent of all voters in the state and 24 percent of all votes cast for Republican House candidates. The 2000 elections, by contrast, were the worst in a generation for the state GOP, although evangelical

Table 10.1   Political Characteristics of White Christian Right Voters

Voter Characteristics	1994 (%)	2000 (%)
Conservative	61	68
Moderate	32	25
Republican	60	73
Christian Right as % of the electorate	17	10
Christian Right as % of GOP vote	24	22

Note: Data from 1994 and 2000 Voter News Service exit poll. Christian Right voters were defined as those who considered themselves "part of the conservative Christian political movement, also known as the religious right." Data from 2000 were weighted to achieve a demographically representative sample.

influence in the party remained strong. In 2000, white evangelical Christians represented 10 percent of all votes cast (a fairly dramatic fall from 1994), but they were still a sizable 22 percent of all Republican identifiers.

As in previous years, belonging to the Christian Right significantly increased one's chances of voting for a Republican candidate. And as in earlier elections, this pro-GOP influence remains robust after one statistically corrects for the effects of education, income, gender, ethnicity, and age (see table 10.2). The logistic regression coefficients in the first column of table 10.2 indicate, for instance, that a forty-year-old, white, non–Christian Right Protestant woman who holds a bachelor's degree and receives a household income of $40,000 per year would have a 38 percent chance of voting for George W. Bush. If this hypothetical voter were the same on all characteristics except that she belonged to the Christian Right, however, her likelihood of casting a ballot for Bush would almost double to 62 percent. Membership in the religious right thus strongly influenced one's vote for president (as well as for U.S. Senate and House candidates) in 2000, but its impact was only about as third as powerful as that for being Jewish (b = −3.171; p < 0.05) and about half as influential as that for being African American (b = −1.855; p < 0.05).

THE CHRISTIAN RIGHT AND PARTY CANDIDATES

Candidates closely identified with the Christian Right have historically done poorly in statewide races. The last candidate to run for statewide office who had strong public ties to the Christian Right was William Dannemeyer, who sought the GOP Senate nomination in 1994 but was easily defeated in the primary by his socially moderate counterpart, John Seymour. Dan Lungren, the party's gubernatorial nominee in 1998, did

Table 10.2 Determinants of Presidential, U.S. Senate, and U.S. House Vote

	GOP Pres. Vote	GOP Sen. Vote	GOP House Vote
Independent variables			
Christian Right	0.973[b]	0.918[b]	0.701[b]
Catholic	−1.176[b]	−0.844[b]	−0.951[b]
Jewish	−3.171[b]	−2.806[b]	−2.052[b]
Other religion	−1.061[b]	−0.562	−0.683
Secularist	−1.594[b]	−0.430	−1.483[b]
Education	−0.095	−0.089	−0.048
Income	0.360[b]	0.298[b]	0.383[b]
Female	−0.889[b]	−0.995[b]	−0.962[b]
African American	−1.855[b]	−1.832[b]	−1.911[b]
Latino	0.096	−0.652[a]	−0.896[b]
Asian	0.501	−0.540	−0.135
Other race	.158	−1.025	−0.177
Under age 30	−0.393	0.039	0.249
Over age 64	0.542[a]	−0.015	0.410
Constant	−0.308	−0.263	−0.544
Model statistics			
Sample size (N)	505	463	426
% correctly predicted	69.7	67.1	67.2
χ^2	124.7[c]	82.4[c]	91.5[c]
Degrees of freedom	14	14	14
Pseudo R^2	.196	.150	.179

Note: Data from 2000 Voter News Service exit poll. Christian Right voters were defined as those who considered themselves "part of the conservative Christian political movement, also known as the religious right." Estimates were obtained by dichotomous logistic regression. Pseudo R^2 was calculated according to Aldrich and Nelson (1984, 56–57). Education ranges from 1 to 5, and income varies from 1 to 6. Cases with missing data were deleted listwise. Data were weighted to achieve a demographically representative sample.
[a]$p < 0.10$, two-tailed test
[b]$p < 0.05$, two-tailed test
[c]$p < 0.05$, one-tailed test

not have any formal ties to the Christian Right but was a Roman Catholic who opposed abortion and favored school vouchers. His pro-choice, anti–school-voucher opponent, Democrat Gray Davis, handily defeated him. Often, in getting favored candidates nominated in the primary, the Christian Right has torpedoed the GOP's chances in the general election.

Two congressional districts in the state highlight both the tensions within the state GOP between social conservatives and moderates and the political liabilities of candidates too closely identified with the Christian Right. In 1996 Republican incumbent Robert "B-1 Bob" Dornan ran against a political neophyte, Loretta Sanchez, in the Forty-Sixth Congressional District race. As in many other Orange County congressional districts, the demographics of District 46 had changed dramatically in the previous decade. What was once a solidly white district in staunchly conservative Orange County had become increasingly Latino and politically moderate (Brinkheroff 2001). Dornan, however, was anything but moderate. He consistently scored perfect scores from the Christian Coalition and the Traditional Values Coalition on their congressional scorecards, was a vocal and persistent opponent of abortion and gay rights, and lashed out against "illegal aliens." In 1996 he lost his race to Sanchez. National party leaders tried to recruit a socially moderate candidate for the district race in 1998, but Dornan won the party's primary election. In that contest, he received financial support from such Christian Right PACs as the Campaign for Working Families, Eagle Forum, California Right to Life Committee, Republican Coalition for Life, and Pro-Life PAC of Orange County. Come the general election, however, Sanchez once again defeated the conservative firebrand.

A similar dynamic was at work in the congressional race in District 22, located primarily in Santa Barbara and San Luis Obispo, two upper-income and socially moderate cities along the coast. This district has historically been a marginal seat in Congress. The seat was vacated and a special election was called when Congressman Walter Capps died in office. The Democrats nominated Capps's widow, Lois, to run, while the Republican primary pitted prolife candidate Tom Bordonaro, who had the support of state and national Christian Right groups, against the prochoice Brooks Firestone, a Republican moderate who was endorsed by such GOP luminaries as Gerald Ford and Newt Gingrich. In the primary, Firestone fell victim to a devastating series of television ads targeting his alleged position on partial-birth abortion. Funded and directed by the Campaign for Working Families (Bathen 1998), a political action committee affiliated with Gary Bauer's Family Research Council, the ads appear to have influenced socially conservative GOP voters to shift their support to Bordonaro (Dionne 1998). In the runoff election, however, Bordonaro proved incapable of beating Capps despite favorable advertising by Bauer's group and the Christian Coalition. In the end, Capps appears to have received not only the votes of Democrats but also of as many as two in five of Firestone's first-round voters. Such socially moderate Republicans seem to have deserted the party's extremist candidate in favor of the more mainstream Democrat (Cannon 1998). Bordonaro repeated his poor performance against Capps in the November general election.

The failure of candidates closely identified with the Christian Right in electoral campaigns does not mean that Republican officeholders are hostile to the agenda of the Christian Right. In fact, the Christian Coalition's scorecard rating of the 1999–2000 roll-call votes for California's twenty Republican House members on "Christian family issues" was a respectable 81 percent. The problem for the Christian Right, and the GOP, is that there are fewer and fewer Republican house members to vote in ways consistent with groups like the Christian Coalition.

The Christian Right also had some success in moving the party's caucus in the state assembly and senate in a more socially conservative direction during the 1990s. Allied Business PAC, a political action committee formed in 1991 by four wealthy businessmen with close ties to the Christian Right, spent $9,000,000 from 1992 to 1997 for Republican Party candidates in state and local races (Bailey and Warren 1998). Allied PAC sought candidates who supported the group's fiscally and socially conservative ideals. Candidates responded by adopting a more conservative platform on abortion, gay rights, and related "family values" issues. One of the group's founders, Rob Hurtt, won a seat in the state senate and became the minority leader in 1994; he served in that post until 1998 (Morain and Ingram 1995). In that year the Republican Party also gained control of the state assembly for the first time in decades.

The intervening years, however, have not been good to the GOP or to socially conservative candidates in the state assembly and senate. The Democrats regained control of the state assembly in 1996 and increased their majority in both houses after the 1998 and 2000 elections. In addition, two officeholders closely identified with the Christian Right, Rob Hurtt and Jim Morrissey, lost their seats in the 1998 elections.

While conservative Christians have maintained fealty to their political principles in state party battles, the Christian Right has been willing to modify those ideals in order to help get socially moderate Republicans elected to office. In 1994, for example, the movement supported dozens of "stealth" candidates who minimized their formal ties to the Christian Right. The Christian Coalition especially took this path, consistently stressing a wide variety of issues in its voters' guides. The 1998 voter guide included such issues as support for a balanced budget amendment and a flat-rate federal income tax. The effect has been to make moderate Republican candidates seem acceptable to conservative Christians. In the end, the Coalition all but endorsed socially moderate GOP candidates Michael Huffington, Matt Fong, and even Pete Wilson in their bids for statewide office.

THE CHRISTIAN RIGHT AND LEGISLATIVE INITIATIVES

Initiative campaigns are the perfect vehicle for Christian Right activism because they play to the political strengths of the movement, which are the enthusiasm and vitality of activists and the interconnection of movement participants through evangelical churches throughout the state (Allswang 2000). While political parties sometimes take a stand on a particular initiative, they provide few of the resources necessary to get an initiative on the ballot or to publicize it for an upcoming election. On sociocultural issues ideological interest groups and wealthy individuals dominate the process. Between 1979 and 2000, for example, the Christian Right was instrumental in placing eight initiatives on the ballot, six dealing with gay and lesbian rights and two with the use of state educational vouchers for public or private schools, including religious schools. The Christian Right has been able to use the initiative process to get some of their key issues on the legislative agenda.

The voucher initiatives were virtually identical; Proposition 174 in 1993 proposed that the state would provide a $2,600 voucher to all school-age children (kindergarten through twelfth grade) to pay for tuition and fees at private schools, including private religious schools. Proposition 38 in 2000 increased the amount of the voucher to $4,000 annually. Both propositions seemed well timed to take advantage of a growing concern about the quality of public education in the state. The Christian Right provided vocal support for both initiatives. The Christian Coalition made a concerted effort to expand beyond their white, evangelical Protestant base to include Roman Catholics, Latinos, and African Americans, whom they argued would benefit most from a voucher system. Despite these efforts, the voters rejected the two voucher initiatives by identical 70 percent-to-30 percent margins.

The Christian Right has been only marginally more successful on propositions dealing with gay and lesbian rights; Proposition 6 in 1978 was the first to deal with this issue. If passed, the proposition would have allowed schools to fire an employee for advocating or practicing homosexuality, and would have prohibited them from hiring gays or lesbians. Lou Sheldon, founder of the Traditional Values Coalition, was the chief architect of this proposition. Proposition 6 failed by a 58 percent-to-32 percent margin. Two other propositions from the 1980s that would have declared AIDS an infectious disease and placed carriers of the disease on a special list were also soundly defeated by the voters. In 2000, the Christian Right did help to secure passage of Proposition 22, the Limit on Marriages Initiative, which mandates that only marriages between a man and a woman are valid and recognized in the state of California. It passed by a comfortable 61 percent-to-39 percent margin.

Securing a voice in the political process has not translated into many policy successes for the Christian Right. Initiatives have been a good way for the movement to raise public awareness about a number of their concerns, but the Christian Right has been frustrated in passing legislation for three reasons. First, the Christian Right has proposed initiatives that appeal to its most ardent and ideological supporters but that tend to alienate the general electorate. Proposition 6 is a good example. Even in 1978, when public attitudes toward gay and lesbian rights were more conservative than they are currently, the voters were not prepared to back a proposition that on its surface seemed to deny gays and lesbians basic legal, political, and civil rights. Similarly, the two AIDS proposals appealed to those within the Christian Right who viewed homosexuality as an aberrant and dangerous lifestyle, but the more moderate California electorate found both of them discriminatory.

Second, because of the ideological nature of the initiatives the Christian Right has proposed, the movement has not been able to move much beyond its limited base of support. The two voucher proposals were so comprehensive in scope that they ended up with very little support outside the Christian Right. Even the California Catholic Conference of Bishops, which runs the most private schools in the state and presumably stood to gain a great deal from the passage of a voucher initiative, declined to take an official position on Proposition 38. Supporters were no more effective at building a political coalition with ethnic minority groups. While a handful of African American ministers and Latino leaders joined the Christian Right in support of Proposition 38, the larger Hispanic and black political organizations opposed it (Rojas 2000). In order to be politically successful, the Christian Right has to build political coalitions with other religionists, but as a rule the initiatives that conservative Christian organizations have championed have not facilitated such alliances.

Finally, the Christian Right has consistently faced a well-organized and financed opposition. Opponents of the voucher initiatives included all the teachers' unions in the state, the state Democratic Party, President Clinton, the League of Women Voters, the Mexican American Legal Defense Fund, the National Association for the Advancement of Colored People, Governor Gray Davis, and many others (Allswang, 2000:185). Raising over $12,000,000 from teachers' unions alone, opponents of Proposition 174 outspent supporters by $24,000,000 to $3,000,000. In 2000, the California Teachers Association PAC raised over $26,000,000 of the $32,000,000 spent to oppose Proposition 3. In this case, however, the proponents were not significantly outspent, as Silicon Valley millionaire Tim Draper contributed over $25,000,000 of the $28,000,000 spent in support of the initiative (California Voter Foundation 2001). The Christian Right has encountered a similarly well-mobilized opposition on its initiatives against gay rights. Both of the AIDS initiatives from the 1980s were opposed by civil liberties groups, gay- and lesbian-rights organizations, the entire California medical community, U.S. Surgeon General C. Everett Koop, Republican Governor Deukmejian, and most of the prominent religious leaders in the state. Opponents of both measures considerably outspent supporters. This is instructive of the larger point that key opponents of the Christian Right, such as feminists, gay-rights advocates, teachers' unions, and environmentalists are politically powerful in California.

The only Christian Right legislative proposal to pass was Proposition 22, the Limit on Marriage Initiative. Changing the tactics it normally used to champion initiatives, the Christian Right expanded its support beyond its evangelical base, raised more money than its opposition, and designed a proposal that appealed to moderate and conservative voters in the state. Two of the four largest donors to the campaign were an evangelical organization, Helping Hands Ministry, and a Roman Catholic one, the Roman Catholic Archbishop of Los Angeles. In all, supporters raised $10,300,000 to $6,100,000 for the opponents. While Proposition 22 was not without controversy, the legislation did not push public policy in California in a far more conservative direction. Same-sex marriages were banned in California before Proposition 22; the initiative simply confirmed that California would not recognize such marriages if they were performed in other states. The success of Proposition 22 thus suggests that the Christian Right can have a legislative impact through the initiative process, but only under certain limited conditions.

The Christian Right and State Public Policy

Despite the political mobilization of Christian conservatives, California's public policy has not become significantly more conservative on the issues of gay rights and abortion. In each of the last three legislative sessions, bills have been passed and signed into law with the support of gay-rights organizations and despite the opposition of conservative Christian groups. In 2001, for example, the legislature passed two bills on hate violence that encourage teachers, administrators, and students to appreciate and respect diversity (Ellis 2000). Governor Davis also signed a bill in 2001 that gave new rights to domestic partners. The law allows couples registered in a domestic partnership to make medical decisions for each other, to sue for wrongful death, to adopt a partner's child, and to use sick leave to care for an incapacitated partner (*San Francisco Chronicle* 2001). In addition, public attitudes have become more liberal on gay and lesbian rights in the past twenty years. Public support for gay marriage, for example, rose from 28 percent to 38 percent between 1977 and 1997, while support for child-custody rights for gays and lesbians increased from 50 percent to 69 percent over the same period.

Nor has the Christian Right been able to have much of an impact on abortion policy at the state level. At present, California has among the most liberal abortion policies in the union (Russo 1995). Public opinion polls do indicate that support for abortion has declined slightly in the past decade, but the public consensus on abortion is so strong that the issue has not been particularly important in state politics over the past twenty years. John Fugatt, executive director of the Christian Coalition of California, admitted as much in an interview with the first author when he noted: "We have no control over the abortion issue; it has been settled for some time now" (Fugatt 2001).

Prospects for the Future of the Christian Right in California

If the past is a prelude to the future, the Christian Right is almost certain to see its social and political influence in California wane in the decades ahead. The reasons are fairly clear. First, the structural weaknesses of the state Republican Party will limit the political impact of any movement that is closely identified with the GOP. As we have argued in the pages above, the Christian Right in California is part and parcel of the state Republican Party. Conservative Christians have become an essential part of the party organization, the party in the electorate, and the party in government. It is possible that the state GOP, in order to become more competitive in a state that is liberal on traditional social values, will try to abandon its ties to the Christian Right. There certainly have been candidates for statewide office who have done just that, though with little positive electoral success. A "clean break" between the GOP and the Christian Right, however, is not likely to happen in the immediate future. Conservative Christians remain a vital party of the state GOP; while dwindling as a percentage of the electorate, white conservative Christians provide considerable resources for the party and its candidates. In 1994 Christian Right voters represented one-quarter of all GOP votes; by 2000 the proportion fell, but only to 22 percent. The constituency of the Christian Right is still too important for the GOP simply to ignore. Having a place at the party table, however, might well prove to be a pyrrhic victory for the Christian Right. It will likely take decades for the Republican Party to crawl out of the hole that it has constructed for itself over the past ten years.

A second problem for the Christian Right is that the core support for the movement has historically come from white evangelical Protestants. The Christian Right has been unable to expand its support among ethnic minorities, but such a cross-ethnic movement is now essential for the movement's future in California. The most notable demographic feature of California in recent decades has been the rapid growth of Latinos and Asians and the decline of Anglos as a percentage of the state's population. California is now a "majority minority state." After the 2000 census, whites made up 47 percent of the state population, Latinos 32 percent, Asians 11 percent, and African Americans 7 percent. Additionally, the minority electorate, particularly among Latinos, has expanded rapidly in the past several decades. While Latinos have historically lagged well behind non-Hispanic whites in voter participation, that situation is slowly changing. The state's demographics, in short, make it virtually impossible that a political movement of white evangelical Christians alone can have a dramatic political impact in California. The capacity of the Christian Right to succeed in the Golden State will be a function of the ability of movement leaders to increase support among Latino, Asian, and African American Christians.

Fortunately for the Christian Right, Latinos, Asians, and African Americans are more socially conservative as a whole than non-Hispanic whites, and they are more likely than non-Hispanic whites to identify with the Christian Right. In the 2000 election, for example, exit polls indicate that 31 percent of Latinos, 23 percent of African Americans, and 17 percent of Asians considered themselves part of the "conservative Christian political movement." Only 13 percent of white voters, by comparison, identified themselves in this way. In that election, Hispanics represented one-quarter (25.5 percent) of all those who identified with the religious right, one in ten (10.2 percent) was African American, and 5.1 percent were Asians. There is, in other words, a Christian conservative constituency in California; it is just increasingly found outside the white, evangelical Protestant world that has historically propelled the Christian Right political movement.

On its surface, a political movement by the Christian Right that crosses ethnic lines seems highly unlikely. For the past several decades the Christian Right has worked hard to increase its presence within the state Republican Party, but that affiliation limits the movement's capacity to mobilize Latinos and African Americans, who vote overwhelmingly Democratic, and Asians, who are slightly more Democratic than Republican. The creation of a new kind of Christian Right that might mobilize Latino, Asian, and African American evangelicals would likely require a new leadership cadre that is not as bound to the GOP or as narrowly focused on the social issues of abortion and gay rights. One first-generation Salvadoran American the second author interviewed at a Pentecostal-oriented, Spanish-speaking church in Los Angeles explained that he had voted for Governor Gray Davis so as not to reward the Republicans for their dirty methods of electioneering. The U.S. resident of twenty years also preferred many of Davis's policies, such as his stand on bilingual education. Though this Latino Pentecostal was not dead-set against voting for a Republican candidate in the future (and actually was fond of Ronald Reagan), he did not see himself supporting the GOP unless they adopted "more just" positions on immigration and welfare reform. Given the extent to which the state's Republicans and the Christian Right have shown themselves hostile to immigrants and welfare recipients, however, such a "kinder, gentler" GOP is not likely to appear anytime soon. For at least the medium term, then, California's Latinos and African Americans are likely to remain solidly in the Democratic fold, despite their socially conservative views.

California will, on the other hand, continue to provide opportunities for any movement that can muster support at the local level. Because the state's institutional structures are porous and open to the mobilization of committed activists, there will always be a place in California politics for a social movement, like that of the Christian Right, that can effectively organize group members for political activism. What remains to be seen is whether a new kind of Christian Right can emerge that will cross ethnic lines in order to take advantage of those institutional openings. Without this attempt to bridge the ethnic divide among evangelical Protestants, any future political movement among evangelical Christians will be limited in impact.

NOTE

1. It is notoriously difficult to design a questionnaire that accurately measures the degree to which one is a member of the Religious Right. The Field Poll defined respondents as religious if they answered positively to one of two questions: (1) whether they had had a born-again" experience, or (2) whether they described religion as being "very important" to them in their own personal lives. The poll then overlaid self-reported political ideology onto this typology, creating three segments of the California public. The religious right were those who were both religious and politically conservative. Religious moderates were those who were religious but who generally consider themselves middle-of-the-road or moderate in politics. Secularists were those who did not qualify as religious according to the Field Poll's definition. One weakness of the poll is that it does not include race as a measurement for identifying members of the religious right. The problem is that many African Americans and Latinos identify themselves as religiously and politically conservative, yet studies of the Christian Right have indicated that as a political movement, the Christian Right is overwhelmingly white. It would be wrong to suggest, therefore, that the religious right represents 21 percent of California's population. A second weakness of the study is that it does not indicate what it means for a person to describe himself or herself as politically conservative, moderate, or liberal.

REFERENCES

Aldrich, John H., and Forrest D. Nelson. 1984. *Linear Probability, Logit, and Probit Models.* Newbury Park, Calif.: Sage.
Allswang, John M. 2000. *The Initiative and Referendum in California, 1898–1998.* Stanford, Calif.: Stanford University Press.
Bailey, Eric, and Peter M. Warren. 1998. "Power PAC Steps out of Spotlight." *Los Angeles Times* (15 June), A3.
Barabak, Mark A. 2001. "State Republicans Search for Beacon amid Gloom." *Los Angeles Times* (2 February), A1.

Bathen, Sigrid. 1998. "The Politics of Abortion." *California Journal* (April): 22–23.

Block, A. G. 1998. "The Wilson Legacy." *California Journal* (November):6–10.

Brinkheroff, Noel. 2001. "GOP Identity Crisis." *California Journal* (June):22–27.

California Opinion Index. 1993. "Religion and Politics" (September).

———. 1997. "Gay and Lesbian Rights Issues" (May).

California Republican Party. 2001. California Republican Party 2000–2003 Platform. www.cagop.org/resources/platform.

California Voter Foundation. 2001. www.calvoter.org.

Cannon, Lou. 1998. "The California GOP: A House Divided." *California Journal* (November):18–21.

———. 2002. "Reagan Rerun?" *California Journal* (April):18–21.

Cannon, Lou, and A. G. Block. 2001. "Can the Grand Old Party Survive?" *California Journal* (February): 30–37.

Conger, Kimberly H., and John C. Green. 2002. "Spreading Out and Digging In: Christian Conservatives and State Republican Parties." *Campaigns and Elections* (February):58–64.

Decker, Cathleen. 2000. "Shift Toward the Left Takes Firm Hold." *Los Angeles Times* (8 November), A1.

Dionne, E. J. 1998. "Internal Strife Hurts GOP Chances." *Denver Post* (24 March), B1.

Dunlap, David W. 1994. "Minister Stresses Anti-Gay Message." *New York Times* (19 December), A8.

Elazar, Daniel J. 1972. *American Federalism: A View from the States.* 2d ed. New York: Thomas Y. Crowell.

Ellis, John. 2000. "Group Opposes Bills as Pro-Homosexual." *Fresno Bee* (14 September), B2.

Fetzer, Joel and Christopher J. Soper. 1997. "California: Between a Rock and a Hard Place." Pp. 135–52 in *God at the Grass Roots: The Christian Right in the 1996 Elections,* ed. Mark J. Rozell and Clyde Wilcox. Lanham, Md.: Rowman and Littlefield.

Field Poll. 1997. "Majority of Voters Continue to Approve of Abortion During 1st Trimester" (March 1997).

———. 2000. "The Expanding Latino Electorate: California's New Latino Voters Differ from Their Predecessors in Many Ways" (May 2000).

Fugatt, John. 2001. Personal Interview with J. Christopher Soper, Long Beach, California, 15 August.

Gerston, Larry N., and Terry Christenson. 1995. *California Politics and Government.* Belmont, Calif.: Wadsworth.

Gilbert, Christopher P. 1993. *The Impact of Churches on Political Behavior.* Westport, Conn.: Greenwood Press.

Green, John C. 2000. "The Christian Right and the 1998 Elections: An Overview." Pp. 1–19 in *Prayers in the Precinct: The Christian Right in the*

1998 Elections, ed. John C. Green, Mark J. Rozell, and Clyde Wilcox. Washington, D.C.: Georgetown University Press.

Hyink, Bernard L., and David H. Provost. 1998. *Politics and Government in California*. Menlo Park, Calif.: Longman.

Kosmin, Barry A. and Seymour P. Lachman. 1993. *One Nation under God: Religion in Contemporary American Society*. New York: Crown Trade Paperbacks.

Los Angeles Times Poll. 2000. "Study #449/Exit Poll. General Election: Nation and California, November 7, 2000." www.latimes.com/extras/timespoll.

Lucas, Greg. 2001. "More State Voters than Ever, and More Without Party." *San Francisco Chronicle* (5 May), A3.

Mayhew, David. 1986. *Placing Parties in American Politics*. Princeton, N.J.: Princeton University Press.

McGirr, Lisa. 2001. *Suburban Warriors: The Origins of the New American Right*. Princeton, N.J.: Princeton University Press.

Meyerson, Harold. 2001. "California's Progressive Mosaic." *The American Prospect* (18 June):17–23.

Morain, Dan, and Carl Ingram. 1995. "Hurtt's Spending Equals His Bold Conservative Agenda." *Los Angeles Times* (24 November), A1.

Nollinger, Mark. 1993. "The New Crusaders—The Christian Right Storms California's Political Bastions." *California Journal* (January):6–11.

Persinos, John C. 1994. "Has the Christian Right Taken Over the Republican Party?" *Campaigns and Elections* 15 (September):20–24.

Peterson, Larry. 1991. "The Dannemeyer-Seymour Race: Do Republicans Face an Unpalatable Choice?" *California Journal* (January):30–34.

Rojas, Aurelio. 2000. "Proposition 38 Pitch in High Gear: Draper in Uphill Push for School Vouchers." *Sacramento Bee* (October 10).

Russo, Michael A. 1995. "California: A Political Landscape for Choice and Conflict." Pp. 168–81 in *Abortion Politics in American States*, Mary C. Segers and Timothy A. Byrnes. Armonk, N.Y.: M.E. Sharpe.

San Francisco Chronicle. 2001. "We've Come a Long Way." 16 October, A16.

Schupparra, Kurt. 1998. *Triumph of the Right: The Rise of the California Conservative Movement, 1945–1966*. Armonk, N.Y.: M.E. Sharpe.

Skelton, George. 2000. "State Republicans Find Waking Up Is Hard to Do." *Los Angeles Times* (13 November), A3.

Soper, J. Christopher. 1995. "California: Christian Conservative Influence in a Liberal State." Pp. 211–26 in *God at the Grass Roots: The Christian Right in the 1994 Elections*, ed. Mark J. Rozell and Clyde Wilcox. Lanham, Md.: Rowman and Littlefield.

Wildermuth, John. 2001. "Moderates Rebuffed in Bid to Lead State GOP." *San Francisco Chronicle* (26 February), A1.

ELEVEN

The Christian Right in the Northwest: Two Decades of Frustration in Oregon and Washington

William M. Lunch

Sɪɴᴄᴇ 1980, ᴛʜᴇ Nᴏʀᴛʜᴡᴇsᴛ ʜᴀs ᴇxᴘᴇʀɪᴇɴᴄᴇᴅ sᴜʙsᴛᴀɴᴛɪᴀʟ economic, cultural, and political change. The region has been affected by the decline of traditional natural resource industries, such as agriculture, timber, and fishing, and the simultaneous rise of an information-based economy. High-tech industry leaders such as Microsoft and Intel grew rapidly to become major employers even as traditional industries—particularly timber and agriculture—suffered a series of setbacks, displacing many workers from familiar rural roots[1] (Warner 1997; Balmer and Lunch 1995). Overall, the region has been strengthened economically and has grown dynamically in population, but for some, the changes have been profoundly unwelcome.

Christian Right activists in the Northwest have reacted against these social, economic, and cultural changes, reinforcing a pattern of opposition that dates back to the 1960s. Indeed, Christian conservatives experienced a painful, almost daily awareness of their marginalization in the new social order. Since the mid-1980s, intense controversies over "social control" issues—from abortion to gay rights to assisted suicide— have been at the center of this reaction. These debates have been especially evident in a series of initiative campaigns in Oregon and in contests for public office in Washington. Most of the initiatives supported by the Christian Right have been rejected, and few of the candidates it backed have prevailed. Indeed, the Christian Right has suffered two decades of almost continuous frustration in both states.[2]

WASHINGTON AND OREGON:
REGIONAL POLITICAL CONVERGENCE

Half a century ago, Washington was one of the most Democratic states and Oregon was solidly Republican, but the two states have slowly converged politically, so that now they are often portrayed in national profiles as innovative political twins, at the edge of the United States both geographically and culturally. Barone and Ujifusa (1999,1323) described Oregon as "an experimental commonwealth and laboratory of reform on the Pacific Rim. . . . Oregon has led the nation with bike trails and Nike sneakers, light rail trams and Pendleton shirts, with assisted suicide and mail-in ballots. . . ." In the same volume, they described Washington: "From Starbucks coffee to grunge music, from America's leading exporter Boeing to America's leading software maker Microsoft, Washington . . . became a national trend setter in the 1990s" (1667). The states may have become political siblings, but are fraternal rather than identical twins.

A good illustration of this convergence is the presidential vote. Both states went Republican in the 1984 Reagan landslide, but then both went Democratic in the next four elections. In 1988, Oregon and Washington backed Michael Dukakis by slim margins and then gave Bill Clinton solid support in 1992 and 1996. Al Gore won both states in 2000: Oregon was a very close contest, Washington somewhat less so. Minor party candidates were a major factor during this period. In both states, Ross Perot won nearly one-quarter of the vote in 1992 and more than one-eighth in 1996. Ralph Nader and the Green Party hurt Gore in 2000. These trends have both encouraged Christian Right activism and thwarted its aspirations.

These patterns illustrate the weakness of traditional politics in the Northwest, reflecting the legacy of the Progressive Era (Mayhew 1986, 188–91). Political parties are weak and open to outside pressure; candidates are chosen in open primaries, and in the case of Washington, a "blanket" primary (where all candidates for either party appear on the same ballot); it is relatively easy to qualify ballot initiatives (especially in Oregon); and ballot access for independent and minor party candidates is relatively easy as well. All these features have influenced the Christian Right's strategy and tactics.

This political convergence arises from notable parallels in the development of Oregon and Washington. In each, there is a dominant metropolis—Seattle in Washington, Portland in Oregon—where an increasingly knowledge-based economy has been vibrant, the population has grown rapidly, growth has been concentrated among the relatively young, and voters are now heavily Democratic. In rural areas with natural resource–based economies and aging populations the Republicans have surged. These trends are strongest east of the Cascade Mountains, where, at most, one-quarter of the regional population resides. It is in these places that the Christian Right has its greatest strength.

There are political buffers between the cities and the countryside, particularly in the suburbs. In Washington, the key suburbs fan out around Seattle, including Redmond (headquarters of Microsoft), Everett, Bellevue, and Bainbridge Island. The Puget Sound area (including the Seattle suburbs, Tacoma, and the state capital in Olympia) leans Democratic, but not as much or as consistently as the central city. In Oregon, the key suburbs are south and west of Portland in Clackamas and Washington Counties (such as Beaverton, where Nike is based). The Willamette Valley, often politically divided, stretches south from Portland to Eugene, just over a hundred miles away. So in close state elections, the Seattle and Portland suburbs and the "buffer zones" in the Puget Sound and Willamette Valley are usually the keys to victory. These voters tend to be conservative on economics but liberal on social control.

The Pacific Northwest states are among the most secular in the nation, as measured by surveys on church attendance and strength of religious attachment (O'Keefe 1996). A recent national survey shows Oregon with 29 percent of state residents categorized as "secular," that is, without religious affiliation (including those who refused to answer questions about their religion); Washington was very similar, at 31 percent. A broad measure of evangelical Protestants found 29 percent in Oregon and 22 percent in Washington. However, the core political support for the Christian Right has been considerably lower, 12 percent to 15 percent in both states. Other religious groups are smaller. Mainline Protestants made up a little more than one-sixth of both states. Catholics were slightly less numerous than mainliners in Oregon and slightly more common in Washington. The Northwest has few racial, ethnic, or religious minorities, although the Latter Day Saints (Mormons) have a presence.[3]

Christian conservatives are very aware of the pluralistic and secular character of the region. In interviews, religious conservative activists often complain about indifference, if not active hostility, of neighbors and coworkers to religious expression and practices. Thus, it is ironic that Northwest politics are dominated by a moralistic political culture with deep historic roots.

Oregon and, to a lesser extent, Washington have been characterized by Elazar (1972) as having a "moralistic" political culture. However, this insightful observation does not tell us *which* policies or values moralists favor. In these states a new definition of political involvement for "moral" reasons has evolved. Three positions on moralism are important in the Northwest: the *new moralists*, the *old moralists*, and the *libertarians*.

The old and new moralists agree that shared values should be influential in the lives of citizens and that such values, enforced by the state, should establish rules and standards for all. But they differ intensely over what those values should be, and thus over the content of public policy. The libertarians, by contrast, reflect a contrasting individualistic conception, present in much western political history and culture, but a minority theme in these states.

Social control policy lies at the heart of the differences between the new and old moralists (see Lunch 1995 for a fuller discussion of social control questions). Such questions concern how much government should intervene to restrict individual behavior deemed threatening to society, limit relationships, and enforce conformity with conventional standards. All governments impose at least some social controls, but the intensity and direction vary. Some social controls apply to everyone—black or white, male or female. Even on a sunny summer day, public nudity is illegal. But many social controls are enforced disproportionately against traditionally subordinate groups, such as African Americans, women, or gays and lesbians.

The ideas of the new moralists, who historically dominated Oregon's political and cultural life, evolved during the postwar era. For many, change began by observing the horrors of World War II, particularly the Holocaust in Europe, guilt over the wartime incarceration of Japanese Americans, and the use of atomic weapons against Japan. These concerns slowly led to support for the civil rights movement among many new moralists, and the environmental and feminist movements later influenced their evolving conception of morality. As a result, they championed the loosening of many traditional social controls and redirected social control policy in other directions.

Well-connected moderate Republicans such as Oregon governors Charles Sprague and Tom McCall, Oregon senator Mark Hatfield, and Washington governor and senator Dan Evans were examples of this new moralism (McKay 1999; Walth 1994; White 1982). Contemporary new moralists tend to be Democrats, including governors John Kitzhaber (D-Ore.) and Gary Locke (D-Wash.) and senators Ron Wyden (D-Ore.) and Maria Cantwell (D-Wash.).

The most prominent adversaries of the new moralists are the old moralists, of which the Christian Right is a prominent example. The old moralists reject the relaxed social control the new moralists welcome, being nostalgic for an earlier time when traditional authority was more widely accepted (Luker 1984; FitzGerald 1986; Coontz 1992). They oppose feminism, affirmative action, legal contraception and abortion, outlooks and policies in which social control has been abandoned or weakened since the 1960s. They particularly oppose policies contributing to changes in the status of women and relaxation of controls over homosexuals (Herman 1997; Kohut 1994). Leaders accept formal equality for racial minorities, but followers often quite openly reject civil rights policies (Lunch 1995).

Many Northwest politicians and group leaders—including antitax activist Bill Sizemore, the 1998 Republican gubernatorial nominee in Oregon—are associated with the old moralist position. In Washington, former U.S. Representative and Senate candidate Linda Smith, and Ellen Craswell, a former state senator and the 1996 Republican nominee for governor, are old moralists.

Libertarians oppose most social controls, just as they do government intervention in the economy, so the Libertarian Party has opposed both public education and laws against drug use. Such strict ideology puts off most voters, but under a more relaxed definition, former senator Bob Packwood might be counted as something of a libertarian. Libertarian views are important to suburban swing voters.

CHRISTIAN RIGHT ORGANIZATIONS
IN THE NORTHWEST

The Christian Right developed special organizations in the Northwest. The Oregon Citizens Alliance (OCA) was organized first, and it encouraged the creation of the Washington Citizens Alliance (WCA) and Idaho Citizens Alliance (ICA). In part because of these groups, other movement organizations arrived later in the Northwest than elsewhere. For example, the Christian Coalition became prominent in Oregon and Washington in the late 1990s, gaining strength as the OCA declined.

During the 1980s and 1990s, groups opposed to legal abortion (and most legal contraception) were active in both Northwest states. Oregon Right to Life was particularly involved, sponsoring an antiabortion initiative in 1990, for example. These organizations were regular allies of the Christian Right.

The Oregon Christian Right

Prior to 1986, the most visible Christian conservative in Oregon was Walter Huss, a fundamentalist minister. In the early 1960s, he published a newspaper described by the *Washington Post* as "both anti-Semitic and anti-black" (Cannon 1978). In 1966, Huss ran against Mark Hatfield for the GOP U.S. Senate nomination, and in 1982 against incumbent governor Vic Atiyeh. He lost both contests overwhelmingly, and in the late 1970s was briefly chairman of the state GOP. In 1990, Huss tried but failed to reverse designation of a major Portland street for Dr. Martin Luther King, Jr.

Huss was an example of the alienation of old moralists from the new moralist moderates, such as Senator Hatfield, who then dominated the state GOP. Such moderation was essential to political success in the state, but it frustrated more conservative Republicans. In 1980, the conservatives found a champion in Congressman Denny Smith, a wealthy former fighter pilot initially elected in an upset in 1980 in a huge congressional district in eastern Oregon. After a new seat was created in 1982, Smith chose to run west of the mountains in the marginal Fifth District in the Willamette Valley. Though he focused mainly on military issues, he was a social conservative, and he encouraged Christian Right political involvement to counter peace and civil rights activists on the left (Barone and Ujifusa 1983).

In 1986, a Baptist minister, Joe Lutz, was recruited to run against Senator Bob Packwood in the GOP Senate primary because of the senator's prochoice position. Lutz exceeded expectations with 42 percent of the vote in a low turnout primary. He and his key supporters believed he—and the Christian Right—had a political future, and he organized the OCA to seek it.[4] Lutz soon developed marital problems that proved fatal to his political aspirations. Lon Mabon, a Vietnam vet who had been something of a hippie until he was converted to fundamentalist Protestant faith, replaced him. Mabon was an effective leader, communicating to potential supporters in church through their ministers. In contrast to the largely personal efforts by Huss, Mabon and his allies institutionalized the OCA and sustained political activity over seven elections, albeit with increasing difficulty in the later years.

Mark J. Rozell and Clyde Wilcox (1997) have emphasized that mobilizing adversaries has been one of the central problems for the Christian Right. By 1994, the OCA had mobilized strong adversaries. Opponents assembled an organization called Basic Rights Oregon (BRO) to oppose Measure Nine, a 1992 initiative sponsored by the OCA to deny civil rights protection to gays and lesbians. BRO was initially organized in the gay and lesbian communities, but with major support from civil libertarians. One consequence was that by 1996, BRO and a related organization called the Rural Organizing Project (ROP) had more members than the OCA and far superior financing.

By 1996, organizational woes were mounting for the OCA. Anti-homosexual initiatives had qualified for the ballot in 1992 and 1994 but were defeated. Mabon began circulating petitions for a third attempt in 1996, but the OCA itself now was rife with internal divisions. A number of former OCA activists broke with Mabon, among them Marilyn Shannon, a state senator initially appointed to her post with OCA support. Shannon quoted Mabon, "I get the message and if [legislators] want to know how to vote, they should ask me," implying that he was divinely inspired (Sarasohn 1996). A key strength of the OCA had been very loyal volunteer petition signature circulators, but many of them abandoned the OCA to gather signatures for other conservative groups, in part because of the organizational disarray.

In 1996, the U.S. Supreme Court declared an anti–gay-rights amendment passed in Colorado to be unconstitutional in *Romer v. Evans* (Herman 1997; see chapter 9). Signatures for the third OCA measure, which had been slow in coming, all but dried up. In July—the deadline for initiative petitions in Oregon—Mabon had so few signatures he did not bother submitting those he had collected. Similarly, in 1998, the OCA did not gather enough signatures to qualify any of the initiatives it was sponsoring. There was talk in political circles that the organization would disappear, but that proved premature. In 2000, Mabon managed to qualify another anti-gay/ lesbian initiative by making common cause with an organizational rival, the Oregon Christian Coalition. However, this measure failed as well.

Most recently, an old court judgment has plagued the OCA. In 1992, a gay-rights activist was injured when physically ejected from an OCA meeting by one of Mabon's aides. She sued and won judgments, against both the aide and the OCA. The aide eventually settled, but Mabon refused to do so, claiming the OCA did not have the money. In

2002, a judge ordered Mabon to submit financial records to examination, but he refused. The judge then ordered Mabon jailed for contempt of court (Hogan 2002). He served time for a number of weeks before finally agreeing to the examination.

The Washington Christian Right

A state chapter of the Moral Majority appeared in Washington shortly after the organization began in 1979, led by a young attorney, Michael Farris, who eventually ran for the lieutenant governor of Virginia (see chapter 2) (Rozell 2001). This chapter was reported to have been the largest Moral Majority affiliate in the nation. But like its counterparts elsewhere, the Washington Moral Majority was in decline by the mid-1980s, and Farris ultimately broke from the national group and reconstituted his state affiliate under a different name.

Christian Right activity was more effectively mobilized by the 1988 presidential candidacy of Pat Robertson. Movement activists organized at the precinct level because Washington selected party convention delegates using the caucus system. Despite their importance, the caucuses attract very few participants—usually no more than 3 percent of those eligible—but those who appear select delegates to successive meetings, culminating in the state party convention, where national party delegates are chosen. Activists pledged to Robertson appeared in large numbers and dominated the 1988 GOP caucuses. A visibly confrontational state party convention resulted at which moderate Republicans were vilified (Strinkowski 1997). Subsequent movement mobilization seemed to emerge from links established during the Robertson campaign rather than from organizational connections through the Christian Coalition, which appeared in the early 1990s.

In 1992, the Washington state party convention was again a scene of confrontations between moderate party leaders and the Christian Right; the latter largely prevailed. Old moralists were still angry over their defeat by prochoice forces in an initiative campaign in 1991. They blamed their loss on the new moralist moderates. Denunciations of the moderates flowed from the podium like spring rain down the Columbia River. The state party platform was rewritten in hyperbolic language, attracting attention even from local television news—it denounced witchcraft (Appleton and Francis 1997).

In Washington in 1994, an organization cloned from the OCA, the Washington Citizens Alliance (WCA), tried to qualify an anti–gay/

lesbian initiative for the ballot but failed. Washington requires a higher signature qualification threshold for initiatives than Oregon does, and the WCA never attracted as many activists as the OCA, perhaps because the Christian Coalition was gaining strength. Moreover, an organization parallel to BRO called Hands Off Washington (HOW) worked to prevent anti–gay/lesbian measures from appearing on the ballot.

CHRISTIAN RIGHT POLITICAL ACTIVITY IN THE NORTHWEST

Political parties are weak in the Northwest, a fact that has allowed Christian Right activists to periodically take control of state party organizations (Oldfield 1996). John Persinos (1994) described this pattern of substantial Christian Right influence in the formal party structures in Oregon and Washington in 1994; his work has been updated by a recent study by Kimberly Conger and John Green (2002). In Oregon, surveys show the Christian Right to have strong party influence, but in Washington, religious conservative influence declined between 1994 and 2002. However, in Oregon, the parties are largely devoid of power, and in Washington, they are only marginally more influential. Thus Christian Right activity has often focused on particular candidates.

One of the key reasons the Christian Right has been so visible in the Northwest has been relatively easy access to the ballot, available through the initiative and referendum—and sometimes legislative referrals (Cronin 1989; Ellis 2002). In recent years, many of the most significant public decisions in the Northwest have been made in the initiative process. Although ballot issues are less common north of the Columbia River, they are important to the politics of both states. Many Christian Right measures have qualified for the ballot, particularly in Oregon. State legislators have taken few of these initiatives seriously, but they appealed to the resentment and fears generated by social, economic, and cultural change.

Candidates in Oregon

The Christian Right in Oregon has supported a number of Republican candidates for office in the past two decades. None closely associated with the movement have prevailed in statewide elections, though some legislative candidates have won. This record of failure started in 1986, when Joe Lutz challenged Bob Packwood in the GOP Senate primary, the campaign that led to the creation of the OCA.

In 1990, the nomination of the prochoice Republican Attorney General Dave Frohnmayer for governor offended the OCA. On social control issues, Frohnmayer was, if anything, a liberal. In a meeting with OCA leaders, Frohnmayer refused to change his positions on abortion, gay rights, or related issues and—perhaps most critically—refused to contribute to the OCA, though his campaign treasury was very full. Mabon, furious, recruited a spoiler gubernatorial candidate named Al Mobley. In November, Mobley took 13 percent of the vote, virtually all of which would have gone to Frohnmayer otherwise. The result was victory for Barbara Roberts, very much a liberal Democrat, who won with 46 percent of the vote.

In 1992, Mabon struck a deal with Bob Packwood, despite repeated threats to run a spoiler against him too. Instead, Mabon quietly accepted contributions at a number of dinners featuring out-of-state GOP senators, funds that were used to mount an initiative campaign (Mapes 1992).

In 1994, the Republican Party enjoyed its best year in half a century. It was, as later became clear, also the high-water mark for the Christian Right in the region. In Oregon, the GOP took control of the state senate for the first time in forty years, won the open Fifth Congressional District with Jim Bunn; kept control in the huge, rural Second District with Wes Cooley; and came very close to winning the suburban-dominated First District near Portland with Bill Witt (Barone and Ujifusa 1995). All these candidates had Christian Right connections (Witt was the founder of the Oregon Christian Coalition).

In 1995, the political season opened earlier than expected, with the resignation of Senator Bob Packwood in September. A special mail-ballot election to fill the remaining years of Packwood's term was conducted in the winter of 1995–96. The winner of the GOP primary was state senator Gordon Smith, a wealthy, conservative Mormon businessman endorsed by the OCA. Smith was widely expected to win the general election but was upset in January 1996, losing by a narrow margin to Democratic Congressman Ron Wyden.

Exit polling showed the key swing voters were suburban Republican and independent women, who defected to Wyden in higher than usual proportions. Smith was seen as antienvironmental and hostile to the aspirations of women. Because the OCA has an image among most voters as malicious and extreme, its endorsement proved damaging to Smith. Smith's campaign manager argued "the OCA's support of Gordon tended to eclipse . . . Gordon's views and record on issues of conscience" (Sarasohn 1996; Schneider 1996).

Soon thereafter, Mark Hatfield chose to retire from the Senate. Hatfield retired, in part, because he would have faced a difficult primary. Bill Witt, a Christian Right leader who had nearly won a congressional seat in 1994, issued a challenge. Hatfield took Witt's challenge seriously. Even though Hatfield, a Baptist, was one of the most religious members of the U.S. Senate, he had become a target for the Christian Right. For public consumption, Witt attacked Hatfield's 1995 vote against the balanced budget amendment to the Constitution, but in both religion and politics Hatfield's ecumenical approach offended much of the Christian Right. Witt ultimately opted out of the Senate race and instead ran again in the First District in 1996, losing by a larger margin.

After Hatfield announced his retirement, Gordon Smith agreed to run again for the Senate but this time announced that he would not accept the OCA endorsement. Mabon was furious and just before the deadline filed to run against Smith in the primary. He may have calculated that his candidacy would attract donors for the OCA, which was then suffering from financial woes. But Mabon's candidacy was an unexpected gift for Smith. It allowed him to largely erase the stain of his former endorsement by the unpopular OCA. The primary against Mabon was offered as proof of his relative moderation, even though his positions on social control issues were considerably to the right of Hatfield or any of the Oregon GOP moderates (Green 1996; Berke 1997).

Smith won the primary easily with more than 75 percent of the vote. Mabon was humiliated, receiving 8 percent of the vote, only marginally ahead of a nuisance candidate who ran in a clown suit. In November, in his second contest for the U.S. Senate in less than a year, Smith repackaged himself as a moderate, narrowly defeating Tom Bruggere, a Democratic high-tech millionaire with almost no political experience (Esteve 1996).

Neither of the Republican freshmen from Oregon elected in 1994 returned to Congress after the 1996 elections. Wes Cooley, from the Second District, was found to have made false claims about his military service; GOP leaders pressured him to resign as a candidate. He was replaced by former congressman Bob Smith, a popular conservative but without ties to the Christian Right. In the Fifth District, Jim Bunn had won in 1994 as a cultural conservative with OCA support, but soon after his victory he divorced his wife and married his young chief of staff. In 1996 the Democrats nominated a strong candidate, and Bunn lost (Barone and Ujifusa 1997).

In 1998, one of the Christian Right's most visible supporters, Bill Sizemore, was the Republican candidate for governor. Sizemore had achieved a level of public prominence as the director of an antitax group called Oregon Taxpayers United (OTU), which institutionalized a coalition of economic conservatives, libertarians, and old moralists. They had sponsored a property tax limit initiative in 1990—Measure Five—which cut local property taxes roughly in half. Sizemore, a Christian conservative, did not start at OTU until 1994 but was deeply involved in 1996 in another antitax initiative, Measure Forty-Seven, which cut property taxes another 10 percent and capped any increases at levels below inflation. In the legislative session in 1997, Sizemore was given extraordinary influence as Measure Forty-Seven was being rewritten to meet constitutional requirements. The revision, known as Measure Fifty, was sent to voters in a special election in spring 1997 and passed.

In 1996, Sizemore had also sponsored a state referendum to reject a transportation package including substantial sums for extension of the light rail system in Portland. Senator Mark Hatfield had secured over $300 million in federal funds, but the required state matching funds were rejected as many rural Oregonians—including many Christian Right supporters—took pleasure in taking a blow at the city. Given that success, Sizemore decided to challenge the popular incumbent governor, John Kitzhaber.

Because of Kitzhaber's popularity, Republicans with more conventional political credentials passed on the race, leaving the GOP nomination to Sizemore. But even before the primary, the *Oregonian* published a series of articles revealing that before becoming a political entrepreneur and initiative sponsor, Sizemore had run two businesses into bankruptcy, leaving huge debts (Baker and Walker 1998). Even before those revelations, Sizemore trailed Kitzhaber badly in the polls; but the *Oregonian* stories made it all but impossible for Sizemore to appeal even to many Republicans. In November, Kitzhaber rolled to victory by a huge margin, winning 64 percent of the vote to 30 percent for Sizemore.

The two most visible Republican candidate statewide contests in 2000 were for secretary of state and attorney general, and both GOP candidates had strong ties to the Christian Right. The secretary of state is the second most important state office because Oregon does not have a lieutenant governor. The speaker of the state house, Lynn Snodgrass, a cultural conservative, won the GOP nomination. She and her allies had staged an intraparty coup and deposed a moderate Republican,

Lynn Lundquist, the speaker during the 1997 legislative session (Mapes 1998). Snodgrass presided over a very divided and ineffective legislative session in 1999. In 2000, she ran against Lundquist in the primary for secretary of state and beat him again. During the general election, she avoided drawing attention to divisive issues such as abortion and assisted suicide, but her reputation followed her. In November, she lost to the appointed incumbent, Democrat Bill Bradbury, who had been in office about a year.

For attorney general, Republicans nominated former state legislator Kevin Mannix. He ran for attorney general in 1996 as a Democrat but was unacceptable to party leaders in part because of his social positions, including opposition to legal abortion and assisted suicide. They recruited a former speaker of the house, Hardy Myers, who defeated Mannix in the primary and went on to win the general election. Soon thereafter, Mannix changed parties and obtained the 2000 GOP nomination for attorney general to face his old nemesis, Myers. Despite outspending the incumbent and running a series of aggressive TV ads, Mannix lost to Myers again.

Candidates in Washington

The Christian Right was even more deeply involved in elections in Washington. Although the movement enjoyed a brief success in the 1994 congressional elections, a destructive factionalism between the old and new moralists seriously harmed the Republicans before and after 1994. During the 1980s, Christian conservatives became increasingly unhappy with Washington's moderate Republican officeholders. This discontent exploded at the 1988 Republican state party convention, polarized by Pat Robertson's presidential campaign. Christian Right activists nominated a fundamentalist state representative, Bob Williams, for governor. In what would become a familiar pattern, Williams and his followers alienated moderate Republicans, particularly in the Puget Sound area. He lost the general election to the Democratic incumbent governor, receiving less than 40 percent of the vote (Strinkowski 1997; Barone and Ujifusa 1989).

There was a rare moment of Republican unity in 1994, and it produced a dramatic victory (Green, Rozell, and Wilcox 2001). There were no statewide contests to inflame the conflict between the new and old moralists, and the two factions worked together. The result was a wholesale reversal of party fortunes in the Washington congressional delegation, going from eight Democrats and one Republican to seven Republicans and two Democrats. Among those defeated was the Democratic Speaker of the House, Tom Foley (Barone and Ujifusa 1995). In addition, the GOP took control of the state house with a gain of twenty-eight seats.

A number of Christian conservatives were elected to the legislature, and three became new members of Congress. In the Third Congressional District, state senator Linda Smith, a militant, populist conservative with strong Christian Right credentials, won the Republican primary in a write-in campaign after an early favorite withdrew. Smith ran as an angry opponent of environmentalists, tapping into the anger of loggers and mill workers who were suffering from the decline in the timber industry. In the Ninth District, Randy Tate, a state legislator strongly associated with the Christian Right, ousted an incumbent Democrat in a close contest. And in the Fourth District, Doc Hastings, a staunch antiabortion Catholic, recaptured a Republican district that had gone narrowly Democratic in 1992.

In 1996 the Christian Right achieved a very high level of visibility in Washington but not success. The Democratic governor, Mike Lowry, did not run for reelection because of a sex scandal, so Republicans had plausible hopes to win. The GOP primary had four contenders; one was former state senator Ellen Craswell, a candidate with close ties to the Christian Right.

Craswell started her political career in 1976, when her husband, Bruce Craswell, declined to run for the state house in their Seattle suburban district. She ran as a traditional fiscal conservative and won, and was later elected to the state senate. Then the Craswells experienced a religious conversion, and Ellen became a visible, uncompromising representative of cultural conservatism. She sponsored a bill, for example, to castrate sex offenders (Appleton and Francis 1997). Although she lost her state senate seat in 1992, Craswell remained a visible figure on the right, thus entering the blanket gubernatorial primary with a strong base.

Many Christian Right activists walked precincts and contacted friends and neighbors for her. This "friends-and-neighbors" campaign, often conducted in church, could work in a relatively low-turnout primary (Guth et al. 1998). Craswell received just over 185,000 votes, first among the GOP candidates but only third overall, with 15 percent of the total. The two leading Democratic candidates, Gary Locke and Norm Sims, together received 41 percent of the vote and the loser, Sims, quickly closed ranks behind Locke. The losing Republican candidates were reluctant to endorse Craswell.

Craswell continued to focus on old moralist themes, to the obvious discomfort of many other Republicans. She attempted to again use the friends-and-neighbors campaign tactics that had worked in the primary, but the size of the general electorate was more than twice as large as in the primary in a state where relatively few voters are regulars at church. As expected, Craswell lost to Locke with 42 percent of the vote. The size of Craswell's defeat helped drag down some Republican legislative candidates, as women voters chose Locke by a two-to-one margin, and 23 percent of GOP voters defected (Strinkowski 1997; Appleton and Francis 1997).

In the Third Congressional District, Linda Smith survived in 1996, if just barely. Despite her customary defiant positions, she seemed popular, and the most prominent Democrats deferred to a little-known college professor, Brian Baird. But Smith had alienated many voters: on election day, she lost to Baird by 2,400 votes. She was rescued, however, by heavily Republican absentees and retained her seat by some 900 votes (Barone and Ujifusa 1997). Randy Tate was not so lucky: his Ninth District returned to its historic Democratic roots in a close contest. In 1997, Tate replaced Ralph Reed as national director of the Christian Coalition. One bright spot for the Christian Right was Doc Hastings's reelection in the solidly Republican Fourth District.

In 1998, Linda Smith aggressively pursued the Republican nomination for the U.S. Senate to run against incumbent Democrat Patty Murray in 1998. State party leaders believed they could win if they nominated a credible candidate, but the most potentially competitive Republicans declined to run. Smith never hesitated. She won the Republican nomination easily. In the general election, however, Smith's views on abortion, contraception, and the environment, plus her confrontational style, hurt her badly in and around Puget Sound. On election day she lost, running slightly behind Ellen Craswell's numbers two years earlier (Nelson 1998b).

After Craswell's loss in 1996, she and her husband, Bruce, left the GOP for the American Heritage Party, a far-right minor party. They briefly hoped there would be a mass exodus of religious conservatives out of the GOP, but the exodus did not materialize. However, in 1998 Bruce Craswell ran as the American Heritage Party candidate in the First Congressional District race to punish the incumbent Republican, Rick White. An economic conservative and a social moderate, White had also had a messy divorce that offended many Christian conservatives. Craswell attracted 6 percent of the vote in a close election, probably contributing to White's defeat (Nelson 1998b). The election was evocative of the OCA's spoiler candidacy in 1990 against Dave Frohnmayer—the Christian Right was again able to defeat a moderate Republican, but the result was a Democratic victory. Meanwhile, the Third District was open because of Linda Smith's senatorial bid. The GOP nominated a very conservative state senator, Don Benton, who had support from the Christian Right, and in the general election, the district returned to its Democratic roots, electing Brian Baird (Barone and Ujifusa 1999).

The 2000 elections continued the erosion of the 1994 Republican gains and revealed the continuing costs of the intraparty strife between the new and old moralists. The Republicans abandoned the pattern of nominating Christian Right figures for statewide office. For governor, they chose John Carlson, a radio talk-show host who had been a lead sponsor of Initiative 200, the 1998 anti–affirmative-action measure. Carlson was something of a libertarian, and though articulate, had no experience in public office. As in Oregon in 1998, there was a popular incumbent governor—Gary Locke—running for reelection in a time of political contentment, so the big names among Republicans passed on the race. For the Christian Right, Carlson was disappointing. For example, he said he opposed legal abortion but then shrugged and admitted that Washington is a prochoice state. Carlson's diffident brand of conservatism, compared with that of Craswell or Smith, turned off Christian Right volunteers. In November, Carlson lost with only 40 percent of the vote, an even worse showing than Craswell's in 1996 (Thomas 2000; Ramsey 2000).

The other major contest in Washington in 2000 was between GOP senator Slade Gorton and Democratic challenger Maria Cantwell. Gorton had served in the U.S. Senate for three terms. He had initially been elected in 1980, lost in 1986, returned in 1988, and won reelection in 1994. Regarded as a moderate, Gorton was never particularly close to the Christian Right. Indeed, he consistently opposed the Christian Right's positions regarding racial and ethnic minorities. The movement offered lukewarm support.

Maria Cantwell had served one term in the U.S. House, losing narrowly in the Republican sweep of 1994. She went to work for one of the high-tech firms in the Seattle area and became very wealthy. After winning the blanket primary among the Democrats, Cantwell spent some $10,000,000 of her own money in what developed as the closest U.S. Senate race in 2000. Gorton was ahead on election day, but there were hundreds of thousands of absentee ballots yet to be counted. It was weeks before the final result was announced, but in the end, Cantwell prevailed by just over 2,000 votes (Ammons 2000). Gorton's defeat created a fifty-fifty tie in the U.S. Senate in 2001.

Ballot Initiatives in Oregon

The Christian Right was especially active on ballot initiatives in Oregon, where it is relatively easy to qualify an issue. Ballot issues were the signature activity of OCA. In 1988, the OCA qualified an initiative to overturn civil rights protections for homosexuals in public employment, after Governor Neil Goldschmidt extended such protections by an executive order. The Oregon political establishment did not take the initiative—Measure Eight—seriously and so only a minor campaign was conducted against it. But to their surprise, Measure Eight passed with 53 percent of the vote. The state supreme court later overturned the law, but this victory signaled the OCA's potential.

In 1990, the OCA sponsored an initiative to outlaw abortion except in very rare cases. Had the U.S. Supreme Court overturned *Roe v. Wade* and returned control over abortion policy to the states, the OCA measure would have rewritten state law to make it much more restrictive than it was prior to *Roe v. Wade* (Craig and O'Brien 1993). The OCA initiative qualified as Measure Eight. At the same time, Oregon Right to Life qualified a parental notification initiative, Measure Ten. Swing voters were uneasy and conflicted but not prepared to ban abortion outright. Opponents were able to tie the two measures together and defeated both.

In 1992, the OCA shifted back to opposing gay rights. Mabon first made a quiet deal not to run a spoiler candidate against Bob Packwood in 1992, as he had threatened to do (Mapes 1992). In return, Republican officials organized a number of fund-raising dinners for the OCA, featuring out-of-state GOP senators. Next, OCA leaders qualified a sweeping initiative to deny legal and civil rights to homosexuals. It became Measure Nine on the 1992 ballot. It described homosexuality as "abnormal, wrong, unnatural and perverse" and compared it to pedophilia, sadism, and masochism. The entire state political and business establishment, along with mainstream clergy, joined with liberal activists to oppose Measure Nine. Oregon voters rejected it by a relatively modest margin of 56 percent to 44 percent.

Despite the loss, Measure Nine was an organizational success for the OCA. The campaign drew more than a million dollars in contributions, most of it from out of state. The debate over the measure dominated the state political agenda in 1992 and contributed to national attention given the Christian Right and the gay/lesbian community (Herman 1997; Gallagher and Bull 1996).

After the defeat in 1992, Mabon adopted a strategy to keep the OCA in the headlines—and keep contributions flowing—sponsoring a series of local anti–gay/lesbian initiatives. These were targeted in rural cities that had favored Measure Nine; Mabon was trying to build support for another initiative in 1994. Of sixteen local anti–gay/lesbian measures in 1993–94, fifteen passed (but in 1995 the state legislature overturned these local laws).

In 1994, the OCA qualified a revised version of Measure Nine, which became Measure Thirteen. It was stripped of much of the hyperbolic language but would have had almost identical consequences. Despite the Republican surge in 1994, Measure Thirteen was defeated—though the vote was closer than in 1992, 48 percent to 52 percent.

Meanwhile, in 1994, new moralists qualified a ballot issue of their own, an assisted suicide initiative. It proposed allowing some terminally ill patients to end their own lives under limited circumstances and was narrowly approved by Oregon voters, 51 percent to 49 percent. Similar measures had narrowly failed in Washington in 1991 and in California in 1992. Christian conservatives and the Catholic Church immediately challenged the assisted suicide law in court. A conservative Republican federal judge with a record of support for old moralist positions granted the plaintiffs an injunction to stop the new law from being implemented. He later ruled the law unconstitutional, and it went into legal limbo (Egan 1997). But in 1997, the Christian Right suffered one of its most embarrassing defeats when the Ninth Circuit Court of Appeals overturned the injunction that had prevented implementation of the assisted suicide law. It appeared that the U.S. Supreme Court would shortly resolve legal ambiguities concerning assisted suicide with a national standard, but in June, the Court left standing various state laws, allowing Oregon's experiment to proceed (Greenhouse 1997).

The Oregon legislature, controlled by Republicans, was meeting at the time; on this issue the majority caucuses were strongly influenced by their Christian Right members. In May and June, quite partisan votes returned the assisted suicide law to voters. In the state house, 88 percent of the votes for rereferral were from Republicans, and in the state senate, 90 percent were. The initiative became Measure Fifty-One in a special election[5] (Green 1997). Such a rereferral by the legislature was almost unique in state history.

The proposed repeal of the assisted suicide law pitted the old and new moralists against each other with clarity and intensity. There were only two measures on the ballot in the special election in 1997, and only Measure Fifty-One was controversial, so the campaign provided a good measure of the support the old moralists could achieve when allied with conservative Catholics. The opponents of the law, heavily financed by the Catholics and the Christian Right, spent more than $4,000,000, almost a record in a ballot measure campaign. New moralists, with temporary support from libertarians—organized as the "Don't Let 'Em Shove Their Religion Down Your Throat" Committee—spent almost a million dollars to oppose Measure Fifty-One. In November, voters strongly reaffirmed their support for the law, with 60 percent voting against repeal.

In 1998, the OCA failed to qualify a new version of its earlier anti–gay/lesbian initiative. This time Mabon circulated petitions for a proposal that would have defined "the family" narrowly, to include only heterosexual couples with children. It would have also banned same-sex marriages, but would have gone much further to prohibit public aid for any nontraditional family, including single mothers with children. A revived attempt to qualify an antiabortion initiative also failed to reach the ballot (Wentz 1998).

However, the OCA qualified another anti–gay-rights initiative in 2000, with the help of the Christian Coalition. This version proposed to prohibit public schools, including colleges and universities, from "encouraging or promoting" homosexuality, but polls showed it was widely perceived as simply the latest reflection of the anti–gay/lesbian sentiments that had been central to the earlier initiatives in 1992 and 1994 (Carter 2000). By a quirk in the numbering system, this initiative was numbered Measure Nine, as in 1992.

In the fall, the Measure Nine campaign was familiar, with the same lineup of liberal activists, mainstream churches, civic groups, and establishment political figures in opposition. The measure was defeated by almost exactly the same result as in 1994, 52 percent to 48 percent. The pattern of the vote was very similar as well. The initiative won in rural counties but lost in most urban and suburban counties. Mabon and the OCA collected a smaller total in campaign contributions—just less than $200,000—than in the earlier elections, and the opponents raised substantially more—$1,300,000—but since public attitudes were largely crystallized in the earlier contests, the campaigns probably changed relatively few minds.

Ballot Initiatives in Washington

Because it is more difficult to qualify ballot initiatives in Washington, they are less common there, but the Christian Right was involved in several high-profile campaigns in the state. In 1991, an initiative by pro-choice activists in Washington proposed to codify into state law the *Roe v. Wade* criteria for legal abortion. Because it appeared that the U.S. Supreme Court was preparing to overturn *Roe*, everyone involved perceived the stakes as very high. In the end, the prochoice initiative was narrowly approved, despite extensive efforts by the Christian Right to defeat it (Hamilton 1991).

Nineteen-ninety-eight was a mixed year for the Washington Christian Right. An initiative ostensibly to ban late-term abortions—Initiative 694—was written ambiguously, so it could have criminalized virtually all abortions, but it was widely rejected. However, Initiative 200, to ban state affirmative action programs, passed easily. The difference was that I-200 drew support not just from the Christian Right but also from the business conservatives and libertarians (Foster 1998). The Christian Right also had a rare success in the 1998 legislature: after Governor Locke vetoed a bill to ban gay and lesbian marriages, the state legislature quickly passed it over his veto (Nelson 1998a).

Two Decades of Frustration

If nothing else, this chronology of Christian Right activity demonstrates the persistence of the movement and the persistent rejection of its preferred policies and candidates, with occasional exceptions, by voters and public officials in Oregon and Washington. Viewed historically, the emergence of the Christian Right was a reaction against profound social, economic, and cultural changes, beginning in the 1960s and exacerbated in the 1980s. For citizens anchored in the natural resource economy of old—timber, agriculture, and mining—this period has not been a happy time. Because the social and cultural changes associated with the rise of Microsoft and Intel have coincided with the painful decline of the old natural-resource-based economy, it is not surprising that there should be an intense political reaction.

However, it is clear that in the Northwest there is little popular support for a return to the status quo ante in social control policy advocated by the old moralists. The high-water mark for the Christian Right in both the region and the nation was in 1994, but when confronted with the prospect of actually returning to old patterns of social control, the public drew back. In the Northwest continued Christian Right activism has had a devastating effect on the Republican Party. Bruce Ramsey of the *Seattle Times* was on target when he suggested in the aftermath of continuing Republican losses in Washington: "[I]n the 1990s, the Republicans ditched the chambers of commerce and became the party of rural, anti-abortion, anti-homosexual pro-gun religious believers . . . [but] Republicans cannot win without carrying some cities and suburbs"(Ramsey 2000). Without much doubt, the Christian Right will continue to have influence in the Republican Party in the Northwest and the nation, but it is very likely to continue to be frustrated in its efforts to achieve its ultimate policy ends.

NOTES

1. The Oregon state cconomist released a report in 1997 showing declines in the timber industry but increases in high-tech employment from the mid-1980s to the late 1990s; the lines crossed in 1996.

2. I have served as the Political Analyst for Oregon Public Broadcasting since 1988. My interest in the religious right grew directly out of my observations as a political scientist and political analyst in the Northwest.

3. The figures cited are from the *American Religious Identity Survey*, conducted by Kosmin, Meyer, and Keyser (2001) but communicated to me by John Green, one of the editors of this volume.

4. The name given the organization originally was the Oregon Conservative Alliance, but it was soon changed to the Oregon Citizens Alliance (OCA) to appear more inclusive.

5. The legislature could have repealed the law, but that would have required the governor's signature. Governor Kitzhaber, a Democrat, threatened to veto a repeal bill. The Oregon legislature, however, can bypass the governor with a referral to the ballot, so the Republicans chose that option.

REFERENCES

Ammons, David. 2000. "Cantwell Wins Last Unsettled Senate Race." *Associated Press* (2 December).

Appleton, Andrew M., and Daniel Francis. 1997. "Washington: Mobilizing for Victory." Pp. 169–86 in *God at the Grassroots, 1996: The Christian Right in American Elections*, ed. Mark J. Rozell and Clyde Wilcox. Lanham, Md.: Rowman & Littlefield.

Baker, Nina, and Brent Walker. 1998. "Sizemore Leaves a Trail of Debts." *Oregonian* (19 April), 1.

Balmer, Donald, and William Lunch. 1995. *Oregon in an Era of Uncertainty.* Corvallis, Ore.: Program for Government Research & Education.

Barone, Michael, and Grant, Ujifusa. 1999. *The Almanac of American Politics, 2000.* Washington, D.C.: National Journal.

———. 1997. *The Almanac of American Politics, 1998.* Washington, D.C.: National Journal.

———. 1995. *The Almanac of American Politics, 1996.* Washington, D.C.: National Journal.

———. 1989. *The Almanac of American Politics, 1990.* Washington, D.C.: National Journal.

———. 1983. *The Almanac of American Politics, 1984.* Washington, D.C.: National Journal.

Berke, Richard. 1997. "Trent Lott and His Fierce Freshmen." *New York Times Magazine* (2 February).

Cannon, Lou. 1978. "Fundamentalist Cleric Altering Oregon's GOP." *Washington Post* (6 October).

Carter, Steven. 2000. "Latest OCA Proposal Makes Ballot." *Oregonian* (1 August).

Conger, Kimberly, and John C. Green. 2002. "Spreading Out and Digging In: Christian Conservatives and State Republican Parties." *Campaigns and Elections* 23 (February):58–60, 64–66.

Coontz, Stephanie. 1992. *The Way We Never Were.* New York: Basic Books.

Craig, Barbara H., and David M. O'Brien.1993. *Abortion and American Politics.* Chatham, N.J.: Chatham House.

Cronin, Thomas E. 1989. *Direct Democracy.* Cambridge, Mass.: Harvard University Press.

Egan, Timothy. 1997. "Assisted Suicide Comes Full Circle, to Oregon." *New York Times* (26 October).

Elazar, Daniel J. 1972. *American Federalism: A View from the States.* 2d ed. New York: Thomas Y. Crowell.

Ellis, Richard J. 2002. *Democratic Delusions.* Lawrence: University Press of Kansas.

Esteve, Harry. 1996. "Smith Scores with Gentler Campaigning." *Eugene Register-Guard* (10 November).

FitzGerald, Francis. 1986. *Cities on a Hill: A Journey through Contemporary American Cultures.* New York: Simon & Schuster.

Foster, Heath. 1998. "Affirmative Action Rules Tossed Out by State Voters." *Seattle Post-Intelligencer* (4 November).

Gallagher, John, and Chris Bull. 1996. *Perfect Enemies.* New York: Crown.

Green, Ashbèl S. 1996. "GOP Backs Off, Shuns Support from OCA." *Oregonian* (9 March).

———.1997. "Suicide Law Returns to Voters." *Oregonian* (10 June).

Green, John C., Mark J. Rozell, and Clyde Wilcox. 2001. "Social Movements and Party Politics: The Case of the Christian Right." *Journal for the Scientific Study of Religion* 40:413–26.

Greenhouse, Linda. 1997. "Court, 9–0, Upholds State Laws Prohibiting Assisted Suicide; Protects Speech on Internet." *New York Times* (27 June).

Guth, James L., Lyman A. Kellstedt, Corwin E. Smidt, and John C. Green. 1998. "Thunder on the Right? Religious Interest Group Mobilization in the 1996 Election." Pp. 169–92 in *Interest Group Politics*, 5th ed., ed. Allan J. Cigler and Burdett A. Loomis. Washington, D.C.: Congressional Quarterly Press.

Hamilton, Don. 1991. "Abortion Foe Stirs Comment." *Oregonian* (7 November).

Herman, Didi. 1997. *The Anti-Gay Agenda*. Chicago: University of Chicago Press.

Hogan, Dave. 2002. "Judge Orders Jail for Leaders of OCA." *Oregonian* (21 February).

Kohut, Andrew. 1994. *The New Political Landscape*. Washington, D.C.: Pew Center.

Kosmin, Barry A., Egon Meyer, and Ariela Keyser. 2001. *American Religious Identification Survey*. New York: Graduate Center of the City University of New York.

Luker, Kristen. 1984. *Abortion and the Politics of Motherhood*. Berkeley: University of California Press.

Lunch, William. 1995. "Oregon: Identity and Politics in the Northwest." Pp. 227–51 in *God at the Grassroots: The Christian Right in the 1994 Elections*, ed. Mark J. Rozell and Clyde Wilcox. Lanham, Md.: Rowman & Littlefield.

Mapes, Jeff. 1992. "Mobley, OCA Consider Independent Senate Race." *Oregonian* (16 January).

———. 1998. "GOP Conservatives Challenge Lundquist." *Oregonian* (8 November).

Mayhew, David R. 1986. *Placing Parties in American Politics*. Princeton, N.J.: Princeton University Press.

McKay, Floyd. 1999. *An Editor for Oregon*. Corvallis: Oregon State University Press.

Nelson, Robert T. 1998a. "Gay Democrats Torn over Murray Support." *Seattle Times* (27 March).

———. 1998b. "GOP Seeking Some Answers after Big Losses." *Seattle Times* (5 November).

O'Keefe, Mark. 1996. "His Own Right." *Oregonian* (13 October).

Oldfield, Duane M. 1996. *The Right and the Righteous*. Lanham, Md.: Rowman & Littlefield.

Persinos, John. 1994. "Has the Christian Right Taken Over the Republican Party?" *Campaigns and Elections* (September):20–24.

Ramsey, Bruce. 2000. "State Republicans: The Wreckage of a Great Party." *Seattle Times* (6 December).

Rozell, Mark J. 2001. "The Reverend Michael Farris: Baptist Social Movement Organizer." Pp. 141–58 in *Religious Leaders and Faith-Based Politics*, ed. Jo Renee Formicola and Hubert Morken. Lanham, Md.: Rowman & Littlefield.

Rozell, Mark J., and Clyde Wilcox. 1997. "Conclusion: The Christian Right in Campaign '96." Pp. 255–70 in *God at the Grassroots, 1996: The Christian Right in the American Elections*, ed. Mark J. Rozell and Clyde Wilcox. Lanham, Md.: Rowman & Littlefield.

Sarasohn, David. 1996. "To Some, Real Mabon a New Revelation." *Oregonian* (15 March).

Schneider, William. 1996. "Women Made the Difference in Oregon." *National Journal* (10 February).

Strinkowski, Nicholas. 1997. "God Among the Evergreens." Paper presented to the 1997 Annual Meeting of the Western Political Science Association, Tuscon, Arizona, March 13–15.

Thomas, Ralph. 2000. "Locke Rolls to Easy Victory." *Seattle Times* (8 November).

Walth, Brent. 1994. *The Fire at Eden's Gate*. Portland: Oregon Historical Society Press.

Warner, Paul. 1997. "Oregon's Changing Economy." Salem: Oregon Office of Economic Analysis.

Wentz, Patty. 1998. "He's Back." *Willamette Week* (11 February).

White, G. Edward. 1982. *Earl Warren: A Public Life*. New York: Oxford University Press.

TWELVE

Citizen Initiative in Maine

Matthew C. Moen and Kenneth T. Palmer

RELEASE OF U.S. CENSUS BUREAU DATA IN 2001 SHOWED northern New England to be the least demographically diverse area of the nation. Similarities among Vermont, New Hampshire, and Maine do not end there. All three states were populated by settlers from England but then gained immigrants from French Canada and southern Europe, giving them a substantial Catholic population. All three share a moralistic political culture, with widespread participation and concern for the welfare of the entire community (Elazar 1984). Each state has a large legislature where districts in the lower chamber sometimes resemble neighborhoods. An annual town meeting remains the governing mechanism in many rural communities.

Despite similar origins, the three states have moved in rather different directions in recent years. Vermont has experienced the most dramatic change. An influx of people from the urban areas of the Middle Atlantic starting in the 1970s reconfigured its politics. Once considered the most Republican state in the nation (because it never voted for a Democratic presidential candidate until 1964), Vermont is now very liberal. In fact, a Voter News survey in the early 1990s showed Vermont had a higher proportion of self-identified liberals than any other state (Nelson 1997). This change is symbolized by Bernie Sanders, who was elected mayor of Burlington in the 1980s as a socialist and has since served as an independent in the U.S. House of Representatives.

Vermont's compactness and unstructured politics have caused state government to adapt relatively quickly to the policy orientations of this new electorate. Vermont has an activist and centralized government focused on issues such as environmental protection (Bryan and Hallowell 1993). On July 1, 2000, Vermont bestowed on same-sex partners the legal benefits of marriage, such as inheritance and insurance benefits. This civil union legislation followed a Vermont Supreme Court ruling in 1999 that failure to provide such protection to gay couples violated state civil rights laws. Public hearings by the Vermont legislature on civil unions drew the highest turnout in the history of the state (Graff 2000), and an organization known as "Take Back Vermont" recruited candidates to run against legislators who supported the civil union law (Goldberg 2000b). But its efforts mostly failed. Democratic governor Howard Dean won reelection despite its opposition, and Democrats prevailed in the senate (but they lost control of the house). Conservatives have since worked with "Take Back Vermont" on a constitutional amendment to overturn the civil union law. While it is possible that conservative groups will slow down, or even reverse, some of the state's progressive policies, Vermont is inhospitable to the Christian Right. Recent data suggest Vermont is one of seven states where the Christian Right is weak (Conger and Green 2002).

On the surface, New Hampshire seems to be more receptive to the Christian Right because it is one of the most conservative states in the nation. It is one of eighteen states where the Christian Right is judged to have a moderate influence within the Republican Party (Conger and Green 2002). New Hampshire remains the only state without a broad-based tax, relying mostly on municipal property taxes to provide limited public services. It was the only northeastern state to favor Republican George W. Bush in 2000. In contrast to those in Vermont and Maine, its Republican members of Congress have operated within the right wing of the party. Senator Bob Smith (R-N.H.) even left the GOP temporarily in 1999 to pursue the presidency on a more conservative platform, while its congressional delegation has supported the Christian Coalition about 90 percent of the time on key votes (Barone and Ujifusa 1999).

Yet, the political conservatism of New Hampshire is usually confined to issues of economic development. Southern New Hampshire in particular is tied to the Boston-area economy, and as many as one-fourth of its part-time state legislators work in real estate (Egbert and Fistek 1993). One scholar suggests the Republican Party lost the 1996 gubernatorial election precisely because its nominee, Ovid Lamontagne, was viewed as having "too many ties to the religious right" (Fistek 1997, 53). Republican leaders do not necessarily see religious conservatives as an asset. This skepticism is confirmed by a survey of interest groups in New Hampshire showing that religious groups account for less than 1 percent of all registered lobbies (Egbert and Fistek 1993).

Maine presents a different situation. Some years ago it was identified as one of only two states in the Northeast with a "substantial" Christian Right presence, defined as 25 percent to 50 percent strength within
the GOP state committee (Persinos 1994). More recently, an exit poll
conducted by CNN in the 2000 presidential race found that 15 percent
of Maine voters identified themselves as members of the "white religious
right." The Christian Right has a clear (but limited) presence in Maine.
Significantly, CNN did not bother to ask Vermont or New Hampshire
voters the exit poll question about religious right identification.

Maine is much more insular than Vermont or New Hampshire.
Figures from 1990 show that 69 percent of Maine residents were born
in the state, compared with 57 percent for Vermont and 44 percent for
New Hampshire (Hornor 2000). Census data released in 2001 show
only 3 percent growth in the state's population in the last decade. Moreover, newcomers bring less change to Maine's political system. They
settle disproportionately in its two southern counties and along its vast
coastline. Less influenced by newcomers are the northern and eastern
regions of the state, as well as the Franco-American towns of central
Maine, such as Lewiston and Waterville. Those areas support conservative positions on social issues more vigorously.

Maine presents a curious situation: the Christian Right's influence
within the state is real but circumscribed in many ways, and yet it continues winning on the salient issue of gay rights. This chapter describes
the role and evolution of the Christian Right in the state over time,
showing how tactical transformation has aided a movement that
remains at the margins of state politics.

The Political Environment

Maine was originally settled by English Protestant religious refugees and
French Catholics, who created closely knit communities (Palmer, Taylor, and LiBrizzi 1992). A result of this ethnic division is that delegates to
the state constitutional convention tried to minimize religious sectarian-
ism. Maine trumpeted religious freedom and made "no distinction"
between religious traditions when it became a state in 1820 (Banks 1970).

Recent data suggest this long-standing ethnic and religious dynamic still exists, with a population composed of 32 percent mainline
Protestants, 25 percent evangelical Protestants, 24 percent Catholics,
16 percent seculars, 1 percent Jewish, and 2 percent other.

The concentration of Franco-Americans in specific regions has miti-
gated conflict. For the most part, the Franco-American communities have
been satisfied with influence in particular regions, and with election of
sympathetic members to the state legislature. Members from those regions
promote French culture and language, but they fall short if their efforts
are seen as promoting division. An example was the decisive defeat of a
pilot project in the 120th Maine legislature (2001–2002) to offer French
in kindergarten classrooms in the Franco-American parts of the state.

The centrist politics of the state also mitigate religious conflict. Historically, those politicians who promote sectarian goals have fared
poorly, as have ideologues from either political party (Moen and Palmer
1997). Separation of religious and political matters is the norm. Current
members of the state's congressional delegation all claim a Protestant
or Catholic affiliation, for instance, but the affiliations are neither
salient nor important to their electoral prospects. Besides, all members
of the delegation are politically moderate, adjusting for party differences. Republican Senators Olympia Snowe and Susan Collins are part
of a core of moderates in their institution. They are fiscal conservatives
but social liberals who hold gay-rights and prochoice positions. Both
voted to acquit President Clinton of impeachment charges, and both
opposed the Christian Coalition about two-thirds of the time on key
votes in recent years (Barone and Ujifusa 1999). First District Democratic Representative Tom Allen is relatively liberal, but he spends time
on naval defense contracts for his district's largest employer, Bath Iron
Works. Second District Democratic Representative John Baldacci
carved out a position as a moderate that he parlayed into the governorship in 2002. Both representatives have opposed the Christian Coalition on key votes almost 100 percent of the time in recent years (Barone
and Ujifusa 1999). Former Independent governor Angus King was likewise a fiscal conservative and social liberal who favored gay-rights and
prochoice positions.

That the state's leading politicians are prochoice makes sense
because Maine is a strong prochoice state. It has experienced virtually
no abortion clinic violence. Some of its local communities have passed
highly restrictive ordinances to minimize picketing by right-to-life
groups (Saucier 1997). Opinion polls demonstrate overwhelming support for a prochoice position (Campbell 1996), and that viewpoint was
reaffirmed in a 1999 vote on "partial-birth" abortions. Maine voters
decisively rejected a proposed ban on that most controversial of all abortion procedures by a margin of 56 percent to 44 percent.

From Temperance to Initiative

Despite centrist political tendencies, Maine has long had a moralistic flavor to its politics. Only in 1990 via citizen initiative were "blue laws" prohibiting Sunday shopping repealed. The temperance movement may be traced to the first Total Abstinence Society, which was founded in Portland, Maine, in 1815. Such organizations wielded considerable influence in Maine politics. In 1851, Maine banned the manufacture and sale of alcohol. This "Maine Law" remained substantially in effect until prohibition was repealed in 1934 (Brunelle 1999). Even today, controversy swirls around closing a handful of state liquor stores that regulate distribution in order to reduce consumption.

The temperance movement is the clearly identifiable origin of the contemporary Christian Right in Maine. The Maine Christian Civic League (MCCL)—the principal Christian Right group in the state—began as a temperance organization in 1897. Over the course of the twentieth century, it lost its raison d'être and much of its membership. It survived in the post–World War II period under the leadership of Benjamin Bubar, Jr., a charismatic minister elected to the Maine House of Representatives at age twenty-one. For three decades, he kept the MCCL together in the face of declining interest, through his personal charisma and his willingness to broaden its agenda to issues like sex education in schools and gambling (Higgins 1998). Still, the "particular obsession" of Bubar and the MCCL was always prohibition (Martin 1980).

The MCCL seemed to be a dying organization at the time the Christian Right was starting to coalesce nationally. It claimed to have 6,500 members and a $126,000 budget, but its eighty-third annual statewide meeting, held in 1980, drew only fifty to sixty elderly participants, some of whom appeared to be disengaged from the events of the day (Martin 1980). The MCCL had only one part-time lobbyist, Laurence Bagley, whose background was school superintendent.

The MCCL benefited from some of the issues raised by national Christian Right leaders in the late 1970s, such as the tax-exempt status of religious schools. Such issues energized supporters. But the MCCL was not well connected to the Christian Right or to leaders such as Jerry Falwell (Wyman 2001). It badly needed a makeover to capitalize on the changing national political environment.

Change came to the MCCL in 1984. Following one year as Ben Bubar's assistant, Jasper Wyman became executive director. He set out to modernize the MCCL's agenda by moving beyond its prohibitionist roots, and he tried to connect it more explicitly to the state Republican Party, consistent with national trends. According to Wyman (2001), the MCCL scored a breakthrough when the Maine Legislature passed the Equal Rights Amendment (ERA) in 1984, subject to statewide referendum. The MCCL teamed up with Maine Right to Life and several conservative political consultants in the state. Funded by Linda Bean—an heir to the L.L. Bean fortune and later a political candidate—the ERA Impact Coalition took the offensive. It successfully tied the ERA to abortion and gay rights. Despite a comfortable win in the Maine legislature, the ERA lost the referendum vote by 63 percent to 37 percent. According to Wyman (2001), "In one swoop we took the League out of the nineteenth century and showed that we were a player in state politics."

Trying to capitalize on that victory, the MCCL collected citizen signatures to put an antiobscenity measure on the 1986 ballot. The measure made it a crime to "make, sell, give for value, or otherwise promote obscene material in Maine." It drew opposition from the normally staid Maine Library Association, which countered with a provocative and effective "book burning" advertising campaign. The obscenity measure was defeated by almost a three-to-one margin. The Christian Right did not push another citizen initiative in the state for nearly a decade.

Instead, Wyman pushed the MCCL toward the established political structure. He became a member of the executive committee of the state Republican Party. He stepped up in 1988 to challenge popular incumbent U.S. senator George Mitchell when some of the more logical Republican candidates already in office refused to do so. He drew only 19 percent of the vote. By the time he sought the Republican nomination for governor in 1994, his political aspirations were putting him at odds with some members of the MCCL, who felt he was undermining the organization. Wyman moderated many of his views on the social issues in response to Maine's centrist tendencies. He incrementally switched from a prolife to a more neutral position on abortion, claiming the battle had to be won in the hearts of individuals. He even criticized his right-to-life allies for their opposition to birth control (Rawson 1995). He repudiated his earlier support for the obscenity initiative (Weinstein 1994). He called for compassion and tolerance for gay people, while keeping up opposition to gay-rights statutes (Moen and Palmer 1997).

After placing third in a crowded Republican gubernatorial primary, Wyman left Maine to work in the Prison Fellowship Ministry program. His efforts to reinvigorate the MCCL were successful, but his attempt to moderate its ideological bent was not.

New MCCL executive director Michael Heath symbolically ended the Wyman era by changing the locks on the doors (Higgins 1998), and he promptly pushed hard to reinvigorate the core conservative constituency. During Wyman's tenure, the motto of the MCCL was "Bringing an Ethical Perspective to the Dialogue Over Public Policy." The new leadership substituted "Ethical" with "Biblical." Yet, since Wyman's departure, the MCCL has struggled. In 1998, several members of the MCCL board of directors went to court to force Heath to open the financial records of the organization. Heath responded at a board meeting by having the local police escort them from the premises; the MCCL subsequently released an audit showing no improprieties (Associated Press 1998). State newspapers had a field day, causing support for the MCCL to drop so much that it could not meet its payroll on three consecutive occasions (Fisher 1998). Its membership was estimated at 3,000, which was less than one-half of its estimated strength in 1980 (Fisher 1998). If this figure is accurate, the MCCL comprises a minuscule .002 percent of Maine's total population, although it has institutional support from churches that give it more clout.

The story took more twists and turns. In fall 1998, Heath announced his intention to leave the MCCL to work for the Family Research Council in Washington, D.C., led by Christian Right leader and Republican presidential candidate Gary Bauer. The move was then delayed amidst allegations of mismanagement at the MCCL. Those ousted from the board of directors and escorted out by the police returned in 1999 with a court order that granted them access to MCCL computers. Subsequently, they considered whether to file a "contempt of court" charge against Heath, who they claimed spirited out a laptop with the most sensitive information when confronted with the court order (Higgins 1999b).

In addition to those difficulties, the Maine Commission on Governmental Ethics and Election Practices cited the MCCL for failing to register as a political action committee, and for contributing illegally to state referendum campaigns (Associated Press 1999). The MCCL was found negligent and received a token fine for its first offense (Higgins 1999b). Michael Heath remains executive director of the MCCL, but its image is a bit tarnished.

The MCCL's struggles in the 1990s opened the door in Maine for the Christian Coalition of Maine (CCM), the state affiliate of Pat Robertson's Christian Coalition of America. CCM is headed by Paul Volle, a long-time Republican activist who served as chairperson of the

Cumberland County GOP and as Linda Bean's campaign manager in her 1992 bid for Congress. According to its webpage, CCM was incorporated by Volle and his wife in 1993 (Christian Coalition of Maine 2002). It claims activism on issues such as gay rights, abortion, educational reform, and public lands in the 1990s, but it was overshadowed by the MCCL until recent years. Volle has a regular presence at the state house in Augusta. In the 120th legislature (2001–2002), he lobbied against gun control, domestic partner benefits, abortion, and restrictions on the citizen initiative process. The CCM webpage states that "because we influence legislation donations are not tax deductible."

The CCM is not identified with the political aspirations of its leaders. It is a vocal lobby with some of the characteristics of a sophisticated "mom and pop" operation. It has teamed up with the conservative allies downplayed by Jasper Wyman during his bids for public office, linking to them electronically and politically; more recently, it forged a tie with (potential rival) Michael Heath and the MCCL on the issue of gay rights. More than any other issue, gay rights captures the transformation of the Christian Right in Maine politics.

GAY RIGHTS IN MAINE, 1977–2002

The 1969 Stonewall riots in Greenwich Village are usually cited as the trigger that made gay rights part of the national agenda. A sizable gay-rights constituency in the southern part of Maine, along with the permeability of the Maine legislature, was key to starting the gay-rights debate in the state back in 1977. A representative from Portland (Maine's largest city, located within Cumberland County) sponsored legislation to include "sexual or affectional preference" in the Maine Human Rights Act. The standard practice of the Maine legislature to consider any bill receiving at least one affirmative vote in a policy committee led to a floor vote. Figure 12.1 summarizes support for gay-rights legislation in the Maine house and senate over time.

The original gay-rights bill (L.D. 1419) was decisively defeated, losing twenty-one to ten in the senate and eighty-eight to fifty-four in the House. Attempts by proponents to rework language in subsequent legislatures failed, at least in the short term. The 109th (1979–80) and 110th (1981–82) Maine legislature voted on bills to insert "sexual orientation" into the Human Rights Act, but they failed in the senate and by larger margins in the house.

Figure 12.1 Support for Gay Rights in the Maine Legislature, 1977–97

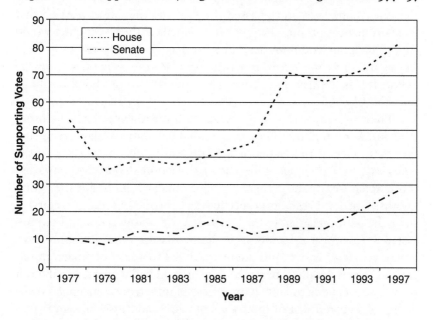

The first break for proponents came in the 1982 elections, when Democrats won 23 of 33 senate seats and 93 of 151 house seats. In the 111th legislature (1983–84), the house voted decisively against the proposal, but the senate passed it eighteen to twelve. Gay-rights advocates started gaining more public support for their cause the following year, when a gay man in Bangor was thrown from a bridge and killed in a highly publicized case (*Bangor Daily News* 1998). Support for including sexual orientation in the Human Rights Act grew steadily in the house thereafter. Yet, the house and senate did not register support at the same time. In three of the next four legislatures, running from 1985 to 1992, one chamber passed a gay-rights bill, but not the other.

Stymied at the state level, the Portland City Council enacted its own gay-rights ordinance in 1992. Opponents gathered petition signatures to force a local referendum, but they lost the subsequent vote. The Lewiston City Council followed suit in 1993, but local voters overturned its decision. That same year the Maine legislature passed a gay-rights bill for the first time. Surprisingly, moderate Republican governor John McKernan killed it by refusing to sign it. Under fire for his handling of state government, he needed to shore up his conservative base (Rooks 1995).

His veto gave gay-rights opponents a reprieve. They were furious that the Maine legislature passed the bill, and they were worried that local ordinances passing through city councils in the larger cities would spread to other communities. They reshaped the gay-rights fight in Maine by launching a citizen petition to place the issue on a statewide ballot. It was the first such effort since the disastrous "book burning" initiative of 1986.

Their strategy was part of a larger shift toward use of citizen initiatives in Maine politics. The state has lenient initiative laws requiring that petitioners gather signatures equivalent to only 10 percent of the votes cast in a previous gubernatorial election. Even more striking, those signatures can be gathered on election day right beside the voting booths. Once a threshold is reached and certified by the secretary of state, the petition is sent to the legislature for consideration; it becomes a statewide citizen referendum if the legislature does not approve it. These relatively easy requirements have led to a rash of citizen initiatives in recent decades, many of which gained ballot access but did not pass. One incentive to launch unsuccessful initiative campaigns is ownership of a current list of thousands of names/addresses of sympathizers. For that reason, as table 12.1 makes clear, the number of citizen initiatives has risen dramatically over time.

Question 1

The objective of gay-rights opponents was to craft a measure that prevented future expansion of the Maine Human Rights Act to include sexual orientation, and to override contravening policies. Drafted by

Table 12.1   Citizen Initiatives in Maine Politics, 1911–2000

Decade	No. of Initiatives	No. Passing
1911–20	1	1
1921–30	2	0
1931–40	2	1
1941–50	1	0
1951–60	0	0
1961–70	0	0
1971–80	8	4
1981–90	14	7
1991–2000	16	7

conservative constitutional scholar Bruce Fein, it was awkwardly (but cleverly) worded:

> Do you favor the changes in Maine law limiting protected classifications, in future state and local laws to race, color, sex, physical or mental disability, religion, age, ancestry, national origin, familial status, and marital status, and repeal existing laws which expand these classifications as proposed by citizen petition?

By ratifying existing classifications, the citizen initiative was neutral in principle, but aimed at homosexuals in practice. By repealing "existing laws," it overturned local gay-rights ordinances, a "hate crimes" statute, and the University of Maine System's provision against discrimination (Young 1995). It was the first initiative of its kind in the eastern United States.

Support for "Question 1" on the 1995 ballot was spearheaded by Carolyn Cosby, a self-described housewife from Portland. Under the rubric of Concerned Maine Families, she gathered more than 60,000 citizen signatures during 1993 and 1994. She raised and spent approximately $75,000, mostly on printed flyers and advertisements (Associated Press 1995). Her rhetorical approach was neutral, saying that she had nothing against homosexuals, and pointing out that the initiative was careful not to single out any particular group (Dunlap 1995). She ran the campaign for Question 1 out of her basement. She even refused assistance from Focus on the Family, the Colorado-based outfit of Reverend James Dobson.

Some religious conservatives disagreed with Cosby's more neutral stance toward homosexuality. Michael Heath of the MCCL teamed up with Paul Madore, who had led the successful petition drive to overturn the gay-rights ordinance passed by the Lewiston City Council. They formed the Coalition to End Special Rights. They criticized Cosby for straying from the issue of homosexuality and took some contributions from Reverend Dobson. His financial assistance was minimal, though, judging by the fact that the group raised and spent only around $30,000 (Hale 1995). The major contribution seemed to be radio advertisements (Weinstein and Vegh 1995). Heath and Madore also received some assistance from the Family Research Council. Spokesperson Robert Knight of the FRC toured through Maine and helped plot out strategy at the request of the MCCL.

Opponents of Question 1 took a different approach. Under the rubric of "Maine Won't Discriminate," they accepted contributions from many outside donors, amassing a campaign war chest of more than

$1 million. They lined up endorsements from leading politicians in the state, including popular Independent governor Angus King. He helped write the television advertisements on which he appeared, arguing that passage of Question 1 would make it hard to attract new business. All four members of Maine's congressional delegation—which included three Republicans at the time—opposed Question 1. So did state groups such as the AFL-CIO, the Chamber of Commerce, the Maine Education Association, the Council of Churches, and the Catholic Diocese of Portland. Large banks and businesses also announced their opposition.

In a salient off-year election with high voter turnout, opponents of Question 1 prevailed. They won eleven of sixteen counties, including populous southern and coastal regions. However, they carried only 53 percent of the statewide vote—a much closer margin than polls or the resource disparity between the two sides suggested.

Gay-rights legislation was not considered in the short second session of the 117th legislature (1996). Both sides needed a cooling-off period. Proponents eagerly awaited the first session of the 118th legislature (1997), though, convinced that momentum from the Question 1 victory would lead to passage of a gay-rights bill.

A Second Initiative

In May 1997, the Maine legislature amended the Human Rights Act to include sexual orientation. This made it illegal to discriminate in areas of employment, housing, access to public accommodations, and financial credit. The bill easily passed on a twenty-five to five vote in the Senate, and on a much closer eighty-two to sixty-two vote in the House. Governor King signed it. For the first time, state government enacted a gay-rights statute.

But gay-rights opponents did not accept this apparently decisive setback. Figuring they would lose in the Maine legislature, they concentrated on building popular support for another citizen initiative. Under Maine law, citizens are free to make any enacted law the subject of a citizen initiative if they present the requisite number of citizen signatures within six months. Gay-rights opponents figured they could easily produce the signatures since they had collected them once before. By using this so-called people's veto, they could outflank and overturn the Maine legislature and governor.

Working together, the MCCL and CCM submitted 65,256 petition signatures only four months after Governor King signed the gay-rights law. In October 1997, Secretary of State Dan Gwadosky certified 58,182 signatures—more than enough to force a referendum. Gay-rights advocates challenged the legality of the petitions, claiming they had been circulated before it was legally permitted. A judge denied the challenge, forcing the governor to call a special election. In November 1997, Governor King scheduled a vote for February 10, 1998.

Everyone assumed the citizen initiative would be hotly contested. The state had zigzagged on gay rights, with both sides suffering reversals of fortune in the 1990s alone. Unanticipated was the worst ice storm in the state's history in the period leading up to the vote, causing thousands of people to lose power for days. Politics was pushed out of the limelight as large parts of Maine were declared a federal disaster area. Interest was also driven down by polling results, which showed consistent majority support for gay rights. The defeat of Question 1 in 1995, the gay-rights statute passed in 1997, and the current polls convinced Maine citizens that the issue was settled. One of the supporters of the revived Maine Won't Discriminate organization noted two weeks before the election that voter interest was low (Pochna and Nacelewicz 1998).

The 1997 citizen initiative was again adroitly worded, so that a yes vote on gay rights actually meant opposition to such rights: "Do you want to reject the law passed by the Legislature and signed by the Governor that would ban discrimination based on sexual orientation with respect to jobs, housing, public accommodations, and credit?" Supporters of this initiative formed an umbrella organization called "Vote Yes for Equal Rights." Much of the public dialogue during the eleven-week campaign was explanation to voters what a yes versus no vote actually meant.

Yet the real story was a muted public dialogue. Given the abbreviated timetable, it was not worth trying to raise much money to spend on advertisements or line up a litany of endorsements. In contrast to 1995, when the Catholic Church opposed Question 1 because it prevented the extension of rights to any new classes of people, the Church sat out this battle focused exclusively on rights for homosexuals (Vegh 1998). Both sides worked on voter turnout. Backers of the citizen initiative had a built-in advantage because they had recently submitted thousands of valid signatures.

The citizen initiative passed in February 1998 by a 51 percent to 49 percent margin. The total turnout was 32 percent less than for the 1995 citizen initiative on gay rights. In a stunning reversal, this time those opposed to gay rights won eleven of sixteen counties. They fared particularly well in the northern and eastern rural areas of the state, as well as the urban Franco-American regions in central Maine. Those favoring gay rights once again fared best in the populous southern and coastal regions, but not in sufficient numbers to overturn lopsided margins in the rural areas.

The vote repealed the gay-rights law, making Maine the first state to do so, and the only New England state without such a law. Newspapers wrote critical editorials, and some gay-rights groups threatened to boycott the state's tourism industry. For their part, gay-rights supporters started preaching tolerance and organizing supporters in the rural areas of the state, with the thought of revisiting the issue (Moen and Palmer 2000).

Interestingly, another citizen initiative with enough signatures in the same year as the gay-rights initiative never went to voters because the Maine legislature enacted it without change. The initiative prohibited legal recognition of same-sex marriage. Two years before Vermont passed its civil union law, Maine explicitly rejected it.

A Third Referendum

Supporters of gay rights were disheartened by the 1998 vote but unwilling to accept defeat. They started a dialogue with the Catholic Church to improve their vote in the traditionally Democratic Franco-American areas. It seemed to pay off. Language was inserted in a reworked gay-rights bill that exempted religious entities. The 119th Maine legislature (1999–2000) passed that bill by a vote of eighty-five to sixty-five in the house and twenty-eight to seven in the senate, subject to approval by referendum in the presidential election of 2000. The higher-salience election was seen as an important corrective to low-turnout special elections. Note the reworked language of the bill, which framed gay rights positively in the context of ratifying legislative action against discrimination:

> Do you favor ratifying the action of the 119th Legislature whereby it passed an act extending to all citizens regardless of their sexual orientation the same basic rights to protection against discrimination now guaranteed to citizens on the basis of race, color, religion, sex or national origin in the areas of employment, housing, public accommodation and credit and where the act expressly states that nothing in the act confers legislative approval of, or special rights to, any person or group of persons?

The campaign to pass the statewide referendum kicked off after Labor Day, with a tour of the Equality Express. It was a motor home painted with patriotic colors and sponsored by supporters of the referendum. They started with a big advantage. An August poll showed 65 percent in favor, 28 percent opposed, and 7 percent undecided (Tuttle 2000).

Opponents conceded that their situation looked grim. They countered with claims that passage of Question 6 was the first step to same-sex unions. They planned a six-day, twenty-city bus tour of their own called "Impact Maine: The Straight Talk Tour 2000." Pasted on the side of the bus was the placard: "We are not Vermont." They held a rally in Augusta to convey the message to voters that the legislature was thumbing its nose at the 1998 special election results. They bypassed the Catholic hierarchy, appealing directly to the laity. Michael Heath of the MCCL, Paul Volle of the CCM, and Paul Madore of the Coalition to End Special Rights all joined forces to launch a coordinated grassroots campaign (Tuttle 2000; Adams 2000). They received a money-raising sendoff in late September from national Christian Right leaders. Reverend Jerry Falwell and Jan LaRue of the Family Research Council argued that the gay-rights referendum was part of a broad agenda including same-sex unions and child pornography (Meara 2000b). An intense (but low visibility) campaign was under way.

The agreement that referendum supporters had made with the Catholic Church began to haunt them. Lay Catholics marched on the Portland diocese headquarters, claiming that "secret negotiations" with homosexuals to win an exemption were unprincipled. They also noted the church was exempt from the statute, but they were not as individual citizens. On the other side, some gay activists announced their intention to vote against Question 6 precisely because it exempted the Catholic Church. They read the vote on partial-birth abortions in 1999 as proof they could win in spite of the church. Still other gay activists complained that the Maine legislature should never have sent the bill out to referendum.

The "Yes on 6" campaign sputtered. A close presidential race brought candidates to Maine as late as the day before the election. Contests for a U.S. Senate seat, two House seats, 186 state legislative seats, and five other referendum issues all vied for the attention of voters. Some of those referendum issues—such as physician-assisted suicide—claimed the lion's share of attention. Those supporting gay rights put up few yard signs. They aired a television commercial only in the last week of the campaign. The Equality Express was reduced to two people driving somewhat ad hoc around rural areas of the state (Haskell 2000b). Although polls showed the margin closing as election day approached, the final poll taken before the election still showed 61.5 percent support for gay rights (Meara 2000a).

The vote turned out differently. Maine voters rejected the gay-rights referendum by 318,846 (50.4 percent) to 314,012 (49.6 percent). The referendum lost in ten of the mostly rural counties while winning in six of the more populous southern and coastal counties. A CNN exit poll in Maine showed the "no" voters were older, male, less educated, Republican, and conservative. Those claiming a religious right identification voted 71 percent against, compared with 46 percent without that identification. Protestants opposed it by 54 percent and Catholics by 55 percent, while seculars supported it with 62 percent. The big surprise was that a much larger turnout did not change the result. Portland and its suburbs passed the referendum by a two-to-one margin, but rural areas rejected it by even larger percentages.

Gay-rights advocates were dumbfounded. They offered a variety of explanations: complacency among activists caused by favorable polls; misrepresentation by opponents of the statute's effect; division over the religious exemption; placement on the ballot; an angry electorate voting down all six referendum measures (Haskell 2000a). Governor King and others convened at the state house the next month for a public "soul searching" about why the referendum lost (Goldberg 2000a).

Michael Heath of the MCCL said the same-sex marriage law adopted in Vermont contributed to victory (Meara 2000a). In retrospect, the campaign theme of "Maine is not Vermont" was shrewd. It reminded Maine voters that civil unions had recently passed in Vermont, and it reinforced the idea that gay-rights protections were merely a precursor to gay marriage. Paul Volle of the CCM also said a "phony compromise" with the Catholic Church contributed to victory (Meara 2000a). Whatever the proper explanation, Maine is currently without a gay-rights law, despite the fact the Maine legislature has approved such a law three times in the last ten years.

Where the gay-rights issue is headed in Maine is unclear. Gay-rights activists are not interested in another referendum fight, having lost two consecutive ones. They prefer that the Maine legislature simply enact a statute, although that seems unlikely in the near future, given the recent "people's veto" of an earlier statute. Gay-rights opponents, on the other hand, call upon the legislature to accept the outcome of two statewide votes, and they demand their opponents collect citizen signatures if they want to make another run at it. Maine remains deeply divided over the issue. About a dozen municipalities (including Portland) have enacted domestic partner benefits, along with such large employers in the state as UNUM Corporation, Maine Medical Center, Anthem Blue Cross Blue Shield, and the University of Maine System. In early 2001, the State Employee Health Commission quietly approved health insurance benefits for domestic partners of state employees, a move that Governor Angus King let stand (Associated Press 2001). The MCCL expressed outrage over a decision made without a public debate, and it started collecting signatures for another citizen initiative. It abandoned that effort in 2002, partly because of the confusion over reversing an administrative policy decision through citizen initiative, and partly because the MCCL was viewed as "overreaching" by trying to deny health benefits to state employees.

CONCLUSION

In our earlier work, we argued the Christian Right had only limited influence in Maine politics (Moen and Palmer 1997, 2000). We believe that conclusion is still a reasonable one. Moderates control the state Republican Party, and even a "substantial" Christian Right influence within it does not say much because it is a loosely organized entity. It has been the minority party in the state legislature for almost all of the past two decades, and one indication of its continued weakness is that it did not field candidates in numerous state legislative races in the 2000 election cycle. Moreover, leading Republican officeholders mostly oppose its social agenda. The few times that candidates drawn from Christian Right ranks have run for statewide office, they lost badly.

Influence within other arenas is also limited. The Christian Right gained control of a handful of school boards as part of its "stealth strategy" in the early 1990s (Morken 1993), but those victories were quickly reversed. In the 120th Maine legislature (2001–2002), only a few senators and about a dozen representatives fit the label "religious conservative." Most of them are Republicans from the rural areas of northern and eastern Maine. They have a weekly meeting devoted to prayer, members' personal concerns, and policy. They pay close attention to the education and judiciary committees, where most of the social issues are referred. They rarely prevail, but they do rework legislation to promote their agenda. In 2001, for instance, a religious conservative on the education committee tried to alter a bill that prohibited teaching about homosexuality, simply to push the bill out of committee to the floor, where it would be publicly debated. Fighting quixotic battles to put "members on record" is reminiscent of the effort of religious conservatives in the U.S. Congress in the late 1970s and early 1980s. In the context of Maine politics, the tactic is calculated to build and maintain citizen support for the referendum campaigns where the Christian Right has been the most successful.

Demographic shifts will erode the power of the more conservative and rural areas of the state when legislative seats are reapportioned in 2003. Census data show that from 1990 to 2000, the most southern county (York) grew 13.5 percent, while the most northern county (Aroostook) dropped 15 percent. In aggregate terms, the First Congressional District, located in the southern part of the state, now has about 60,000 more people than the Second District. Policymakers aware of this massive shift often speak of the "two Maines."

The political implications are considerable. Southern Maine should pick up about two state senate seats and eight to ten house seats. This will intensify regional funding battles but also create a more sympathetic statewide climate for a liberal politics. Young people from rural areas are leaving the state in droves, with concomitant declines in the fishing, forestry, and agricultural sectors; in contrast, the urban service and technological centers of southern Maine are growing. The six counties supporting the gay-rights referendum in 2000, for instance, grew an average of almost 10 percent in the last decade.

It is hazardous to predict exactly when the long-standing feud over gay rights will be settled. The state seems almost evenly divided on the issue, and its moralistic political culture has been unable to diffuse it. Each side has used whatever tactics best amplify its strengths. Yet recent population shifts imply eventual passage of gay-rights legislation, as the rural and conservative eastern and northern regions slowly lose ground to the urban and liberal southern and coastal areas. Issues straddling the "two Maines" are particularly resistant to solution, but the changing demographics indicate that Maine will eventually include sexual orientation in its Human Rights Act, as other New England states have done.

The Christian Right in Maine has changed as the state of Maine has changed. For almost ninety years, the MCCL was a temperance organization drawing its support from the conservative churches in the rural areas. It had to change or fade into irrelevancy. Jasper Wyman changed it in the 1980s, expanding and moderating the agenda of the MCCL.

He also placed it more squarely within the established political structure. In the 1990s, the adaptation extended to citizen initiative and referendum battles, where the Christian Right can work outside a mostly unsympathetic Republican Party and a Democrat-controlled Maine legislature. It has twice narrowly reversed the Maine legislature on gay rights. Curiously, it has the most unlikely allies in protecting a lenient citizen initiative process from statutory change. The Green Party—concerned with forestry practices in the state—defends citizen initiative because it regularly pursues statewide referenda on clear cutting. Hemp advocates also pursue citizen initiatives, helping to pass a 1999 initiative allowing patients with specific illnesses to grow and use small amounts of marijuana with doctor approval. Religious conservatives sometimes have peculiar bedfellows in Maine.

The Christian Right has achieved notable but narrow victories in two statewide votes on gay rights. It lost one other on gay rights and one on partial-birth abortion. A 2001 fund-raising letter sent by Americans United for the Separation of Church and State identified "threatening legislation" under consideration in forty-three of the fifty states. Maine was one of the seven with no issues pending. The Christian Right's ability to increase its clout amidst the state's centrist politics and demographic changes is limited. Most Mainers just do not subscribe to its agenda.

ACKNOWLEDGMENT

The authors wish to thank John C. Green for providing data on religious affiliations in Maine, and Jonathan R. Thomas for his excellent research assistance.

REFERENCES

Adams, Glenn. 2000. "Gay Rights Bill Faces Uphill Fight." *Bangor Daily News* (7 September).
Associated Press. 1995. "Gay Rights Funds Outstrip Anti-Gay Coffers 10 to 1." *Portland Press Herald* (2 November).
———. 1998. "Christian Civic League Says Audit OK." *Bangor Daily News* (10 September).
———. 1999. "Christian Civic League in Violation." *Bangor Daily News* (15 April).

————. 2001. "Maine Domestic Partners Get Benefits." *Bangor Daily News* (10–11 March).

Bangor Daily News. 1998. "Milestones in the Gay-Rights Debate in Maine" (4 September).

Banks, Ronald F. 1970. *Maine Becomes a State.* Middletown, Conn.: Wesleyan University Press.

Barone, Michael, and Grant Ujifusa. 1999. *The Almanac of American Politics 2000.* Washington, D.C.: National Journal.

Brunelle, Jim. 1999. "History of Maine." Reprinted in *Senate and House Registers 1999*, State of Maine, 119th Legislature, 49–55.

Bryan, Frank, and Ann Hallowell. 1993. "Vermont: Interest Groups in a Rural Technopolity." Pp. 323–45 in *Interest Groups in the Northeastern States*, ed. Ronald Hrebenar and Clive S. Thomas. University Park: Pennsylvania State University Press.

Campbell, Steve. 1996. "Poll: Mainers on the Issues." *Portland Press Herald* (29 September).

Christian Coalition of Maine. 2002. www.ccofme.org.

Conger, Kimberly H., and John C. Green. 2002. "Spreading Out and Digging In: Christian Conservatives and State Republican Parties." *Campaigns & Elections* (February):58ff.

Dunlap, David W. 1995. "After Bitter Debate on Gay Rights, Maine Will Vote in Referendum on Discrimination." *New York Times* (5 November).

Egbert, Robert, and Michelle Anne Fistek. 1993. "New Hampshire: Tradition and the Challenge of Growth." Pp. 199–222 in *Interest Group Politics in the Northeastern States*, ed. Ronald Hrebenar and Clive S. Thomas. University Park: Pennsylvania State University Press.

Elazar, Daniel. 1984. *American Federalism: A View from the States.* 3d ed. New York: Harper & Row.

Fisher, Frank. 1998. "Money Troubles for Civic League." *Bangor Daily News* (9 September).

Fistek, Michelle Anne. 1997. "Is the Granite Grip of the Republican Party Cracking?" Pp. 37–54 in *Parties and Politics in the New England States*, ed. Jerome M. Mileur. Amherst, Mass.: Polity Publications (special issue of *Polity*).

Goldberg, Carey. 2000a. "Maine Governor and Gay Rights Supporters Pose a Question." *New York Times* (8 December).

————. 2000b. "Vermont Residents Split over Civil Unions Law." *New York Times* (1 September).

Graff, Christopher. 2000. "Civil Unions Debate Voted Vermont Top Story." *Bangor Daily News* (26 December).

Hale, John. 1995. "Mainers Face Off on Gays." *Bangor Daily News* (28–29 October).

Haskell, Meg. 2000a. "Lack of Money, Clear Opposition Doomed Yes on 6." *Maine Times* (16 November).
———. 2000b. "Questions About Question 6." *Maine Times* (26 October).
Higgins, A. Jay. 1998. "Civic League Struggles with Bubar's Legacy." *Bangor Daily News* (24–25 October).
———. 1999b. "Heath Faces Accusation of Contempt." *Bangor Daily News* (27 January).
Hornor, Edith. 2000. *Almanac of the Fifty States: Basic Data Profiles with Comparative Tables.* Palo Alto, Calif.: Information Publications.
Martin, Lucy L. 1980. "Maine's Premier Conservative Group: Has the Christian Civic League Gone Soft?" *Maine Times* (7 November).
Meara, Emmet. 2000a. "Failure Looms for Gay Rights." *Bangor Daily News* (8 November).
———. 2000b. "Falwell Campaigns Against Gay Rights Ordinance." *Bangor Daily News* (25 September).
Moen, Matthew C., and Kenneth T. Palmer. 1997. "Maine: Slow Growth in the Pine Tree State." Pp. 223–37 in *God at the Grassroots, 1996,* ed. Mark J. Rozell and Clyde Wilcox. Lanham, Md: Rowman & Littlefield.
———. 2000. "Maine: Which Way Should Life Be?" Pp. 271–86 in *Prayers in the Precincts: The Christian Right in the 1998 Elections,* ed. John C. Green, Mark J. Rozell, and Clyde Wilcox. Washington, D.C.: Georgetown University Press.
Morken, Hubert. 1993. "Religious Identity Concealment as Political Strategy: Shades of Prudence or Deceit?" Paper delivered at the annual meeting of the American Political Science Association, Washington, D.C., 2–5 September.
Nelson, Garrison. 1997. "Vermont's Politics Transformed: How Come It Got Fixed When It Wasn't Broke?" Pp. 56–76 in *Parties and Politics in the New England States,* ed. Jerome M. Mileur. Amherst, Mass.: Polity Publications (special issue of *Polity*).
Palmer, Kenneth T., G. Thomas Taylor, and Marcus A. LiBrizzi. 1992. *Maine Politics and Government.* Lincoln: University of Nebraska Press.
Persinos, John. 1994. "Has the Christian Right Taken Over the Republican Party?" *Campaigns & Elections* (September):21–24.
Pochna, Peter, and Tess Nacelewicz. 1998. "Low Voter Turnout Could Doom Gay-Rights Laws." *Maine Sunday Telegram* (25 January).
Rawson, Davis. 1995. "Wyman Picks Religion over Politics." *Waterville Morning Sentinel* (3 September).
Rooks, Douglas. 1995. "No Room Left for Jasper Wyman in Maine." *Maine Times* (7 September).
Saucier, Roxanne Moore. 1997. "Bangor Requests Picketing Hearing." *Bangor Daily News* (3 January).

Tuttle, Jeff. 2000. "Gay Rights Drive Kicks Off in Bangor." *Bangor Daily News* (14 September).

Vegh, Steven G. 1998. "Diocese Clarifies Official Position on Gay-Rights Vote." *Portland Press Herald* (30 January).

Weinstein, Joshua L. 1994. "Wyman Bucks Stereotypes to Reshape Image." *Portland Press Herald* (7 May).

Weinstein, Joshua L., and Steven G. Vegh. 1995. "Vote Puts Maine Center-Stage in Gay Rights Battle." *Portland Press Herald* (5 November).

Wyman, Jasper. 2001. Telephone interview with author, 11 April.

Young, Christine. 1995. "Question 1: The Effects." *Lewiston Sun-Journal* (5 November).

The Meaning of the March:
A Direction for Future Research

Clyde Wilcox, Mark J. Rozell, and John C. Green

ONE PURPOSE OF THESE CASE STUDIES OF CHRISTIAN RIGHT activity from 1980 through 2000 is to help scholars in a broader endeavor to join empirical work with normative assessments of the movement's impact on American politics. Because the political goals of the Christian Right provoke so much controversy, it has been a challenge to describe its activities accurately, let alone to assess its consequences fairly. Indeed, much of the literature evaluating the movement is polemical, including that of movement advocates (Reed 1996; Minnery 2001), inside (Thomas and Dobson 1999) and outside (Diamond 1998; Boston 2000) critics. However, as the cases in this book illustrate, our collective understanding of the movement is now sufficiently advanced to ask a critical question with some hope of arriving at a useful answer: Is the Christian Right good or bad for democracy? In its "marching toward the millennium" has the movement improved or impeded the broader purposes of American politics?

After two decades of activity, it is useful to step back and assess the impact of the Christian Right on American democracy. As scholars have rushed to embrace the importance of civil society, some have asserted that a citizenry involved in political groups is always an asset to democracy. But seldom has any set of groups generated more controversy than the contemporary Christian Right.

Critics of the movement charge that it has mobilized into politics a group of religious bigots who lack the norms of civility and tolerance and who despise the very idea of compromise and cooperation. The movement is portrayed as undermining democracy by elevating the importance of an unrepresentative group of activists in the political process, intimidating opponents, and polarizing political discourse. The source of the movement's greatest strength—the certitude of its members that they are doing God's work (Wilcox, Jelen, and Linzey 1991)— is seen as its greatest problem. Individuals bent on doing God's work are unlikely to find common ground with those who oppose them.

Yet supporters of the movement claim that it has enabled evangelical and other conservative Christians to become involved in politics, thereby adding new voices to the political discussion. They argue that the process of political engagement has inevitably taught these activists the norms of civility and tolerance and schooled them in the need for compromise and cooperation.

Mark Warren (2001) argues that such groups can assist or impede democracy in a number of complicated ways. Political groups can enhance the democratic capabilities of individuals, provide for an improved debate in the public sphere, and enhance the performance of government institutions. He suggests that some types of groups are more likely to have positive effects in these spheres than others.

Warren would classify the Christian Right as a set of associations that seek to create exclusive group identity. Many movement organizations have explicitly sought to create among conservative Christians the essential ingredients of a group consciousness—a common identity, a common set of political grievances, a common framework for blaming the political system and enemies for those grievances, and support for collective action as a solution (see Green 1999).

Warren sees such groups being especially likely to enhance some but not all aspects of democracy. He thinks that members of these groups are likely to increase their efficacy and political knowledge, and in some cases they can enhance political skills as well if the group entertains sufficient internal debate. But these organizations do little to help citizens enhance their ability to deliberate in politics, largely because the homogeneous nature of the groups does not lead to significant disagreements. And these organizations do little to foster greater civic virtues, such as tolerance and civility. Warren understands associations like those in the Christian Right as enhancing public deliberation by adding issues to the public debate and by representing the differences that are part of American social life. But they do so at the expense of representing the commonality of political life.

Warren's account would seem to be consistent with a mixed evaluation of the impact of the movement, enhancing some of the capacities of its members without leading to more tolerance, increasing the representativeness of the political system by emphasizing differences and conflict. These theories have yet to be tested, of course. The one attempt to apply the framework to the movement in a single state generally supported the framework in most but not all of its predictions (Wilcox 1999).

Moreover, Warren hints that the impact of groups on democracy depends critically on the social and political ecology in which they act. Thus, if the Christian Coalition worked closely with the National Rifle Association and the Chamber of Commerce, there might be more of a chance that those who joined the group would enhance their ability to deliberate. Such a notion would hark back to Truman's (1951) argument for the important function of crosscutting group memberships, which has had recent confirmation by Mutz (2002). In contrast, if the movement is active in an area where there is substantial and united opposition to its goals, then the civic virtues of tolerance and civility might be especially unlikely to be fostered, as movement activists come to define an "anti-Christian enemy." In a culture war, there may be less incentive to negotiate (Green et al. 1996).

Our previous work on the Christian Right at the state level offers a good opportunity for a systematic investigation of the impact of the movement. The next step in our research agenda is to begin to explore the impact of the movement on democracy in the states, with a special focus on the mediating role of group ecology. Recent research by Gray and Lowery (2000) suggests that the density and diversity of state interest group ecologies can influence the policies produced by states. We suspect that it can influence the impact of specific types of groups on democratic functioning as well.

The lessons from the case studies in this book will help us in this more ambitious undertaking. From them we learn that the concentration of religious conservatives, the openness of the political system (and especially the parties), and the density of opposition groups all influence the successes and failures of the Christian Right in states. These factors will be important as we select states for closer examination in the next stage of the project.

However, these cases are important in their own right, for they detail the rich diversity of the paths that the Christian Right has marched on its way to the millennium. Similar diversity undoubtedly exists for other types of social movements in the states, including liberal movements that are composed of feminists, gay and lesbian activists, and environmentalists. Surely, these marches affect one another, forcing detours in some cases, head-on clashes in others, and perhaps in a few cases, a time of marching together.

References

Boston, Robert. 2000. *Close Encounters with the Religious Right.* Amherst, N.Y.: Prometheus Books.

Diamond, Sara. 1998. *Not by Politics Alone.* New York: Guilford Press.

Gray, Virginia, and David Lowery. 2000. *The Population Ecology of Interest Representation.* Ann Arbor: University of Michigan Press.

Green, John C. 1999. "The Spirit Willing: Collective Identity and the Development of the Christian Right." Pp. 153–68 in *Waves of Protest: Social Movements Since the Sixties,* ed. Jo Freeman and Victoria Johnson. Lanham, Md.: Rowman & Littlefield.

Green, John C., James L. Guth, Corwin E. Smidt, and Lyman A. Kellstedt. 1996. *Religion and the Culture Wars: Dispatches from the Front.* Lanham, Md.: Rowman & Littlefield.

Minnery, Tom. 2001. *Why You Can't Stay Silent.* Wheaton, Ill.: Tyndale House.

Mutz, Diana. 2002. "Cross-cutting Social Networks: Testing Democratic Theory in Practice." *American Political Science Review* 96:111–26.

Reed, Ralph. 1996. *Active Faith.* New York: Free Press.

Thomas, Cal, and Ed Dobson. 1999. *Blinded by Might.* Grand Rapids, Mich.: Zondervan Press.

Truman, David B. 1951. *The Governmental Process: Political Interests and Public Opinion.* New York: Knopf.

Warren, Mark. 2001. *Democracy and Associations.* Princeton, N.J.: Princeton University Press.

Wilcox, Clyde. 1999. "The Christian Right in Virginia: A Mixed Blessing for Civil Society." Paper presented at conference on Democracy and Civil Society, Georgetown University, Washington, D.C., 15–16 June.

Wilcox, Clyde, Ted G. Jelen, and Sharon Linzey. 1991. "Reluctant Warriors: Premillenialism and Politics in the Moral Majority." *Journal for the Scientific Study of Religion* 30:245–58.

CONTRIBUTORS

ALLAN J. CIGLER is Chancellor's Club Teaching Professor of Political Science at the University of Kansas. His research and teaching interests include interest groups, participation, and political parties. He is the coeditor of *Interest Group Politics* (now in its sixth edition) and *Agriculture Groups*, and has recently published *Perspectives on Terrorism*.

JOEL S. FETZER is assistant professor of political science at Pepperdine University. He is the author of *Public Attitudes toward Immigration in the United States, France, and Germany*. His forthcoming book with Chris Soper is *Muslims and the State in Britain, France, and Germany*.

CHRISTOPHER P. GILBERT is associate professor of political science at Gustavus Adolphus College, St. Peter, Minn. He is the author of *The Impact of Churches on Political Behavior* and has written on religion and political behavior, religion and third parties in the United States, and the political activities of Episcopalian and Lutheran clergy.

JOHN C. GREEN is professor of political science and director of the Ray C. Bliss Institute of Applied Politics at the University of Akron. He is the coauthor of *The Diminishing Divide: Religion's Changing Role in American Politics* and *The Bully Pulpit: The Politics of Protestant Clergy*. He is coeditor of *The State of the Parties* and *Prayers in the Precincts*.

JAMES L. GUTH is the William R. Kenan, Jr. Professor of Political Science at Furman University, Greenville, S.C. He is coauthor of *Religion and the Culture Wars: Dispatches from the Front* and *The Bully Pulpit: The Politics of Protestant Clergy*. His work on religion and politics has appeared in numerous journals and collections.

MARK JOSLYN is an assistant professor of political science at the University of Kansas. His research interests include campaigns and elections, political psychology, and public opinion.

LYMAN A. KELLSTEDT is professor of political science (emeritus) at Wheaton College and visiting professor of political science at Furman University. He is coauthor of *The Bully Pulpit* and *Religion and the Culture Wars* and is the author of a number of articles on religion and politics.

JAMES W. LAMARE is professor of political science at Florida Atlantic University. He is the author of *Texas Politics: Economics, Power, and Policy* (7th ed.).

BURDETT A. LOOMIS is professor of political science at the University of Kansas. He has written extensively on legislatures, interest groups, and public policy. He is the author of *The Contemporary Congress* (4th ed.), coauthor of *The Sound of Money*, and coeditor of *Interest Group Politics* (6th ed.).

WILLIAM M. LUNCH is professor of political science at Oregon State University and the political analyst for Oregon Public Broadcasting. He has published a number of articles concerning American politics, elections, public opinion, and environmental, health, and science policy. He is the author of *The Nationalization of American Politics*.

MATTHEW C. MOEN is dean of the College of Arts and Sciences at the University of South Dakota. Prior to that position, he served as professor and chairperson of the Political Science Department at the University of Maine. He is author of *The Christian Right and Congress* and *The Transformation of the Christian Right* and many other works on the Christian Right and on Maine politics.

KENNETH T. PALMER is professor of political science at the University of Maine. He is coauthor of *Maine Government and Politics* and many other works on state politics and intergovernmental relations.

JAMES M. PENNING is professor of political science at Calvin College, Grand Rapids, Mich. He is coeditor of *Sojourners in the Wilderness: The Christian Right in Comparative Perspective*, coauthor of *Evangelicalism: The Next Generation*, and the author of a number of articles on Michigan politics.

DAVID A. M. PETERSON is an assistant professor of political science at Texas A&M University. His research interests are political behavior, political psychology, and elections.

JERRY L. POLINARD is professor and chair of the Department of Political Science at the University of Texas-Pan American. He is the coauthor of *Electoral Structure and Urban Politics* and *State and Local Politics*.

DONALD P. RACHETER is professor of political science at Central College in Pella, Iowa, and president of the Public Interest Institute in Mt. Pleasant, Iowa. He is coeditor of *Limiting Leviathan, Federal Government in Principle and Practice*, and *Politics, Taxation, and the Rule of Law: The Power to Tax in Constitutional Perspective*.

MARK J. ROZELL is professor and chair, Department of Politics, at The Catholic University of America. He is coauthor of *Second Coming: The New Christian Right in Virginia Politics*, and coeditor of *God at the Grassroots, 1996*, and *Prayers in the Precincts*.

RICHARD K. SCHER is professor of political science at the University of Florida and the author of *Politics in the New South* (2d ed.).

CORWIN E. SMIDT holds the Henry Chair and serves as the executive director of the Paul Henry Institute for the Study of Christianity and Politics at Calvin College. He is coauthor of *The Bully Pulpit: The Politics of Protestant Clergy*, coeditor of *Sojourners in the Wilderness: The Christian Right in Comparative Perspective*, and editor of *In God We Trust: Religion in American Political Life*.

J. CHRISTOPHER SOPER is professor of political science at Pepperdine University. He is the author of *The Challenge of Pluralism: Church and State in Five Democracies*. His forthcoming book with Joel Fetzer is *Muslims and the State in Britain, France, and Germany*.

C. DANIELLE VINSON is an associate professor of political science at Furman University. She is the author of a forthcoming book on local media coverage of Congress and has written articles on media and politics and campaign finance in South Carolina elections.

KENNETH D. WALD is Research Foundation Professor of Political Science and director of the Center for Jewish Studies at the University of Florida. He is author of *Religion and Politics in the United States* (4th ed.), coauthor *of The Politics of Cultural Differences: Social Change and*

Voter Mobilization Strategies in the Post New Deal Era (2002), and coeditor of *The Politics of Gay Rights* (2000).

CLYDE WILCOX   is professor of government at Georgetown University. He is author of *Onward Christian Soldiers: The Christian Right in American Politics*, coauthor of *Second Coming: The Christian Right in Virginia Politics*, and coeditor of *God at the Grassroots, 1996*, and *Prayers in the Precincts*.

ROBERT D. WRINKLE   is a professor in the Department of Political Science at the University of Texas-Pan American. He is the coauthor of *Electoral Structure and Urban Politics* and *State and Local Politics*. His current research interests include public policy, electoral structure, and minority politics.

ROBERT ZWIER   is provost and professor of political science at Malone College. Prior to that position, he served as vice president for academic affairs at Colorado Christian University. He has written *Born Again Politics*, as well as several articles on religious interest groups in American politics.

INDEX

Page numbers in italics refer to tables and figures.